# BLACK GIRLS' LITERACIES

Bringing together the voices of leading and emerging scholars, this volume highlights the many facets of Black girls' literacies. As a comprehensive survey of the research, theories, and practices that highlight the literacies of Black girls and women in diverse spaces, the text addresses how sustaining and advancing their literacy achievement in and outside the classroom traverses the multiple dimensions of writing, comprehending literature, digital media, and community engagement. The Black Girls' Literacies Framework lays a foundation for the understanding of Black girl epistemologies as multi-layered, nuanced, and complex.

The authors in this volume draw on their collective yet individual experiences as Black women scholars and teacher educators to share ways to transform the identity development of Black girls within and beyond official school contexts. Addressing historical and contemporary issues within the broader context of inclusive education, chapters highlight empowering pedagogies and practices. In between chapters, the book features four "Kitchen Table Talk" conversations among contributors and leading Black women scholars, representing the rich history of spaces where Black women come together to share experiences and assert their voices. A crucial resource for educators, researchers, professors, and graduate students in language and literacy education, this book offers readers a fuller vision of the roles of literacy and English educators in the work to undo educational wrongs against Black girls and women and to create inclusive spaces that acknowledge the legitimacy and value of Black girls' literacies.

**Detra Price-Dennis** is Associate Professor of Education at Teachers College, Columbia University, USA.

**Gholnecsar E. Muhammad** is Associate Professor of Middle and Secondary Education at Georgia State University, USA.

# How to Expanding Literacies in Education
Jennifer Rowsell and Cynthia Lewis, Series Editors

For more information about this series, please visit: www.routledge.com/Expanding-Literacies-in-Education/book-series/ELIE

# BLACK GIRLS' LITERACIES

## Transforming Lives and Literacy Practices

*Edited by Detra Price-Dennis*
*and Gholnecsar E. Muhammad*

Routledge
Taylor & Francis Group

NEW YORK AND LONDON

First published 2021
by Routledge
605 Third Avenue, New York, NY 10158

and by Routledge
2 Park Square, Milton Park, Abingdon, Oxon, OX14 4RN

*Routledge is an imprint of the Taylor & Francis Group, an informa business*

© 2021 Taylor & Francis

The right of Detra Price-Dennis and Gholnecsar E. Muhammad to be
identified as the authors of the editorial material, and of the authors for
their individual chapters, has been asserted in accordance with sections 77
and 78 of the Copyright, Designs and Patents Act 1988.

*Library of Congress Cataloging-in-Publication Data*
A catalog record for this book has been requested

ISBN: 978-0-367-19962-3 (hbk)
ISBN: 978-0-367-19965-4 (pbk)
ISBN: 978-0-429-24439-1 (ebk)

Typeset in Bembo
by Apex CoVantage, LLC

# CONTENTS

# SERIES EDITOR INTRODUCTION

The *Expanding Literacies in Education Series* features books that highlight the changing landscape and explore new directions and theoretical tools in literacy studies as it is transforming education—including material, embodied, affective and global emphases, digital and virtual worlds, and transcultural and cosmopolitan spaces. Some books in the series locate emerging literacies in practices that extend or trouble their historical uses and functions. Others cross disciplinary borders, bringing new epistemologies to bear on evolving practices that question the very foundations of literacy scholarship. Polemical and forward-looking, encompassing public and vernacular pedagogies as well as formal education, these books engage researchers, graduate students, and teacher educators with new and emerging theoretical approaches to literacy practices in all of their complexities, challenges, and possibilities.

In this collection, editors Detra Price-Dennis and Gholnecsar E. Muhammad offer literacy researchers and educators a close look at what literacy has meant for Black girls historically and contemporaneously, as well as a groundbreaking vision for what literacy can aspire to be for communities seeking and enacting justice in the future. As Marcell Haddix stated in her 2019 Presidential Address for the Literacy Research Association, Black girls' literacies not only sustain Black women's communities but serve as a "rhetorical strategy to define who we are and what we believe as a Black feminist community. We name ourselves for ourselves by ourselves." At a time when many of us, in our writing, research, teaching, and thinking, are taking action to interrupt the racism inherent in our institutions and imaginations—including our research methodologies, our syllabi, and our thinking—this book is a North Star.

We knew we wanted *Black Girls' Literacies: Transforming Lives and Literacy Practices* (BGL) for the series from the day we read the *English Education*-themed issue on BGL (2016) and the transformative framework outlined by Muhammad and Haddix in the issue's lead article. This book refuses anti-Blackness and offers Black girls joy, intellectual acuity, historical agency, community, and criticality. The book addresses BGL in four sections that focus on creating spaces for BGL, language and literacy BGL practices, Black girlhood as represented in literature, and digital BGL literacies. One of the brave and beautiful components of the book is the Kitchen Table Talks at the end of each section, where the authors of each chapter in the section gather around a symbolic kitchen table with a featured Black feminist scholar to expand on the section themes through dialogue that touches on ideas, feelings, and personal connections. In this way, the book's format reinforces its content and message of love and community across generations of Black women. As the editors themselves write in their introduction, "Black girls deserve literacy practices that are designed to advance their academic success, identity development, sociopolitical consciousness, and joy." We could not agree more! There is so much for literacy researchers and educators to gain from this book, and we look forward to sharing *Black Girls' Literacies* with readers far and wide.

Cynthia Lewis and Jennifer Rowsell

## References

Haddix, M. (December, 2019). This is us: Discourses of community within and beyond literacy research. Presidential Address at the 69th meeting of the Literacy Research Association, Tampa, Florida.

Muhammad, G. E., & Haddix, M. (2016). Centering Black girls' literacies: A review of literature on the multiple ways of knowing of Black girls. *English Education, 48*(4), 299–336.

Seeley-Ruiz, Y. (Ed.) (2016). Black girls' literacies [Special issue], *English Education, 48*(4).

# INTRODUCTION

## Centering Black Girls' Ways of Knowing: Past, Present, and Future

*Detra Price-Dennis and Gholnecsar E. Muhammad*

For centuries, Black women leading thinkers such as Sojourner Truth, Ida B. Wells, Phillis Wheatley, and Anna Julia Cooper have taught Black women that what counts as being literate has always been tied to social, political, economic, and historical contexts. The same reality is true for Black girls today. The social and academic success and well-being of Black girls in school contexts cannot be achieved without educators. Literacy educators are in a particular position to engage the literacy and literary traditions of Black girls and womanhood to help their students combat the harsh realities they may face. Additionally, Black girls deserve literacy practices that are designed to advance their academic success, identity development, sociopolitical consciousness, and joy. This edited volume features the research of literacy and English educators who work with practicing teachers, pre-service educators, and Black girls and women. Their research traverses the multiple literacies of writing, comprehending literature, digital media, and community engagement. The authors in this volume draw on their collective yet individual experiences as Black women scholars and teacher educators to share ways to transform the identity development of Black girls within and beyond official school contexts. To this end, each author connects their thoughtful work to the Black Girls' Literacies Framework.

### What Is the Black Girls' Literacies Framework (BGLF)

The BGLF is composed of six components that are useful and necessary for engaging Black girls in literacy pedagogies across grade levels and contexts. These components include an understanding that Black girls' literacies are:

1. Multiple
2. Tied to identities

3. Historical
4. Collaborative
5. Intellectual
6. Political/Critical

## Black Girls' Literacies Are Multiple

Black girls do not practice literacies in isolation. Their literacies are multiple in both practice and theoretical orientations. Historically, Black women would come together to read, discuss literature, write about literature, and then speak (and often debate) about the concept found in the literature read. Thus, they were engaged in literacy practices that were intertwined and interwoven. As an extension to traditional literacies that focuses on reading, writing, thinking, and language development in seclusion, Black girls thrive when they are collectively practiced together.

## Black Girls' Literacies Are Tied to Their Identities

As Black girls read, write, and think, they are defining their identities, which includes the ways in which others perceive them. Identity development is intricately woven into practices of literacy and they engage in a deeper sense of self. Identities are ever-changing and dynamic; therefore, as girls are practicing literacies, they are in a constant state of shaping and reshaping the ways in which they see their lives. Examples of identities include racial, ethnic, cultural, gender, kinship, academic/intellectual, personal/individual, sexual, and community selves. Young people especially need opportunities in literacy pedagogy not only to explore multiple facets of self-identity but also to learn about the identities of others who are different from them. Typically, each researcher who centers Black girls in their studies has somehow focused on identity.

## Black Girls' Literacies Are Historical

Black girls' literacies are embedded in history. Specifically, they are wrapped up in the histories of African people and Black women. Throughout centuries, Black women's writings have been connected to each other in the concepts written about and the ways in which they have written for self- and collective advocacy. Royster (2000) refers to this historical connection to the zamani (meaning past) dimension of Black women literacies. She found that Black women have drawn upon the writings of other Black women to shape their own writings, and their literate self-expressions are similar to the writings of other Black women. Black women were introduced to one another through their writings, and their language provided comfort and mentorship for readers. This connection is intricately woven into the culture and is then conveyed across generations of women and girls.

## Black Girls' Literacies Are Collaborative

Black girls' literacies are collaborative in nature, and they advance in their education when they work together. Collaboration is more than just working in groups or pairs; it is also a shared understanding of collective responsibility.

## Black Girls' Literacies Are Intellectual

Black girls' literacies are highly intellectual and connected to learning new concepts and knowledge. Intellect or knowledge is what we learn or understand about various topics, concepts, and ideals. Black women have used writing as an intellectual exercise, and as they were reading, writing, speaking, and thinking, they were seeking knowledge.

## Black Girls' Literacies Are Political/Critical

Criticality is the ability to read print and non-print text to understand how power, oppression, and privilege are present. As Black girls engage in reading, writing, thinking, and speaking, they are doing so to make sense of how authority is held in texts, communities, and the wider society. This calls readers to think outside of themselves, including the cultural identities and values that they have come to know, and to consider multiple standpoints—including those of marginalized groups. Sociopolitical and critical literacy also calls for seeing, reading, and naming the world the world to make sense of inequality and social justice. This goes beyond deep thinking (which I refer to lower case "c" critical); with *Criticality* (upper case "C"), students are pushed to read between the lines and seek to understand what is not in print (Muhammad, 2020).

Developed from Gholdy's (Gholnecsar E. Muhammad) research, the framework undergirds the understanding of Black girl epistemologies as multidimensional, multi-layered, nuanced, and complex. This framework was gleaned from decades of research and studies of Black women and girls' literacy practices. The genealogy of the BGLF is drawn from historical research and the intellectual thought traditions of Black female leading thinkers, which is largely absent in dominant narratives around what counts as knowledge in education research.

## Why Black Girls' Literacies Matter

In recent years, influential organizations like the African American Policy Institute, Colorlines, the National Coalition on Black Civic Participation, and the

NAACP Legal Defense Fund, among several others, have released reports on the "state of the union" for Black women and girls in our society. The statistics in these reports are horrifying and should move fellow citizens of Black women and girls, and specifically educators, to take action against these harsh realities. It should alarm the public that 12% of Black girls in pre-kindergarten through 12th grade received an out-of-school suspension during the 2011–2012 school year.[1] Moreover, we should be disturbed by the fact that the suspension rate for Black girls is six times higher than their White female counterparts.[2] Educators in schools across the nation should be concerned that Black girls are three times more likely to attend schools that do not offer the full range of college preparatory courses, and where most teachers fail to meet all state requirements for certification or licensure.[3] Researchers are very clear that race is a primary factor that has shaped contexts causing these disparities.

As with Black boys, Black girls are being educated during the age of mass incarceration. Zero tolerance policies and school-to-prison policies executed by security officers and other school personnel directly affect their chances for academic and social success in school. Black girls often find themselves in schools where violence—intellectual violence through excessive testing or actual physical violence—is the norm. On October 26, 2015—the same day the Obama Administration and the Council of the Great City Schools announced that the emphasis on standardized testing that has occurred in public schools for decades was not effective and was "potentially harmful"—the world witnessed a South Carolina police officer body slam a 16-year-old Black girl and fling her across the classroom. Despite these realities of intellectual and physical violence leveled against them, Black girls show up to school with the intent not only to survive, but also to thrive in a climate where the odds are heavily stacked against them. They and their families still believe in schools and the promise of education.

Given the reawakening of racial violence against Black people, and in particular Black women and girls, across the nation, the timeliness of this edited volume is significant. As more research continues to reveal a "separate and unequal" school system for Black girls and their induction into a national school-to-prison pipeline, it is important for educators to lead the charge both to understand that these inequalities exist, and to create strategies and actions to interrupt them. We hope that the readers of this edited volume will gain a fuller vision of the role of literacy and English educators in the work to undo educational wrongs against Black girls and women and to create inclusive spaces that acknowledge the legitimacy and value of Black girls' literacies.

We created this volume to directly address the absence of attention on Black girls' literacies in classrooms. Currently, there is a scarcity of scholarship on the literacy development of Black girls in research journal articles and books for pre- and in-service teachers. Researchers and school leaders have instead focused largely on the reading and writing of Black boys or on White populations of students. Venus Evans-Winters (2005) writes,

> In social science and educational research, the African American female adolescents' experience, in particular, has been left out, ignored, whited out (subsumed under White girls' experiences), blacked out (generalized within the Black male experience) or simply pathologized.
>
> *(Evans-Winters, 2005, p. 9)*

The first part of the explanation speaks to Black girls being situated within the same experiences of White female youth. Although there may be developmental similarities in gender and age between the two groups, it is important to note differences that exist among Black and White female students. One example of an existing difference between the two groups is the ways in which they have been socialized within society. Historically, Black women and girls have been viewed as "subhuman," sexually promiscuous, too loud, and misbehaved (Morris, 2007; Richardson, 2002; Smith, 1982). As young Black girls position themselves within this context, they come to have unique literacy experiences and distinct differences in how they interact with the classroom environment (Grant, 1992; Richardson, 2002). Furthermore, race, class, and gender are intersecting constructs used to make meaning of text and the world. If Black girls experience any of these constructs differently than a White female, it is important to critically examine this population independently. Research has found that teachers systematically respond differently to Black girls compared to White girls, usually focusing more on social and behavior skills with Black girls instead of academic aptitude as with White female students, which may affect their literacy experiences and consequently ignore them altogether (Evans-Winters & Esposito, 2010; Martin & Smith, 2017; Morris, 2007).

The focus has also been on Black boys in education and literacy development. While not to understate their needs, it is important that educational experiences of Black girls are not overlooked, ignored, or overshadowed due to the focus on Black males' education (Frazier-Kouassi, 2002; Rollock, 2007). Educators have gained a large amount of knowledge about reading and outcomes of Black males, but questions still linger about the literacy achievement of Black girls. Educators cannot solely examine one group of students within a race (such as Black boys) when seeking to find ways to improve the educational progress of an entire population. Black girls achieve only at *slightly* higher rates than Black males in reading and writing, but there remains a significant need to improve reading and writing achievement for Black youth overall.

The lack of empirical data we have about the rich and sophisticated literacy practices of Black girls raises questions about the deficit discourses used to describe their academic achievement. Being excluded from the gendered and racial educational research narrative leaves Black girls on the outside of initiatives and programs to help them develop positive racialized-gender identity. This exclusion also means that educators, namely literacy and language educators, do not have a strong sense of the unique ways of knowing and learning. This is further perpetuated by the misrepresentation of Black girls in and outside of schools. Research and media platforms have represented Black girls in false and incomplete ways, focusing largely on pathological issues of obesity, sexually transmitted diseases, and teen pregnancy. Internet searches on Black girls' education and literacies typically brings forth information on sexuality, juvenile delinquency, and dropout rates rather than their educational experiences and the instruction that frames their learning. This leads to the point that these particular social issues and injuries overshadow research such that the concentration is not on pedagogy or how they experience and practice literacy. Additionally, these narratives are told absent of Black girls' voices or their ways of knowing.

Across the chapters in this volume, we argue that counter-narratives and texts are needed to provide truth and understanding in the lives of Black girls, who make up a large population of school classrooms. Given the reductive narrative about Black girls' literacy achievement that is used to justify and frame academic exclusionary practices that masquerade as interventions, along with the disjointed ways in which others have defined Black girlhood, many of the contributors in this volume have created curricular interventions and/or programs to cultivate students' identities, literacies, and social activism through multiliteracies.

We are excited that this edited volume is the first to bring together the work of Black women literacy scholars and researchers speaking and writing truth to the literate lives of Black girls in classrooms. Each author is working to change dominant narratives on Black girls in education and to advance theoretical and empirical research on Black girls' literacies. The volume will serve as a significant resource for educators, researchers, and policy makers on ways to improve practices and educational spaces to advance literacy achievement for Black girls and, thus, for all youth.

## Overview of the Edited Volume

The authors of the edited volume describe approaches to cultivating Black girls' literacies within and beyond school contexts, specifically approaches that counter the harmful conditions that Black girls face in school and that bolster the gendered, racial, and cultural knowledge they bring with them to school. Each chapter comes together to provide readers with a comprehensive view of the historical and contemporary issues impacting Black girls' literacies. The volume represents a comprehensive literature review on Black girls' literacies in the fields of literacy and English education and in education research more broadly. It situates Black girls' literacies within the broader conversations about an inclusive, social justice-oriented education. The volume also highlights transformative and empowering pedagogies that draw on 21st century literacies and digital technologies to position Black girls as creators and knowledge producers in the classroom and beyond. Taken together, each chapter in the volume contributes to a collaborative and dialogic project from Black women literacy educators and researchers, all deeply committed to ensuring that the needs and interests of Black girls are central in the agenda to advance literacy education for all students.

The kitchen table represents, physically and symbolically, an inclusive space for Black girls and women to come together, to be seen, to be heard, and to just be. The kitchen table signifies the rich history of our foremothers and grandmothers who sat at the kitchen table, where, beyond gossip and social talk, women bare their souls and receive healing and affirmation in the company of their sisters. We embrace the notion of "sitting at the kitchen table" as a reflection of our collective desire to transform spaces by sharing our experiences and asserting our voices.

The edited volume is organized into four sections. It begins with a brief introduction from the volume editors that discusses the significance of the Black Girls' Literacies Framework (BGLF) (Muhammad & Haddix, 2016) to the related theme and synthesizes the focus of each chapter; it ends with kitchen table dialogue between the section contributors and a leading Black woman scholar in that area. Chapters are organized across these four sections: Creating Spaces for Black Girls' Literacies; Black Girls' Language and Literacy Practices; Reading Black Girlhood in Literature; and Centering Black Girls' Digital Literacies. Chapter authors in the first section, Creating Spaces for Black Girls' Literacies, theorize and concretize the construct of Black girls' spaces as a necessary condition for Black girls' literacies to thrive. Each author highlights theoretical and empirical research on what it means to create spaces by, for, and with Black girls and women. Section 2, Black Girls' Language and Literacy Practices, includes studies of the linguistic practices and literacy practices of Black girls and women. Chapter authors in Section 2 explore dominant discourses (see Richardson for reclaiming of Gee's theory) on what it means to be a Black girl through the discourse study of their linguistic and literacy practices. This exploration of Black girls' identities through language and discourse is inclusive of race, gender, sexuality, class, and religion, among other identity markers. Section 3, Reading Black Girlhood Literature, features current research on Black girls and women's reading and meaning-making practices and the representation of Black girls' literacies in literature and texts. The chapter authors disrupt monolithic treatment of Black girls' identities through the study of literature and text representations that offer an intersectional understanding of Black girlhood and womanhood. They underscore the importance of Black girls seeing their whole selves reflecting back in the texts they read both within and beyond school curricula. In the fourth section of the volume, Centering Black Girls' Digital Literacies, the chapter authors present work that looks at the ways Black girls are creating and engaging with digital tools and social media as critical literacy practices. The featured scholarship in this section emphasizes how digital literacies empower Black girls to counter dominant narratives about Black girls and women within mainstream spaces and to generate knowledge outside of school-sanctioned expectations. The collection concludes with an afterword by Dr. Elaine Richardson and a postscript from the Black Girls' Literacies Collective (Reprint, Research in the Teaching of English, 2018).

As Black women scholars and teacher educators, we write and edit chapters in this text in solidarity, sisterhood, and love. We are mindful that our own editing and approach must be in the same spirit of sisterhood that Black girls need in schools and classrooms. Editing this volume was a labor of love and pain as we continued to see assaults and murders of Black women and girls in society and within schools. Yet, we remain hopeful when we see the continued progress and striving of sister scholars and teachers as they work tirelessly to share the voices and needs of Black women and girls. Therefore, we hope that this is a contribution to create better experiences for Black girls across spaces, because they deserve a full and quality life so that they are able to reach their full potential and magic.

## Notes

1. National Association for the Advancement of Colored People Legal Defense Fund "Unlocking Opportunity for African American Girls, A Call to Action for Educational Equity", 2014
2. Ibid.
3. National Coalition on Black Civic Participation, Black Women's Roundtable Report, 2014

## References

Collective, B. G. L. (2018). In dialogue. *Research in the Teaching of English, 53*(2), 173.

Evans-Winters, V. E. (2005). *Teaching Black girls: Resiliency in urban classrooms* (vol. 279). New York: Peter Lang.

Evans-Winters, V. E., & Esposito, J. (2010). Other people's daughters: Critical race feminism and Black girls' education. *Educational Foundations, 24*, 11–24.

Frazier-Kouassi, S. (2002). Race and gender at the crossroads: African American females in school. *African American Research Perspectives, 8*(1), 151–162.

Grant, L. (1992). Race and the schooling of young girls. *Education and Gender Equality*, 91–113.

Martin, J., & Smith, J. (2017). Subjective discipline and the social control of Black girls in pipeline schools. *Journal of Urban Learning, Teaching, and Research, 13*, 63–72.

Morris, E. W. (2007). "Ladies" or "loudies"? Perceptions and experiences of Black girls in classrooms. *Youth & Society, 38*(4), 490–515.

Muhammad, G. E. (2020). *Cultivating genius: An equity model for culturally and historically responsive literacy*. New York: Scholastic.

Muhammad, G. E., & Haddix, M. (2016). Centering Black girls' literacies: A review of literature on the multiple ways of knowing of Black girls. *English Education, 48*(4), 299–336.

Richardson, E. (2002). "To protect and serve": African American female literacies. *College Composition and Communication*, 675–704.

Rollock, N. (2007). Why Black girls don't matter: Exploring how race and gender shape academic success in an inner-city school. *Support for Learning, 22*(4), 197–202.

Royster, J. J. (2000). *Traces of a stream: Literacy and social change among African American women.* Pittsburgh, PA: University of Pittsburgh Press.

Smith, E. J. (1982). The Black female adolescent: A review of the educational, career and psychological literature. *Psychology of Women Quarterly, 6*(3), 261–288.

# SECTION 1

# Creating Spaces for Black Girls' Literacies

# 1

# EXPLORATIONS OF LITERACY AND BLACK GIRLHOOD IN OUT-OF-BOUND SPACES

*Erica Womack*

## Where Can Black Girls Go to Simply Be?

Black girls are increasingly finding ways to fully exploit their ways of knowing and behaving on their own and in spaces of their own choosing; therefore, it is necessary to understand and consider how literacy can look in all-Black, all-female centered settings. In Muhammad and Haddix's (2016) conceptualization of Black girls' literacies, they underscore the function of literacies in self-actualizing identity construction in Black girl settings. They define these Black and female spaces as *literacy collaboratives* or "socially constructed spaces to improve and advance literacy development among a group of learners with varying identities, experiences, and literacy experiences" (Muhammad & Haddix, 2016, pp. 412–413; Tatum, 2013). These are spaces in which Black girls possess power and permission to name themselves for themselves. Unfortunately, this kind of affirming Black girl identity formation and literacy engagement often goes unrecognized and unrealized in traditional classroom spaces (Evans-Winters, 2011; Fordham, 1993; Morris, 2007), hence the critical need to shift Black girlhood from the margin to the center (hooks, 2000) of the curriculum. It is also true that this shift often happens in the private sanctums of other Black people or in what I refer to as *out-of-bound spaces*. In this chapter, I highlight the voices, identities, and literacies of Black girls in *out-of-bound spaces*, which I define as individually and collectively constructed spaces that offer a sense of belonging, bonding, safety, seclusion, and interconnectedness by and for Black girls.

Collins (2009) believes such out-of-bound sites constitute "safe space" (p. 111) where Black girls can simply be, without apology or question. Traditionally, the Black church and other Black organizations have served as physical representations of safe space, yet Black female friendships, Black mother–daughter relationships, and Black women and girls' day-to-day conversations provide security as well (Collins, 2009; hooks, 1993). The same is true of creative expression (e.g., music, art, and literature), which is often emblematic of the deep intricacies and intimacies that exist between and amongst Black girls (Collins, 2009). Collins asks, "if we [Black women and girls] will not listen to one another, who will?" (p. 114).

In this chapter, I address how Black girls ascribe meaning to their own lives in out-of-bound spaces and the ways in which educators and researchers can foster such spaces to uplift and actively resist oppression as it pertains to the lives of Black girls. I consider the following questions: *How does the notion of out-of-bound space figure into the lives of Black girls?* and, *How do Black girls "do" literacy (or the ways in which Black girls read, write, speak, move, and create) in such spaces?* I address the role(s) educators and researchers can play in supporting the development of these spaces (along with Black girls' literacy practices) in classrooms and beyond. I draw from my study of an out-of-bound space (i.e., a reserved area of the library) I co-constructed with Black girls over a period of two years. In this space, I facilitated dialogue with Black girls around topics of race/ism, school, friendship, intimacy, misogyny, and more as we also sought to disrupt public ideologies of Black girls (e.g., unladylike, abrasive, defiant). As such, our use of literacy practices—reading, writing, speaking, listening, moving, grooving, creating, and viewing—resulted in our own critical self-awareness and in the construction of a much broader narrative of what it means to be young, female, and Black.

## The Hush Harbor: Where Black Women Go to Simply Be

Though Black women have always dared to speak and write publicly—often in the presence of openly hostile and threatening environments—their individual and collective need for privacy has remained strong. In the comfort and seclusion of Black women's clubs, community organizations, literary societies, and sororities, as well as the kitchen, front porch, and church pew, Black women found greater assurance in their voices being heard and in their humanity being acknowledged (hooks, 1993; Nunley, 2004, 2011; Richardson, 2013). Within such confines, Black women collectively marshaled against gender-, race-, and class-based exploitation. It was there, in the presence of other Black female bodies, that the seeds of activism, engagement, togetherness, and love were sown. In these historically named "hush harbors" (Nunley, 2004, 2011), the intersections of language, literacy, and spatiality were most significant; it was where many Black women and girls first learned to read and write, and it was there that many first claimed their right to free speech.

To that end, the Black hair salon is, perhaps, the finest example of what a contemporary Black female hush harbor or out-of-bound space looks and feels like (Majors, Kim, & Ansari, 2009; Nunley, 2004, 2011). These are spaces in which Black women gather to affirm one another's being and to see visions of themselves in one another as "they form prime locations for resisting objectification as *the* [emphasis added] Other" (Collins, 2009, p. 111). In Black hair salons, Black *is* beautiful. Majors (2015) emphasizes the role of the Black hair salon in preserving African American discourse and language and the implications these kinds of communal exchanges have for how Black students may best learn. In these kinds of spaces, Black students are seen as active producers of meaning as opposed to active consumers of materials. The author thus articulates the need to restructure the classroom as safe space for non-mainstream literacies and languages to live and thrive.

Undoubtedly, social media platforms like Facebook, Instagram, YouTube, and Tik Tok have made it much easier for Black girls to negotiate space and speech in a variety of ways (Price-Dennis, 2016; Greene, 2016), while the boundaries between public and private are left tenuous at best. Yet for the alternative, hidden, suppressed, unacknowledged, and/or marginalized literacies of Black girls, the security of the hush harbor or out-of-bound space is there. Oftentimes, these are the only spaces in which the reading, writing, speaking, performing, and envisioning of Black girls is accounted for. Each of the following studies offers possibilities for engaging Black girls in oppositional readings of Black female identity and for co-designing spaces to address their needs and interests on topics ranging from love, school, and beauty to pain, hardship, and healing.

## Out-of-Bound Spaces in the Lives of Black Girls

In a year-long study of urban high school female youth, Wissman (2009/2011) explored the intersectionality of youth agency, literacy, and gender in an elective writing course entitled "Sistahs." Wissman found that although these young women (most of whom are African American) recognized the hampering effects of gender role constructions, the formal educational spaces to challenge these ideologies did not readily exist. In the "Sistahs" course, however, the girls actively constructed a space that supported their ways of both seeing and being in the world. It was there that the girls in Wissman's study confronted limiting gender roles and expectations through photography and poetry as they redefined prevailing notions of beauty, strength, and intellect as well as various misconceptions of young urban minoritized women.

Similarly, Thein and Schmidt (2017) created an after-school book club, Strong Girls Read Strong Books, to support the literacy and identity development of a diverse group of elementary school-aged girls. Book club leaders were encouraged to engage in critical witnessing (or a deep kind of listening to stories of pain and trauma) to challenge their own assumptions and biases about what it means for girls to read, write, tell stories, and collaborate with others. In this space, Rhonda, a biracial undergraduate book club leader, was forced to grapple with her misconceptions of Daniela, a Black 4th grader, as a book club participant (e.g., questioning Daniela's actual reading of the book, viewing Daniela as resistant for reading apart from the group). Nevertheless, as the semester went on, Rhonda grew to see Daniela's literary understandings, journal writings, and poetry from a strength perspective instead.

The Black girls in Muhammad's (2012/2015) study exercised writing as a tool of resistance akin to the vibrant Black female literary societies and liberation movements of the nineteenth and twentieth centuries. Muhammad formed this literacy collaborative of Black girls, ages 11–17, at a large urban Midwestern university to explore how a co-constructed, self-affirming space (in comparison to traditional academic spaces) contributed to the girls' identity formation and literacy engagement. By bringing a historicized view to the course content, Muhammad encouraged the girls to recognize their work as part of the broader Black woman tradition that includes Anna Julia Cooper, Harriet Jacobs, and Toni Morrison, among many others. Muhammad found that the girls delighted in the freedom to express their authentic selves in this space—to not have to doubt who they were, what they said, and what they believed. Muhammad then contends that culturally relevant text selection coupled with interactive writing exchanges are key to creating self-affirming spaces for Black girls to learn.

Brown's (2009/2014) Saving Our Lives Hear Our Truths (or SOLHOT) after-school program is another example of the kind of relationships that can emerge when critical and affirming dialogue (hooks, 1993) occurs within an out-of-bound space. In SOLHOT, Black girlhood is not only celebrated by both women and girls but also treated as part of a lifelong experience. As members of SOLHOT, Black women and girls used reading, writing, singing, rapping, dancing, and acting to connect to one another and their histories and to construct counternarratives of Black female literacies and identities. To engage in this work, Brown (2009/2014) and the other adult women employed a hip-hop feminist pedagogy to resist and transform popular belief about Black women and girls.

When Black girls have lacked the physical space and support for empowerment, digital outlets have also become necessary. When Kynard (2010) and a group of college-age Black women found themselves in need of both, they elected to form their own digital posse, or "cyber sista-cipher" (p. 34). Kynard likens these digital spaces to the "hush harbor," replete "with plotting, scheming, and planning that no one else in the institution seemed to imagine was happening" (p. 34). As members of this digital sistahood, these women were able to engage in frank discussions about their places in the university and in the world at large. Not only that, this out-of-bound space afforded them opportunities to reconstruct images of Black girlhood.

As the examples in the aforementioned research studies indicate, these all-Black and/or all-female spaces are not only spaces out-of-bound, but opportunities for Black girls to live, learn, love, and laugh together openly and honestly. Collins (2009) believes such spaces serve a greater purpose as sites of resistance that also offer Black girls' opportunities to combat the daily assaults on Black girlhood (see also, Morris, 2019). These assaults include the marginalization, misrepresentations, and physical assaults on their bodies in society. Collins further asserts that some topics may be off limits to those who are not Black and/or not female, as these are spaces created for us by us. Yet, the fragile nature of these spaces cannot also be denied. Wissman's "Sistah" space, for instance, was shut down after one year and the women in Kynard's research had little place else to meet but online and in secret. For these reasons, Collins urges us (and those who ally with us) to remain vigilant in understanding how Black girls may be "empowered and disempowered, even within allegedly safe spaces" (p. 132).

## Planning Our Black Girl Out-of-Bound Space

My research into how out-of-bound spaces figure into the lives of Black girls and how they "do" literacy in such spaces is drawn from data collected during a two-year period in which I worked with Black girls between the ages of 14 and 21 for 90 minutes once a week. The girls and I met in a reserved section of a library that is part of a network of libraries located within a large metropolitan city in the Midwest. Our space consisted of a room with a whiteboard, TV cart, several long tables, multi-colored plastic chairs, and mostly bare, off-white walls. We were typically seated around a large table facing one another with the digital camcorder positioned behind and/or beside us in order to capture what was taking place in each of our activities.

During our weekly sessions, I facilitated most of the activities—meaning I often selected what we read or the prompts we responded to, which included: 1) analyzing fiction and non-fiction literature, media ads, and music videos, 2) writing autobiographical pieces, poetry, and reader responses, and 3) interrogating representations of race, class, and gender as a way to center the girls' experiences. Later in the year, I introduced the girls to the concept of autoethnography[1] and we each designed self-selected and self-reflective projects in order to strengthen our understanding of self and the world around us. The girls and I collected literacy artifacts related to our topics (e.g., photographs, text, video, images, etc.) and created culminating digital products (using such digital tools as Prezi and Pinterest) to share with family and friends. Additionally, it was important that I be just as critical of my own lived experience as a Black girl and exhibit the same level of vulnerability as the girls did themselves. Reflecting upon my experiences helped me to remember the essence of Black girlhood—to see the girls as more than just participants and to recognize myself as more than just a researcher.

To best address my research questions—*How does the notion of out-of-bound space figure into the lives of Black girls?* and *How do Black girls "do" literacy in such spaces?*—I relied on data from: note-taking in a research journal, videotaped recordings of weekly meetings, videotaped interviews with participants (see Appendix A), writings by participants, and other literacy artifacts that were utilized or produced (e.g., readings, journals, collaborative work) in our meetings. Because I facilitated most of our activities, I wrote down everything I could recall in my journal immediately following each meeting—what happened that day, a (preliminary) analysis of what happened, and what to consider in the coming week(s) based upon what took place during that particular meeting. Nevertheless, the overarching goal of each session was to be mindful of what the girls stated they were interested in and to use that information to inform our activity for that day.

I looked at data primarily from the standpoint of these three young women: 1) Chyvae,[2] a 15-year-old high school sophomore who attended a magnet alternative high school across town, 2) Jordan, a 15-year-old high school sophomore who attended a predominately White suburban high school and who later transferred to a more racially diverse STEM school, and 3) Nikayla, an 18-year-old high school dropout. Chyvae, Jordan, and Nikayla were each chosen as focal participants because of their higher rate of attendance, range in personality, and use of literacy in this space. I held a minimum of two 30-minute interviews with each of the young women that shed light on their lived experiences, their engagement in various literacy practices (i.e., reading, writing, and speaking acts), and how these practices framed their perceptions of themselves and the world around them.

I used a narrative analysis approach that Riessman (2008) identifies as "a family of methods for interpreting texts that have in common a storied form" (p. 11) to analyze how the girls do literacy in this space. With this approach, emphasis is placed on "what," "how," and "why" a story is being told in a particular way. According to Riessman (2008), thematic narrative analysis is the most common form of narrative analysis, where individuals' stories are kept "'intact' by theorizing from the case rather than from component themes (categories) across cases" (p. 53). Furthermore, one's analysis of data is generally based upon pre-existing theory.

I began my analysis by examining each girl's literacy artifacts as a whole—I reread each of the artifacts multiple times and created thematic categories in light of prior theory related to race, space, and literacy in the lives of Black women and girls. I then drew possible conclusions that could best address my research questions. I coded and triangulated data from the interviews, videotaped recordings of meetings (including literacy artifacts utilized during the meetings), and my researcher journal to consider how the notion of out-of-bound space figures into the lives of Black girls and how Black girls "do" literacy in such spaces. In the next section, I present findings based on my participants' literacy engagements in our out-of-bound space.

## Black Girl Doing Literacy in Out-of-Bound Spaces

### Nikayla

I can recall Nikayla seeming only slightly interested when I approached her about my study, and thus I was pleasantly surprised when she arrived at our first meeting. With her voice barely above a whisper, Nikayla shared that she and her family had recently moved from Chicago, Illinois, and that because she had been expelled from a nearby high school, she was now being home-schooled. Most significantly, Nikayla revealed that she had been a recent victim of sexual abuse. Although we were technically strangers, I imagined Nikayla felt some sort of connection to the group and/or sense of comfort in being within an out-of-bound (i.e., all-Black and all-female) space. Perhaps Nikayla also took solace in the fact that she was there to speak, and we were there to listen. Nonetheless, Nikayla remained somewhat of an enigma for the remainder of the year—she spoke very little in our meetings and remained rather mum during her initial interview.

It is largely through Nikayla's writing that I got to know her better. In one of our written exchanges, for example, Nikayla shared how much she enjoys performing for others:

> Nikayla Monroe my break was great i chilled with my family and friends and threw a lil party and dance all threw the night then me and my brother rapped for my family I love rapping i have three notebooks full of raps i love music and i love doing shows and dancing but now i'm just trying to get a group together.
>
> *(Nikayla, journal, Winter 2010)*

I then responded by gently nudging her to share her talents with the rest of us:

> First off, keep writing and growing as a writer. I think or should I say I know you have great potential. I think I already told you my favorite [poem] out of these is "Me, Myself, and I." Hopefully, we can grow to all want to read our work aloud for one another. Maybe next quarter, as we're still in the process of getting to know one another. I'm hoping that you will choose to do so as I'm sure you'll get positive feedback from the group . . .

Because I also wanted the girls to engage in alternative approaches to writing, I introduced them to autoethnography and proposed that they film their autoethnographic work. We decided to drive to a nearby park to film, and with TT[3] behind the camera, Nikayla revealed her most intimate feelings about her body and its impact on her relationships with others:

NIKAYLA: . . . [White women] don't really have responsibility.

TT: So what kind of responsibility?

NIKAYLA: Just everything. Got to deal wit the name-calling and—. Because I matured faster, faster than what I supposed to. And I always got that I was a fast little girl. And I was (inaudible) cause my breasts was bigger (laughs) then ah, then the normal 10-year-old and so I was always called the little fast little girl. Didn't nobody parents want they kids hanging out wit me cause I matured quicker than they did. So they thought I was having sex and stuff and no. My mama! Y'all must—I'm like they must not look at my mom. (TT laughs). And that's basically what—to me what black females have to go through now is the name-calling and people talking about us. And stuff like that.

*(Nikayla, park interview)*

For several weeks thereafter, TT and I helped Nikayla and the other girls to develop autoethnographic products through the use of Windows Movie-Maker and PowerPoint, and at our very last session for the year, Nikayla bravely stood to share her autoethnography with family and friends. Once we began meeting again the following year, Nikayla seemed much more self-assured and outspoken around the other girls, many of whom were several years younger. No longer shy or timid, she took on the role of sage, eager to pass on her own knowledge and experience, which included "giving [the other girls] advice on smoking, relationships, getting out of the streets . . . like school and work" (Nikayla, initial interview). Because Nikayla wished for others to learn from her mistakes, she later volunteered to facilitate a few of our group sessions and crafted her own writing prompts for us to consider: "How would you rate yourself and why?" (on a scale of 1–10, with 1 being the lowest and 10 being the highest) and "What type of guy fits you?" Though Nikayla had designed these questions with specific participants in mind, I concluded that these questions were also derived from her own personal struggles with confidence and esteem. Nikayla rated herself a 5½ or 6 (and admitted she would have rated herself lower in the past) whereas most of the other girls rated themselves a 7 or 8. I appreciated Nikayla's honesty and thoughtfulness, however, as these were the kind of emotional and analytical responses that arose in the safety and seclusion of our space.

## Chyvae

Unlike some of the other girls, Chyvae seemed comfortable in her own skin and willing to expose both her assets and flaws to the rest of us. Her willingness to open up became evident the day she shared aloud her body map:[4]

People say—Okay, I put for brain [pointing at the head on her body map] they say, "It's empty." I'm loco. I don't think. I'm stupid. I'm crazy. I'm an idiot. I'm insane, slow, and evil, but nice. My eyes—everyone says they're pretty. My nose—adorable freckles and nosy. My mouth—they say I talk a lot. Need to say how I feel. They say I can sing. They say I can't sing. They say I have a smart mouth. They say I'm sarcastic and I'm silly . . . Then my heart, the nice side. Everyone says I'm sympathetic. Well, I think I'm sympathetic. And then some people say I'm too nice. And I'm say I'm too nice.

As we finished discussing our body maps, conversation later turned to Chyvae's racial identity and "her really light eyes." Chyvae claimed that her mother was biracial and referred to her a second time as "that woman who gave birth to me," which inevitably prompted further questions from the other girls:

JORDAN:  You seem to have some strong hostility against her. Want to talk about it?

CHYVAE:  I don't like her because she's not on drugs and she's not dead, but yet she doesn't want to take care of her children. So therefore she's in the right state of mind. Nothing is wrong with her. But she don't wanna take care of her child—her children. Her five kids that she made with one man.

AMORA:  That's the same thing wit my aunt. That's how she is. She got five kids. They were all together. They were married. She just told him she couldn't do it no more, so she left.

CHYVAE:  . . . She can handle it. I know she can . . . I mean, there's nothing wrong with her. . .

CJ:  Do you live wit your grandparents?

CHYVAE:  I live with my grandma, but yet again, my dad takes care of us. Like he comes over. He makes sure everything's alright. He goes and gets food and everything.

*(conversation during weekly session)*

Given that Chyvae also possessed the gift of gab, I would sometimes encourage her to record rather than share her thoughts aloud, as in the case below:

> Today's Upsetting Situation
>
> Today this girl ask me if I still liked girls. Like omg wtf wow like did she really just ask me that. I told her straight up "I never in my life liked girls." She gonna tell me I'm lying. Woah this trick just crossed the line. She lucky I'm not like the rest of these immature girls out here or she would've got slapped . . . The situation stuck in my head all day. I really hope that whore don't go around spreading rumors. I was never lesbian or bisexual. I only have, is, and will like boys and men when I'm older. Never have I told anyone I like girls. That's not me. No offense to anyone who is. I have no problem with people who are bisexual or lesbian. I'm upset because she for one ask me that in front of all her friends . . . I wish I wasn't so nice and just slapped that rat.
>
> *(Chyvae, journal exchange)*

Because I wanted Chyvae to know I valued her experiences, I responded back to her a week later:

> Wow. I see why you were so fired up to talk last week. I'm glad you wrote all of this down. Perhaps, it got you to calm down. At least I hope. Are

you sure this girl wasn't trying to test you in some way, to see what your reaction might be? I have never experienced anything like that before, so I wouldn't know exactly what to tell you. I guess kids are bolder these days. . .

On another note, I am so happy that you decided to join us. I see that you have a lot of keen insights on life and I think it is really important for the others to hear your perspective on how to relate to people of . . . Keep sharing! We're listening! Write me back when you can.

*(journal exchange)*

In my response, I also praised Chyvae's awareness of and appreciation for diversity. Chyvae's respect for differences was due in part to her school's racially diverse student population. Chyvae understood the importance of relating to all types of people and of using language so as not to offend others. I witnessed Chyvae's stern reaction to June and Jordan's use of the words "dumb" and "retarded" when she stated: "Y'all are mean . . . Y'all should be a little more nicer. Y'all can use other words like 'mentally challenged' . . . you know. Everyone is dumb in something." Like Nikayla, Chyvae took hold of these opportunities to learn with and teach to her peers. For Chyvae, it was important that our space offered opportunities to testify, but to also correct and challenge others' assumptions when necessary.

## Jordan

Like Chyvae, Jordan rarely shied away from opportunities to talk. Jordan was the first volunteer to share her body map and began with the following disclaimer: "So I mean like this big [word] 'ugly' [written in the middle of her body map] wasn't meant to be that big. It just turned out to be that big." Jordan continued by stating, "But, yeah, *people* [emphasis added] say I'm pretty, a sassy bitch, fake, people tend to call me, 'June,' my sister a lot, nice, loud-mouthed, hostile, intelligent, easy-going, crazy, beautiful, impulsive, loud, obnoxious, angry, feisty, lazy, stubborn, big-headed." The other descriptions Jordan did not read aloud included: nappy, cool, talkative, and fat. And though Jordan told us she felt none of these descriptions were negative, I wondered how many of these labels she had internalized.

I later discovered that Jordan and her twin sister, June, deeply resented growing up in predominantly White neighborhoods. During one particular group session, I had asked the girls to develop a list of 20 questions related to their autoethnographic topics and to share these aloud in a read-around.[5] Rather than focus on "I-centric" questions (as did most of the other girls), Jordan chose to draft questions that help her to further explore the mindset of her White peers. When Jordan asked: "Why do White people wear shorts in the winter?" or "Why do White people think it's okay to say, 'Nigga?,'" she is perceiving her White peers (or "White people") as Other or (their thoughts and behaviors) as different from her(s) as a young Black woman. Yet embedded within these questions is the idea that she has been "Othered," particularly when she asks: "Why are they [her White peers] so fascinated by my hair?," "Why do White boys hook up and talk to me in private, but deny it in public?," and "Why are White people obsessed with the 'ghetto booty?'" Jordan's questions also reveal her encounters with everyday racism and her desire to resist such thought and behavior (Collins, 2009).

I sensed that Jordan was struggling to find her identity as a Black girl in majority-White environments. Yet I also sensed her struggles were part of the reason why she seemed unaffected by her engagement in what some might consider "risky" behavior. Every week, Jordan and her sister shared tales of experimenting with drugs and alcohol, sneaking out of their bedroom windows, or hanging out on campus with the college crowd. And every week, at least one of them ended up on punishment. The girls, too, were not shy about expressing their disdain for their parents, despite the fact that their father drove nearly half an hour to bring them to the library each week. And their mother seemed to be at a loss on how to handle them as she often called or texted me for updates. Not wanting to break June and Jordan's trust, however, I chose not to divulge too much about what they wrote or talked about in our meetings.

Because I experienced my own frustration with the twins, I frequently stayed after to express my feelings to TT. Likewise, Amora, Nikayla, and Shey (each of whom participated in both years of my study) voiced their concerns regarding June and Jordan's "immaturity" and behavior. Though Amora and Nikayla were willing to offer the twins advice (e.g., regarding relationships, "how they feel about themselves," "the definition between respect and disrespect"), Shey wondered whether I might ask the twins to leave. For these reasons, I worried about the negative energy June and Jordan brought to our group. Too often I felt as though my plans were being derailed and I became not only a researcher, but disciplinarian as well.

Nevertheless, I kept reminding myself that June and Jordan came to the sessions for a reason—not for me, TT, or even the session topics, but rather to satisfy their own needs as Black girls to be in the company of other Black girls and to be in a space where their thoughts and opinions mattered. In our out-of-bound space, they did not have to worry about fitting in, talkin' or actin' White, being "authentically" Black, or having the right look; here, they could just be.

Mid-year Jordan transferred to a new school with a STEM (science, technology, engineering, and math) focus and a more racially and economically diverse student population than her previous one. Before long, Jordan's grades and relationships with her parents began to improve. In our group sessions, Jordan smiled a lot more and contributed to our discussions more readily. At the same time, Jordan also began to embrace her own individuality. She was no longer just "June's sister," "the twins," or "*one of* the twins"; Jordan was now simply Jordan.

Perhaps this shift in attitude also led to her change in topic, since Jordan found she was no longer interested in exploring her experiences in predominantly

White schools. For months, Jordan had been unable to settle on a topic, however, that all changed the day she, Ms. A (one of the after-school library homework helpers), and I began to discuss our feelings about our (Black) hair:

ME: All of it is good. . .
JORDAN: My hair's not good hair.
ME: Find the right stylist.
Ms. A: That's what you think.
ME: I think I told you guys I haven't had a perm in like two years.
MS. A: . . . The sad thing is that we don't know how to treat our hair in its natural state. We think we got to go somewhere else, but we were born with it. We should know how to care for our hair ourselves.
ME: Right. I agree.
JORDAN: I don't know how to care for my hair.
ME: Look that can be your topic—HAIR!

*(Conversation during weekly session)*

Though Jordan's emotional wounds cut real deep (as evidenced all the way back to the presentation of her body map), she fortunately agreed to choose her hair as the subject of her autoethnography. Jordan used our out-of-bound space as a place to process the collective pain and pride that many Black women and girls have experienced with their hair. But, more importantly, Jordan utilized our space to begin her own process of healing.

## Bearing Witness to Black Girls' Literacies, Love, Joy, and Healing

In reviewing one of my original research questions, *How does the notion of out-of-bound space figure into the lives of Black girls?*, I find that our out-of-bound space fostered: 1) the sharing of intimate, often painful details of one's life and 2) concern for others' well-being. In this space, I witnessed laughter, tears, chatter, giggles, giving, and taking. But above all, I witnessed a genuine act of love. Therefore, our out-of-bound space became a space that honored our innermost thoughts and desires and affirmed our beings. Given the levels of mental, emotional, spiritual, and physical anguish that many Black women and girls experience, hooks finds dialogue to be the best remedy: "It is important that black people talk to one another, that we talk with friends and allies, for the telling of our stories enables us to name our pain, our suffering, and to seek healing" (pp. 16–17). The power of our space resonated in the fact that Nikayla opted to reveal one of the most traumatic experiences of her life, even with knowing very little about us. Each of the girls also viewed our out-of-bound space as a place for sharing their deepest struggles with body image and with negotiating race, class, gender, and sexuality outside of our space, in particular. In our written exchange, Chyvae shifted from disbelief to worry to anger in how her sexuality had been "labeled" by a peer, stating that "I really hope that whore don't go around spreading rumors."

In our out-of-bound space, the girls expressed their authentic feelings about themselves and those around them. For these reasons, Chyvae and Jordan each felt open to discuss their estrangement from certain family members. Jordan's simple inquiry, "You want to talk about it?" also demonstrated how concerns for one another were borne out of this space. Likewise, Nikayla and others advocated on Jordan and her twin sister's behalf and were willing to find other ways to re-engage them in our group by asking "how they fe[lt] about themselves" and "the definition between respect and disrespect." Nikayla aimed to uplift rather than ostracize other Black girls—behaviors she admitted were mostly foreign to her past. Nikayla also wished to use her experiences to help the twins and others to "get . . . out of the streets" and learn from her mistakes. In other ways, Chyvae expressed concern for the twins' use of offensive language and suggested inoffensive terminology instead.

In reference to my second question, I find that these Black girls primarily "do" literacy through: 1) written exchange, 2) visual representation, and 3) *collective processing* in our out-of-bound space. In our space, I encouraged the girls to write to me and to one another, and it was only through our written exchange that I discovered Nikayla's passion for writing, rapping, and performing. Writing afforded Chyvae other means of channeling her frustrations; however, our exchange also provided me with insights on why she felt these emotions. We could not just record our thoughts for our own consumption, but rather needed to relay our thoughts to each other. We also could not just draft questions on paper without also reading them aloud to each other. The same is also true for Nikayla, as she developed her own writing prompts with the intent to share with others within our space.

Visual representations were also critical to how we "did" literacy by working against competing ideas and images of Black girls. For example, Chyvae's body map illustrates how she understands herself and, in turn, how she is understood by others, which Collins (2009) says "question[s] not only what has been said about African women [and girls] but the credibility and the intentions of those possessing the power to define" (p. 126). In our out-of-bound space we used digital media—camcorders, Windows MovieMaker, PowerPoint—as tools to both question and challenge the inequities around us. Nikayla, for instance, used a camcorder to document how her body had been constructed as deviant or abnormal.

I discovered that as we each sought to unpack our own individual experiences, we were at the same time engaged in a *collective* processing of those same experiences. I refer to these shared understandings as such in that our processing engendered more than just self-reflexivity, but also collective consciousness-raising. I found this dynamic to be reflective of the interactions between and among myself and the girls, for we in many ways authored one another's stories as we endeavored to speak and write our own. Chyvae decided to explore the effects of her mother's absence early on in the year, and as she began to share her story, I noted how other participants like Amora shared their understandings of similar experiences with their own family members. Hearing both Chyvae and Amora's stories thus contributed to our collective understanding of the complex nature of motherhood and mothering. I also noted how Nikayla's struggles with confidence and self-esteem impelled her to develop writing prompts and to process her own feelings of self-worth through the experiences of others.

The notion of collective processing, however, is most evident with Jordan, Ms. A., and myself. We each collectively processed our experiences and understanding of Black hair, which ultimately influenced Jordan to explore the topic of hair for her autoethnography. Similar to Nikayla, Jordan was interested in understanding her hair struggles within a larger collective of Black women and girls who have internalized negative beliefs about themselves (see also hooks, 1993) and who have also found ways to resist these previously held notions by collectively working through their struggles.

## Bringing Black Girls In-Bound in Education and Research

I defined out-of-bound spaces as "individually and collectively constructed spaces that offer a sense of belonging, bonding, safety, seclusion, and interconnectedness." In out-of-bound spaces, Black girls read, write, speak, move, and create against gender-, race-, and class-based exploitation. These are spaces in which Black girlhood thrives; yet, I argue that many classroom spaces do not exhibit such characteristics. Therefore, this study has implications for the role educators and researchers can play in supporting the development of these spaces (along with Black girls' literacy practices) in the classroom and beyond. Moving such work in-bound (i.e., in classroom spaces) then encourages all—Black girls, their teachers, and their non-Black and/or female peers—to work collectively to disrupt the "single story" (see Adichie, 2009) of Black girlhood.

Often in the rush to get through the content or lecture, teachers may ignore the time and the space Black girls (and indeed, all youth) need to interrogate their lives and the world around them. Even as a former high school English teacher, I, too, neglected to establish an ethic of caring, comfort, and connection as the cornerstone of my pedagogy. It was not until I began working with these young women that I gained clarity and a better sense of my role as a researcher and as an educator. The Black girls in my study engage in resistance toward common stereotypes of Black girlhood with regard to hair, body image, and intellect. I am arguing, then, that these kinds of resistance practices deserve our support within and outside of the classroom. Because Black girls are already thinking about these issues, out-of-bound spaces are often essential. Based on the themes I uncovered previously, I offer these suggestions for creating out-of-bound spaces for and with Black girls:

- Seek Black girls' input on what such spaces can look like
- Create opportunities for Black girls to share their stories and to offer and receive encouragement from others who look like them
- Engage in reading, writing, and speaking experiences with Black girls both in and outside of the classroom walls for purposes of acknowledging and actively resisting oppression
- Encourage Black girls to create counternarratives through visual representations of themselves and the world around them
- Encourage Black girls to question themselves and the world around them and to process their understandings as a collective

Teachers must, then, ask: *How can out-of-bound interests and activities be brought in-bound (i.e., in classrooms) for and with Black girls? How can such spaces create opportunities for Black girls to talk and for me to listen? How might the creation of such spaces impact girls as learners? How can I contribute to Black girls' sense of belonging, bonding, safety, seclusion, and interconnectedness within the classroom? What can I do to help ease the strain of Black girls' oppression?* Furthermore, *how can I work to ensure Black girls leave my classroom with a healthy sense of self?* For those of us teaching and learning with Black girls, Brown (2009) makes clear that our task is quite simple: "At the risk of romanticizing Black girls, I think we should listen more. Period. They keep telling us. Know That!" (p. 6). The creation of out-of-bound spaces, then, serves as a worthy endeavor by which to listen to the stories of and by Black girls.

# APPENDIX A

## Sample Interview Questions

- Tell me about yourself.
- How would you describe your school experience?
- What do you like to read about?
- What do you like to write about?
- What is your relationship like with other Black girls?
- How would you describe the past year?
- What goals did you set in the last year and how successful were you in meeting these goals?
- What goals will you set for yourself for the upcoming year?
- What did you get out of being a part of my research study?
- How would you define autoethnography?
- What did you learn from doing your autoethnography?
- Why did you choose to focus on _____ for your autoethnography?
- What more did you learn about yourself?

# Notes

1. Autoethnography is a form of narrative inquiry that combines theory, therapy, description, analysis, concern, and critique (Camangian, 2010; Ellis & Bochner, 2000) and a process of reflection that encourages thinking around the positioning of self within society.
2. Pseudonyms are used for all participants in this study.
3. TT [pseudonym], a Black female doctoral student and colleague, was also added as co-researcher to my study as I felt she would offer a fresh perspective given her interest in youth and community activism.
4. For this activity, I asked the girls to trace their bodies on the floor using a large sheet of butcher paper. I then instructed the girls to write down words and symbols that represent their self-perceptions and how others might view them.
5. For this activity, I instructed the girls to take turns reading aloud one question from their list (without stopping) until each one of them reached the end. Further, I requested that they complete the read-around before asking about and/or responding to one another's questions.

# References

Adichie, C. (2009). *The danger of a single story*. www.ted.com/talks/chimamanda_adichie_the_danger_of_a_single_story.html.

Brown, R. N. (2009). *Black girlhood celebration: Toward a hip-hop feminist pedagogy*. New York: Peter Lang Publishing.

Brown, R. N. (2014). *Hear our truths: The creative potential of Black girlhood*. Urbana, IL: University of Illinois Press.

Camangian, P. (2010). Starting with self: Teaching autoethnography to foster critically caring literacies. *Research in the Teaching of English*, *45*(2), 179–204.

Collins, P. H. (2009). *Black feminist thought: Knowledge, consciousness, and the politics of empowerment*. New York: Routledge.

Ellis, C., & Bochner, A. P. (2000). Autoethnography, personal narrative, reflexivity: Researcher as subject. In N. K. Denzin, & Y. S. Lincoln (Eds.), *Handbook of qualitative research* (2nd ed., pp. 733–768). Thousand Oaks, CA: Sage.

Evans-Winters, V. E. (2011). *Teaching Black girls: Resiliency in urban classrooms* (2nd ed.). New York: Peter Lang.

Fordham, S. (1993). "Those loud Black girls": (Black) women, silence, and gender "passing" in the academy. *Anthropology and Education Quarterly*, *24*(1), 3–32.

Greene, D. T. (2016). We need more "us" in schools!: Centering Black adolescent girls' literacy and language practices in online school spaces. *The Journal of Negro Education*, *85*, 274–289.

hooks, b. (1993). *Sisters of the yam: Black women and recovery*. Cambridge: South End Press.

hooks, b. (2000). *Feminist theory: From margin to center*. Cambridge: South End Press.

Kynard, C. (2010). From candy girls to cyber sista-cipher: Narrating Black female color consciousness and counterstories in and out of school. *Harvard Educational Review*, *80*(1), 30–52.

Majors, Y. (2015). *Shoptalk: Lessons in teaching from an African American hair salon*. New York: Teachers College Press.

Majors, Y., Kim, Y., & Ansari, S. (2009). Beyond hip-hop: A cultural context view of literacy. In L. Christenbury, R. Bomer, & P. Smagorinsky (Eds.), *Handbook of adolescent literacy* (pp. 343–359). New York: The Guildford Press.

Morris, E. (2007). "Ladies" or "loudies"?: Perceptions and experiences of Black girls in classrooms. *Youth & Society, 38*(4), 490–515.

Morris, M. W. (2019). *Sing a rhythm, dance a blues: Education for the liberation of Black and brown girls.* New York, NY: The New Press.

Muhammad, G. E. (2012). Creating spaces for Black adolescent girls to "write it out." *Journal of Adolescent & Adult Literacy, 56*(3), 203–211.

Muhammad, G. E. (2015). The role of literary mentors in writing development: How Black women's literature support the writings of African American adolescent girls. *Journal of Education, 195*(2), 5–14.

Muhammad, G. E., & Haddix, M. (2016). Centering Black girls' literacies: A review of literature on the multiple ways of knowing of Black girls. *English Education, 48*(4), 399–436.

Nunley, V. (2004). From the harbor to da academic hood: Hush harbors and an African American rhetorical tradition. In R. Jackson, & E. Richardson (Eds.), *African American rhetorics: Interdisciplinary perspectives* (pp. 221–242). Carbondale: Southern Illinois University Press.

Nunley, V. (2011). *Keepin' it hushed: The barbershop and African American hush harbor rhetoric.* Detroit: Wayne State University Press.

Price-Dennis, D. (2016). Developing curriculum to support Black girls' literacies in digital spaces. *English Education, 48*(4), 337–361.

Richardson, E. (2003). *African American literacies.* New York Routledge.

Richardson, E. (2013). Developing critical hip hop feminist literacies: Centrality and subversion of sexuality in the lives of Black girls. *Equity & Excellence in Education, 46*(3), 327–341.

Riessman, C. (2008). *Narrative methods for the human sciences.* Thousand Oaks, CA: Sage Publications.

Tatum, A. W. (2013). Fearless voices: Engaging a new generation of African American adolescent male writers. New York: Scholastic.

Thein, A. H., & Schmidt, R. R. (2017). Challenging, rewarding emotion work: Critical witnessing in an after-school book club. *Language Arts, 94*(5), 313–324.

Wissman, K. (2009). Reading and becoming living authors: Urban girls pursuing a poetry of self-definition. *English Journal, 98*(3), 39–45.

Wissman, K. (2011). "Rise up"!: Literacies, lived experiences, and identities within an in-school "other space." *Research in the Teaching of English, 45*(4), 405–438.

# 2

# "OUR STORIES ARE UNIQUELY BEAUTIFUL"

## Black Girls' Preamble Writing in Literacy Collectives

*Francheska Starks, Latasha Mosley, Maya White, and Gholnecsar E. Muhammad*

### Contemporary Views of a Historical Tradition

African American literary societies, such as those founded in Philadelphia, Pennsylvania, in the early 1800s were protected spaces that provided Black Americans access to resources such as reading rooms and libraries to enrich their visions of their histories and identities, to enhance their intellectual repertoire, and to develop their literacy-based knowledge and skillset (Muhammad, 2012, 2020). Within African American literary societies, command of Eurocentric and dominant literacies was viewed as a tool of subversion and recognized for its potential to forward an agenda of liberation for Black people (Bacon & McClish, 2000). Black women in the United States of America have used literacy practices within literary societies to resist oppression, heal themselves, and educate their communities for more than two hundred years. Much of Black women's work to cultivate shared literacy practices and awaken ideas of liberatory resistance was traditionally done collaboratively and in community with other Black women. African American literary societies functioned as safe and productive spaces for Black women and girls, and they embodied the core of educational values within Black communities, even as Black Americans were simultaneously denied access to education through effects of systemic racism such as slavery and segregation.

Some of the most well-known Black women literary collectives, such as the Combahee River Collective (CRC), have cultivated emancipation through literacy and collective learning and organizing, and have transformed the critical thought of political social movements. The CRC and its co-founders, Barbara Smith, Beverly Smith, and Demita Frazier, created a coalition that was committed to addressing the interrelated oppressions that Black women faced. Beginning in 1974, the Collective gathered to build a political agenda to address racist, gendered, and other intersecting oppressions. Later, in 1976, the women began to occupy its space as a study group for Black women, where they shared readings, writings, and ideas.

The CRC functioned very similarly to historical African American literary societies, as a consciousness-raising advocacy group for Black women, which promoted a stance that acknowledged Black women's intellectualism and literacy practices. This radical group desired an amalgamation of liberatory literacy practices toward the freedom of Black women and similarly oppressed groups. However, in the curation of confronting the oppressions that plagued generations of people of color, the Combahee River Collective (2014) recognized that the work of true liberation had to begin with "us."

The founders confronted the politics of feminism and the Black liberation struggle of the 1970s and 1980s in the Combahee River Collective statement (1983). The Collective built its politics and development of true liberation on a foundation of acknowledging one's whole humanity. The Collective states,

> The most general statement of our politics at the present would be that we are actively committed to struggling against racial, sexual, heterosexual, and class oppression, and see as our particular task the development of integrated analysis and practice based upon the fact that the major systems of oppression are interlocking.
>
> *(p. 271)*

The CRC held the agenda to confront hegemony with the pursuit of freedom from the intersectional identities of one of the most vulnerable and oppressed groups in existence, Black women.

The Combahee River Collective was among many consciousness-raising collectives that enacted liberation through literacy (e.g., Black Women Organized for Political Action, The National Black Feminist Organization, and the National Alliance of Black Feminists). The writers and thinkers of the Collective cultivated safe spaces for articulating and practicing liberation in order to abstain from internalized suppression and external oppression. Their need to share literacies and acknowledge their humanity was indeed a praxis of Black feminism. Black feminist literacy spaces and collaborative literature such as *Introduction to the Black Woman: An Anthology* (2000), edited by Toni Cade Bambara, and *Home Girls: A Black Feminist Anthology* (2000), edited by Barbara Smith, cultivated safety, consciousness, and endearment of Black women's voices within a movement that recognized the relation between Black women's personal lives and experiences and their political participation.

Black women's literacy collaboratives present opportunities for reflection, the expansion of identities, and the challenging of traditional boundaries (McHenry, 2002), which may be especially important for Black youth. Literacy collaboratives involving girls in reading and writing have gained increased attention in childhood and adolescent literacy research. Muhammad and Haddix (2016) elaborate on the connectivity of literacy collaboratives and practices that organize advanced educational spaces and communities for the purposes of growth and affirmation. Muhammad (2015) specifically delivers a unique perspective to uphold research centering the voices of Black girls and honoring the historical framework of African American literary societies. The elements of the Black Girls' Literacies Framework designed by Muhammad and Haddix (2016) profess the levels of radiance and creativity necessary to enhance standardized and oppressive pedagogies. Literacy spaces are gifts of collective learning, imaginative in praxis, and they carry the potential to create liberated realities.

## A Black Girls' Literacy Collective: Black Girls WRITE!

In the spirit of Black women's literacy spaces, this chapter continues the discussion of Black women and girls' collectives and the importance of creating contemporary literacy spaces for Black girls today. We do this through our analysis of preambles, a tradition within Black women's literacy collectives. Preamble writing is embedded in a history of Black women's literary collaboratives of the 19th century. Similarly, Black women of the past wrote out a powerful statement that would speak to their identities, literacies, and the social change that was desired in society. In an 1831 example, the women of the Female Literary Association of Philadelphia wrote:

> Conscious that among the various pursuits that have engaged the attention of mankind in the different eras of the world, none have ever been considered by persons of judgment and penetration, as superior to the cultivation of the intellectual powers bestowed upon us by the God of nature. It therefore becomes a duty incumbent upon us as women, as daughters of a despised race, to use our utmost endeavors to enlighten the understanding, to cultivate the talents entrusted to our keeping, that by so doing, we may in a great measure, break down the strong behavior of prejudice, and raise ourselves to an equality with those of our fellow beings, who differ from us in complexion, but who are with ourselves, children of one Eternal Parent, and by his immutable law, we are entitled to the same rights and privileges; therefore, we, whose names are hereunto subscribed, do agree to form ourselves into a society for the promotion of this great object, to be called "The Female Literary Association of Philadelphia."

In this chapter, we share several powerful statements written by groups of elementary and secondary aged Black girls over the past ten years—girls who participated in a collaborative called *Black Girls WRITE!*

Black Girls WRITE (Writing to Represent Our Identities, Our Times, and Our Excellence)! is a literacy collaborative that I (Gholdy) developed in 2010 in Chicago, Illinois, while I was a doctoral student. At the time, I was studying

19th-century Black literary societies as a part of my dissertation research and also worked as a graduate assistant for Alfred Tatum's literacy program for Black males. Tatum's program was called the African American Adolescent Male Summer Literacy Institute. This was a five-week program where teenage Black boys from all over the Chicago area came together to read, talk, listen, debate, and write. I was in awe of the brilliant pieces of writings by the participants. The collaborative nature created a brotherhood among Tatum and the young men. A community space formed of kinship, identity, intellect, development of their writing skills, and, might I add, *love*. They found joy and love with reading various texts and wrote short stories, poetry, children's books, and the first chapter of their novel. As I witnessed the literary presence of the young men (aged 12–17) (who referred to each other as Brother Authors), I knew I was in the company of Black excellence. Soon, community members began to ask, *What about the Black girls?* Because my soul-work and research centered on Black girls, Tatum charged me with developing a collective. From that moment onward, I have been creating spaces for Black girls to see themselves and each other—to see, (re) claim, and (re)member the brilliance, excellence, and urgency in their histories, identities, literacies, and liberation (or HILL for short). We too called each other Sister Authors, and the girls were from 10 to 18 years old. We gathered for several weeks during the summer months. We met each week for approximately four days to read powerful and provocative texts (written throughout time by Black women). We read print texts but also social con-*texts*, or the world as text. This led to rich discussions, sometimes debates, critical listening, sometimes crying/ healing, and writing. As I developed these spaces, I had four learning goals or pursuits in mind:

1. To cultivate their knowledge of themselves and the complex nature of Black girlhood/womanhood (Identity)
2. To cultivate their reading, writing, thinking, listening, and speaking skills (Skills)
3. To cultivate new knowledge (Intellectualism)
4. To cultivate their understanding of equity, power, and anti-oppression (Criticality)

I called these four goals the Historically Responsive HILL (responding to students' histories, identities, literacies, and liberation) model (Muhammad, 2020). Framing Black Girls WRITE! in this way not only led to engaging in literacy practices for the sake of joy but also created social awareness and social change. We read from Black women authors from the local community as well as writings from Sister Authors throughout time, such as Gwendolyn Brooks, Ida B. Wells, Frances Ellen Watkins Harper, Sojourner Truth, Alice Walker, Maria Stewart, and Jacqueline Woodson (to name a few). These texts were layered with multimodal texts such as primary source documents, images/photos, videos, songs/

lyrics, and performances. Our readings were followed by discussions and "author warm-ups" where we practiced writing skills. We studied the genres read, engaged in research, and then wrote the same type of writing. We wrote different types of compositions, including included poems, narratives, short stories, public addresses, protest writings, and open letters.

In each first session, the girls would collectively pen a preamble. A preamble is a preliminary or introductory statement. It is like a manifesto, where the girls individually wrote out statements that spoke to the identities, purpose, and power of their pens. Then the girls collectively combined their lines and agreed on what their preamble would be. Each preamble started with the collective, *We, the Sister Authors*, to express a solidarity and collectivity among one another. The girls would stand and recite this preamble at the opening and closing of each session.

In the example mentioned earlier of the members of the Female Literary Association of Philadelphia, the members name themselves and the problems in the world. They are calling out injustice and calling others to action for social change. Following this history, the girls in Black Girls WRITE! wrote powerful statements of their own. In this chapter, we present four preambles across the past ten years, make meaning, and reflect on the girls' words. These preambles are useful artifacts that help to tell the world who Black girls are. Further, these statements are informative for others, namely those who teach Black girls, to learn what they need in learning spaces. As Black women teachers and scholars, we reflect upon the preambles through the lens of the Black Girls' Literacies Framework, as the framework was partly developed from my work in creating such spaces.

## Naming Ourselves, (Re)claiming Our Histories, Writing Our Futures

### From the Sister Authors of Black Girls WRITE! 2010

> We, the Sister Authors, write for then, now, and later to honor those before us and inspire those who are yet to come. We write because we will not allow those who aren't us to speak for us, judge us, or to tell our stories. We all bleed blood but society has chosen to look only at our skin color. In order for the world to hear our voices, we must be brave enough to let them be heard, so we write to advocate for change. While we are young, Black and female, we are individuals. Our stories are uniquely beautiful. We cannot hold it in, we will write it out.

In the opening line of their preamble the Black Girls WRITE! 2010 collective, a group of Black girls, ages 14–17, demonstrate their unwavering commitment to using their writing as a way to advocate for themselves and to elevate the voices of Black women and girls who have been silenced or ignored. Viewing their work as a part of the lineage of African American women activists such as Sojourner

Truth, and contemporarily with the Combahee River Collective (CRC), they began a quest undertaken by generations of Black women and girls before them to unapologetically re-write their narratives. Sister scholars began their journey by situating their writing within a historical and collective struggle for liberation.

The Black Girls WRITE! 2010 collective viewed their writing as a form of power and used their pens as a declaration against the pervasive censuring of Black women and girls' thoughts and actions in both schools and the larger society. They refuse to relinquish agency over their stories, stating "we write because we will not allow others who aren't us . . . to tell our stories." They also understand how both verbal and written literacy practices such as *speaking* and *telling* have been used to create false narratives of Black girlhood. Thus, they use their writing as a tool to refute these falsehoods and transfix a society that they suggest has "chosen to look only at our skin color." It is evident that the Sister Authors' awareness of the sociocultural and political forces that attempt to disempower Black girls is essential to their reading of the world around them.

The Sister Authors who participated in Black Girls WRITE! in 2010 use their preamble to profess a need for "the world to hear our voices" and "to advocate for change." The collective goals expressed by the Sister Authors stand in sharp contrast to what is asked of students, in an age of standards and accountability, in traditional K–12 public classroom settings. However, the Black Girls WRITE! collective demonstrates the potential of adolescent youth to critically evaluate the world and actively work toward its reimagination. As Black Girls WRITE! reveals, fostering criticality is possible through the use of communal space where young and older scholars can collaborate to discuss and re-write the world around them. Furthermore, in order for these needs to be accomplished, the girls argue that bravery and courage is required when they "write it out." They see this bravery as fuel to help them advocate for change for the present and future generation of girls like them.

As Sojourner Truth asked in her notorious speech, "Ain't I a woman?," these Sister Authors dared to declare that their stories of embodied intersectionality are worthy of being told. As they state, "while we are young, Black and female, we are individuals. Our stories are uniquely beautiful." They draw on the strength of Black women writers and thinkers such as the Combahee River Collective whose work emphasized the intersection of these identities and activism for Black women. Their Black girlhood not only fueled their work but expressed the urgency of their stories being told, as the uniqueness of Black girlhood experiences often gets lost in the monoliths of Black girl experience. These stories "cannot be held in."

Emblematic of the Black Girls' Literacy Framework, this preamble demonstrates criticality and intellectualism, as its writers analyzed their individual issues and connected them to larger issues affecting Black girls throughout society. Through the creation of a shared preamble, the girls collaboratively write their truths. Their political awareness allowed them to see how power is used to create false narratives and pushed them to transform these conditions. By declaring their purpose and not allowing others to fashion their narratives, the Sister Authors are defining themselves beyond society's perceptions of them, which are often based on their skin color and gender alone. I wonder the potential impact of engaging in this type of liberatory writing for other Black girls if we make space for this reimagination in our schools. As our Sister Authors of 2010 have shown us, writing is a means of self-definition, a way for our voices to be heard among the noise. Not only do they inspire us to write it out, they also push us to encourage others to write for the generations yet to come.

## From the Sister Authors of Black Girls WRITE! 2012

> We, the Sister Authors, are here to encourage all our sisters to be brave, share our stories and not to fear those without knowledge about us. Together we shall clear a path for those who come later. We will write to ignite a spark in our fellow sisters in order to bring unity among us. Our writing is to entice society with our minds. We write with intelligence, passion and personality. Only we can tell our stories. We are smart and can strive to be anything we want although society projects us as all the same. Today we will change the way we are defined. We will write to not only leave an impression on paper but also on society.

Black Girls WRITE! 2012 collective produced this preamble and, in so doing, expressed their solidarity with Black women who have come before them, those are currently present, and those yet to come in the future. The Sister Authors encourage all Black girls and women to be brave and to share their stories, illuminating truth for those who may be miseducated or ignorant about their lives. They use the term "sisters" to demonstrate collectivism, community, and collaboration. In the same opening line, I found it interesting that they intentionally used the word "brave" in their language, as that implies the presence of some type of danger or pain. This pain could result from society's invisibility and hypervisibility of Black girls. In other words, Black girls are typically overlooked and overshadowed in the narratives of girls or Black boys, but in schools, they are often extremely visible and punished for their behavior. The word brave could also speak to the misrepresentations, racism, and sexism experienced by Black girls.

The Sister Authors also express, "together we shall clear a path for those who come later." Here, they are not just present-minded but are also thinking of future generations. Again, they see themselves as a sisterhood collective. The next lines explain the purpose of their pens, and they give several purposes for their writing. These include writing to "ignite a spark with our fellow sisters," to "entice society with our minds," and to tell their stories through intelligence, passion, and their personalities. Here, their writing/literacies serve multiple purposes. In schools, we often see writing responding to a prompt that can be disconnected from the lived experiences of Black girls. But their pens have authentic purpose. They show the cognitive and sociocultural benefits writing offers. This shows how their literacies are multiple. They show that they never remove the self from writing practices, which embodies the importance of identity. Their writing is also political and grounded in criticality, as they express that Black girls are the only ones who can tell Black girls' stories. The use of the word intelligence shows the BGLF of the component intellectualism. They proclaim that they are brilliant, and while many would call this a counter-narrative, we see it as an original narrative. Black women and girls have always seen themselves as beautiful and smart, even when the world has not. The girls here express that society sees them in monolithic ways, but they are combating this by proclaiming the complexity in their identities. Black women have written for these same purposes and these similar ways traditionally and throughout time. This relates to the component of the Black Girls' Literacies Framework that Black girls' literacies are historical.

They conclude with the words, "Today we will change the way we are defined. We will write to not only leave an impression on paper but also on society." These lines signify action in their words and movement. They express that they will not just sit idly by and allow false and negative stories to be told about Black women, but will instead use their pens in powerful ways to interrupt and disrupt the negative views of Black girls. They write for social change. The Sister Authors seek to change the world and society with the minds and their pens.

## From the Sister Authors of Black Girls WRITE! 2014

We, the Sister Authors, will use our pens to transform the world around us. We write to start a revolution of peace, justice, and equality with a keen mind of who African American Muslim girls are, who they can be, and what they can become. We will go through the journey together, knowing that there is strength in numbers. Our voices will harmoniously shatter any glass ceiling, as eloquently as we define eloquence as loudly, as we define volume, and as powerful as we define power. Hand in hand, toe to toe. We owe it to our ancestors, our daughters, ourselves, and to the world to illustrate our outlooks, our struggles and our various stories. With our empowering youthfulness, magnificent glowing dark skin, proud Islamic faith, we stand to let the world hear us. We refuse to stay mute.

The Black Girls WRITE! 2014 collective preamble invokes a revolutionary and necessary call to action for Black girls' liberation. The Sister Authors call out their purpose, clearly and definitively, to mutate the interpretations of who African American Muslim girls are becoming. The girls proclaim their full humanity through volume, power, and depth. They employ language that addresses issues of sociopolitical containment and a dire need for social change from the world. Sister Authors of 2014 demonstrate the Black Girls' Literacies Framework with a specific emphasis on identity. The collaborative identities with which they identify are youth, African American, Muslim, girls, daughters, writers, and revolutionaries. Their identity is expressed vividly in the power of what they call to do with their writing and the power of their intersecting identities to accomplish and overcome their realities with eloquence.

Their first line of the preamble is a direct call to action: "We, the Sister Authors, will use our pens to transform the world around us. We write to start a revolution of peace, justice, and equality with a keen mind." This speaks to the intellectual and political/critical need for a transformation into a state of liberation. The Sister Authors center their identity as a proclamation of revolutionizing, overthrowing current social order in favor of an equitable order of a world that uplifts peace and acknowledges Black Muslim girls. It a clear statement that evokes courage and attention to our Black Muslim girls. The Sister Authors' intellectualism is rooted in their collective consciousness, which reflects their common goals as African American Muslim girls and change agents. This consciousness is grounded in their proud Islamic faith, and their spirituality is definitive in collective awareness. The Sister Authors of 2014 state, "We will go through the journey together," "We define eloquence . . . We define volume . . . We define power," and the best one, "We refuse to stay mute," speaks to the collaborative and intellectual concepts from the Black Girls' Literacies Framework. The girls are defining their agency with radical resistance and sacred connectivity to their faith and integrity. The strength of the Sister Authors' collective identity and their definition of power and agency in the preamble dismantles the hegemonic narratives that attempt to manipulate or dismiss the liberation of Black Muslim girls. Through defining their power, the girls are addressing the issue of space for Black girls to express their creativity and freedom (Muhammad, 2016). The issue of space for Black Muslim girls draws on the linear techniques of literacy and learning that Black students experience. The Sisters Authors' statement, "Our voice harmoniously shatters any glass ceiling," elaborates that boundaries are not necessary or embodied in the writing, text, sound, and spirit they produce as African American Muslim girls.

The girls speak deeply to the political and critical issues of Islamophobia, sexism, and racism as they address their identity in coherence with revolutionizing. Muhammad and Haddix (2016) state, "Their literacies were tied to power, mis-representations, falsehood, and the need for social transformation" (p. 326). The Sister Authors connect their literacies and sacred obligation to their lineage. The girls state, "We owe it to our ancestors, our daughters, ourselves, and to the world to illustrate our outlooks, our struggles, and our various stories." Here they reference their lineage as an extension of self to discover and defend their literacies. Their lineage adds importance to the historical framework highlighted as a component of Black girls' literacies. Their obligation to "illustrate our outlooks" connects the historical and collaborative concepts, by which their unique epistemological standpoint as Black Muslim girls becomes the autonomous curator of their living experiences. The authors signal in their preamble the importance of collaboration to attain justice. The Sister Authors are aware of collective unity, stating, "We will go through the journey together, knowing that there is strength in numbers." The preamble implies that their writing will not be isolated or objectified from the experience of Black Muslim girls or their community. The purpose is clear in not only its intellectual understanding of the injustices linked to the Black Muslim girl standpoint, but also how injustices affect their lives intergenerationally, personally, and publicly. The Sister Authors of 2014 are intellectually and critically grounded to dismantle deficit ideologies by resonating their truth and power.

### From the Sister Authors of Black Girls WRITE! 2018

> We, the Sister Authors, will promise to push the boundaries of our existence to learn from the past, act on our present and improve our future. We can teach others as our history has taught us. By putting our pens to paper and our voices to action, we can defy all stereotypes put on Black girls by society. As Black girls, we will replace guns with pens and revive the broken spirits within ourselves and our race to break through societal barriers. We, as Black queens, will build kingdoms with our language using the strong identities of our Sisters as pillars of guidance. We are more than enough. Remember, nothing is placed upon us that we cannot handle. We will not allow the chains of injustice to tie us down. We must strive to be the living embodiment of Black excellence. We will juxtapose ignorance with our intellect and fight through our struggles and challenges through the power of words. We are smart and strong, and we express our feelings by writing.

The Sister Authors of this preamble demonstrate their commitments to self-definition and resistance through language that asserts their views about themselves and other Black girls ("We are more than enough," "We are smart and strong"). They exemplify awareness of their marginalization and objectification through their ability to name the stereotypes assigned to them by society. In their preamble, the Sister Authors identify oppressions that work against Black girls and work collectively to introduce the purpose of their group, which is to address their concerns about representation and justice through their intellect and action. Members of the writing collective use a sophisticated practice of drawing upon the tools of historical Black women ("our ancestors") and the function of their literary societies as models for developing their plans to redefine themselves. Participants of the Black Girls WRITE! 2018 collective signify their understanding of the legacy of literacy and activism of Black women who came before them by practicing historically informed social activism. They plan to look to their ancestors, whom they also refer to as "Sisters," for guidance as they work toward self-definition. Sister Authors also empower themselves by viewing their own work through this historical lens. For example, they recognize the power of the written word and suggest that they will use what history has taught them (through other Black women's writings) to teach others, presumably through their own writings. Further, the Sister Authors of this preamble demonstrate actions of resistance by denouncing stereotypes of Black girls and women, such as in the line, "we can defy all stereotypes put on us by society" and vocalizing their desires to reclaim what they feel has been lost ("revive the broken spirits") and their determination to grow toward a self-determined purpose ("build kingdoms with our language"). They recognize their marginalization, yet assert their privileges of a rich historical lineage, as well as literacy skills (their abilities to read and write) to fight both *for* themselves and *against* inequitable systems. Sister Authors signify the gravity of the battle in which they plan to engage with words such as "fight," "strive," "break," and "push." It is clear that they do not take their task lightly, and in assessing the situation understand that their resistance may require force and opposition. Ultimately, they plan to use language as a tool with which to build the futures they envision for themselves and other Black girls and women.

As suggested by the Black Girls' Literacies Framework, Black girls' literacy practices as a collective can be described as multiple, tied to identities, historical, collaborative, intellectual, and political/critical. Most prominent in this preamble are the authors' representations of identity, their use of historical context to inform their current writings, which are tied to their intellectual capacities, their willingness to address the stereotypes that they experience in their social interactions and observations, and their collaborative practice of drafting the preamble to introduce their group's purpose. This preamble is a presentation of Sister Authors' perceptions of themselves, their understanding of how they are viewed by society, and the conflicts between the two views.

Sister Authors' writings are tied to their identities in ways that seek to reclaim definitions of Black girls and Black girlhood. They name themselves as queens who are strong, smart, and expressive. Through intellectual endeavors of reading and writing about historical Black women who have also worked to reclaim their identities, Sister Authors contextualize the writing of this preamble within what has been done historically by other Black women like Maria Stewart (1879) and Anna Julia Cooper (2000). Therefore, this preamble exemplifies an intellectual prowess toward researching, understanding, and applying knowledge from historical texts, as well as a willingness of the Sister Authors to position themselves as students of the historical Black women that they have studied. This preamble addresses critical issues by both naming stereotypes as a threat to the self-definition of Black girls and recognizing these issues as being tied to larger social systems. Their recognition of broad-scale marginalization and oppression signifies an intentional politicization of their writing. The Sister Authors provided an example, through this preamble, of Black girls' literacies and recognize the power of writing, of putting "pen to paper" to invoke changes within the societies in which they live.

## Moving Forward in Solidarity, Resistance, and Hope

For almost a decade, participants in Black Girls WRITE! have collectively enacted the practices of Black girls' literacies by writing manifestos of solidarity, hope, social and political awareness, and resistance. Through studying the historical struggles and successes of the generations of Black women and girl authors before them, each year, the Sister Authors used these lessons as guidance and inspiration for their own compositions. Their preambles serve as insight into what is possible when we create spaces for Black girl excellence.

Sister Authors followed in the footsteps of Black women before them, often beginning their preambles by defining themselves according to their multiple, intersecting identities of race and gender (Lorde, 1985) and refusing to prioritize one identity over the other. Additionally, they each used their sociopolitical awareness, which was fostered in part by their interactions within the Black Girls WRITE! collective, to analyze and challenge stereotypes of Black girlhood. Developing fictive kinship connections with their fellow Sister Authors both past and present supported Black Girls WRITE! collective participants as they engaged in a collective call for the dismantling of social oppressions and societal transformation. The Sister Authors of Black Girls WRITE! used their authentic voices to demonstrate intellectualism and to articulate their hopes and dreams— bravely declaring through their writing that Black girls' lives and stories matter.

As Muhammad and Haddix (2016) suggest, Black girls often practice literacy in ways that are historical, multiple, intellectual, tied to their identities, collaborative, and reflective of and in response to social and political issues. Therefore, it is imperative for educators to be intentional about providing opportunities for them to cultivate their intellect and skills in ways that are not reflected in the organization of traditionally structured literacy programs. Efforts to design literacy experiences that support Black girls' literacies must be informed by an awareness of the elements that are characteristic of their expressions.

Additionally, educators should offer opportunities for collaboration as part of their literacy instruction through multifaceted communications. Educators must strive to develop an awareness and understanding of their students' identities, meaningful historical references, and their social/political concerns. To this end, educators must first recognize the intellectual potential of Black girl students, then provide cognitively rigorous opportunities for them to cultivate their literacy practices and also model effective forms of collaboration. Although students may excel when given the opportunity to work in community with others, they may need support in forming effective and efficient partnerships. As an example, in the Black Girls WRITE! collective, participants formed collaborative groups that centered on the common interest of a social concern. Black Girls WRITE! facilitators supported participants with establishing group norms and determining goals for their collective writing and activism. Similarly, writing programs and curriculum guides should acknowledge the various ways that Black girls engage in literacy practices through their content design. Although not all lessons/content may reflect each aspect of the Black Girls' Literacies Framework, considerations of curriculum design that would allow students to incorporate/ express aspects of their identities, reflect on their historical references, address social and political concerns, and work collaboratively would support the literacy engagement of Black girls.

The Black Girls' Literacies Framework, when used as a foundation for literacy programming and spaces, provides personal and intellectual development opportunities for all students, not just Black girls. The preambles in this chapter provide evidence of the critical thinking, reading, and writing that can occur when the aspects of the Black Girls' Literacies Framework are used to design literacy instruction. The Sister Authors who participated in constructing each preamble gleaned wisdom and understanding from historical figures such as Toni Morrison, Audre Lorde, bell hooks, and countless other Black women who acted as their counterparts in continuing the work to emancipate themselves and others through collective learning and organizing.

## References

Bacon, J., & McClish, G. (2000). Reinventing the master's tools: Nineteenth-century African-American literary societies of Philadelphia and rhetorical education. *Rhetoric Society Quarterly*, *30*(4), 19–47.

Cade, T. (2000). Introduction to the black woman: An anthology. In B. A. Crow (Ed.), *Radical feminism: A documentary reader* (pp. 423–426). New York: NYU Press.

Combahee River Collective. (1983). The Combahee river collective statement. In B. Smith (Ed.), *Home girls: A Black feminist anthology* (pp. 264–274). New Brunswick, NJ: Rutgers University Press.

Combahee River Collective. (2014). A Black feminist statement. *Women's Studies Quarterly*, 271–280.

Cooper, A. J. (2000). *The voice of Anna Julia Cooper: Including a voice from the south and other important essays, papers, and letters.* Lanham, MD: Rowman & Littlefield Publishers.

Lorde, A. (1985). *I am your sister: Black women organizing across sexualities.* Albany: Kitchen Table, Women of Color Press.

McHenry, E. (2002). *Forgotten readers: Recovering the lost history of African American literary societies.* Durham: Duke University Press.

Muhammad, G. E. (2012). The literacy development and practices within African American literary societies. *Black History Bulletin*, *75*(1), 6–13.

Muhammad, G. E. (2020). *Cultivating genius: An equity model for culturally and historically responsive literacy.* New York: Scholastic.

Muhammad, G. E., & Haddix, M. (2016). Centering Black girls' literacies: A review of literature on the multiple ways of knowing of Black girls. *English Education*, *48*(4), 299–336.

Smith, B. (Ed.). (2000). *Home girls: A black feminist anthology.* New Brunswick, NJ: Rutgers University Press.

Stewart, M. W. (1879). *Meditations from the Pen of Mrs. Maria W. Stewart:(Widow of the Late James W. Stewart) Now Matron of the Freedman's Hospital, and Presented in 1832 to the First African Baptist Church and Society of Boston, Mass.* Blair, NE: Enterprise Publishing Company.

# 3

# BLACK WOMEN AND GIRLS SOCIAL ACTIVISM TRADITION

## Critical Media Literacy and the Black Girls' Literacies Framework

*Sherell A. McArthur*

## What We Can Learn From Black Women Traditions of Speaking Truths

Historically, Black women have spoken truth to power in various forms of media. In one of the earliest examples, Maria W. Stewart, known as the first Black woman political writer in the 1800s, was a social activist and lecturer who spent her life advocating for the more complete representation, education, and civil rights of Black people, particularly of African American women. She did this through the publishing of pamphlets that advocated for Black women to know themselves and to engage with politics and social activism. Black women's active resistance to racism and sexism was central to her platform, and these ideas rang through the public address, "What If I Am a Woman?" In this address, delivered in 1833 to the *free* Black community in Boston, she spoke about the struggles she carried as a Black American woman, subordinated in her identities as a woman and Black in the 1800s, as well as about her inner strength, which was the basis of her hope as an activist. Within her speech, she emphasized that Black women were as capable as Black men and argued for equal pay for women's labor. During this time and throughout her political writings, she boldly encouraged other Black women to center their rights and advocate for them, by practicing their highest intellectual capabilities as sociopolitical participants in society. She felt that the pursuit of high intellectualism would give them the tools to resist oppressions and the typecast image of the subservient woman (Richardson, 1987).

In movements since Stewart's activism, Black girls and women are actively engaged in sociopolitical pursuits. Their work of activism involves working to bring social change and shifting oppressive policies that do not serve people of color well. Black women and girls are pushing, resisting, and organizing

(Lemieux, 2014; Williams, 2015; Jackson, 2016; Brown, 2017). They are standing up when others cannot or will not. Black women and girls today are continuing the work of Black women of the past by engaging in social action and activism. Given the current sociopolitical climate of racism and the need for change, I argue that within school contexts, K–12 educators should foster activism by centering the histories and identities of the students in our classrooms and honoring and centering their lived experiences. By using their pens, minds, revolutionary pursuits, and activist spirits, Black women have always been a part of and led movements in the United States to bring about justice for all. They were instrumental in the suffrage movement (Wheeler, 1993) and the Civil Rights Movement (Barnett, 1993), and are the most consistent voting demographic in the U.S. (Harris, 1999). Throughout history, Black girls and women have been strong activists, disrupting narratives the media (once newspapers and now through television and social media platforms) convey about Black girlhood and womanhood by sharing their truths. Therefore, centering Black girls' lived experiences through critical media literacy enables Black girls to counter the stereotypes that haunt society's collective consciousness about Black women and girls with genuine stories of Black girlhood. Critical media literacy "encourages learners to define relationships of power and question social norms" (McArthur, 2019, p. 686). Because children and young adults are learning from multiple media sources, like television, video games, and social media, educators must be diligent in mediating the influence of what they learn from those media. Whether or not teachers introduce or acknowledge media in their classroom, it finds itself in classrooms through student cell phones and conversations, and students find themselves socialized through their engagement with it. Educators can use curriculum and instruction as a site of transformation by being deliberate and intentional in their pedagogy to empower students to effect change. Educators can do this by connecting students to the rich cultural histories they are a part of. Critical media literacy therefore can be seen as a transformative pedagogy (McArthur, 2016; Tisdell, 2008). This transformative pedagogy will enable schools to cultivate critical thinkers who pursue individual and collective good by encouraging youth to take up issues that are important to them and that are in need of transformation.

Black women's historical activism is an impetus for critical media literacy and social change today. To explore the work of Black women who model for and push us to dismantle oppressive structures to advance equity for all, we can look to the Black Girls' Literacies Framework, constructed by Muhammad and Haddix (2016) in an effort to advance the literacies of Black girls. They state "if we reimagine an English education where Black girls matter, all children would benefit from a curricular and pedagogical infrastructure that values humanity" (Muhammad & Haddix, 2016, p. 329). This framework is significant to Black girls and critical media literacy as it provides structure on *how* to engage in transformative pedagogy, utilizing critical media literacy that encompasses the six key elements of Black girls' literacies aids in creating socially empowered critical thinkers. Muhammad and Haddix (2016, p. 325) list those elements as:

1.  Multiple
2.  Tied to identities
3.  Historical
4.  Collaborative
5.  Intellectual
6.  Political/Critical

In this chapter, I unpack critical media literacy and discuss how it can encourage activism by showing examples of a Black girl-centered program that fosters social activism using the Black Girls' Literacies Framework.

## What Is Critical Media Literacy?

Critical media literacy is how we gain access, analyze, critique, and create media; it enables us to understand the role of messaging in media and media in society (McArthur, 2019). Media penetrates every area of our everyday life, so our deep immersion in media prevents us from being uninfluenced by it (Hinchey, 2003). We do not have a choice about whether our students will be engaged in media consumption, so our choice about teaching students to be media literate should be an obvious one. In other words, because youth are naturally exposed to media, they need to learn how to mediate and understand these forms of texts in the classroom. In *Teaching to Transgress*, hooks (1994) supports this point and asserts, "the classroom becomes a dynamic place where transformations in social relations are concretely actualized and the false dichotomy between the world outside and the inside world" (p. 195). It is the understanding of the role of the classroom, and thereby the teaching and learning within it, that makes critical media literacy pedagogy transformative. Paugh (2014) states that with critical media literacy,

> students are positioned to use literacy as part of a social community, both real and imagined, in ways that prepare them not only to be 21st century workers but more importantly to be 21st century citizens, innovating and creating new relationships that keep social justice and equity at the forefront.
>
> *(p. 3)*

Since critical media literacy encourages the questioning of social norms and defining relationships of power, students taught critical media literacy skills are better positioned to see, and right, social inequities. Media literacy educators, therefore, offer students the opportunity to practice becoming critical readers of the world around them. They generate dialogue about the impact of media in shaping the way we think and view ourselves and others (Morrell, 2014). Critical media literacy instruction helps students research, analyze, and critique social conditions of their everyday lives and the world around them. It encourages critical thinking and production of multimodal literacies. The practice of media literacy promotes reflexivity in media consumption habits and urges students to analyze the messages they are receiving. Educators have the opportunity to develop pedagogies that employ advances in technology and to understand the saturation of media around us to reconceptualize how literacy is understood and taught (Luke, 2000).

Critical media literacy is especially vital for Black girls. Media representations of Black girlhood, both as entertainment and in the news, are largely subtractive and dehumanizing. For example, in October 2015, at Spring Valley High School in South Carolina, a cell phone camera video showing a school resource officer dragging a Black girl out of her seat in a classroom went viral on social media sites. Various news outlets reported this assault with commentary such as "we don't know what occurred before the video" to insinuate that there would be sufficient reason for an adult male to manhandle a female student. In November 2017, at a charter school in Nashville, Tennessee, two Snapchat videos were posted of a Black Muslimah's hijab being snatched off of her head by a teacher. In both videos, the student is covering her face, with one video caption referring to how pretty the teacher thought her hair was and the other caption referring to the student having all of her hair covered up. The blatant disrespect for the student in South Carolina's physical and emotional well-being and the Tennessee student's identity, culture, and faith demonstrate the physical and emotional assault Black girls experience in schools. Schools are institutions of violence against Black girls, and centering their histories and lived experiences in the classroom provides socioemotional places for them to address or affirm the complexities of their identities (McArthur, 2018). Black girls' lives matter, however; the way their lives are represented through the media, whether on television, in music, in print, or on the news, sends the message to Black girls and others that they, in fact, do not matter—that their lives are not valuable. And those watching media tend to take up those messages and enact them in ways that are demonstrated in the examples of the two students. Critical media literacy is transformative for Black girls because it is not simply an exercise in reading and writing; it is a mode through which Black girls learn how to push back and (re)write who they are. Critical media literacy education should not be viewed as an ancillary add-on to curriculum but as the basis of civic education in the twenty-first century. Educators not employing critical media literacy are missing real opportunities for addressing key aspects of our social, political, and economic landscape. This approach provides a framework to advocate for social justice; however, social justice and activism are not explicit aims. Therefore, I argue for the use of critical media literacy as a means not only to educate, empower, and encourage Black girls to deconstruct media but also to use their voices, pens, and digital platforms to advocate for social change.

## Critical Media Literacy Pedagogy

In our current sociopolitical climate, where many youths are joining the Black Lives Matter movement, protesting until university presidents resign (like the University of Missouri president in November 2015), marching until policies are changed (from the violent death of Breonna Taylor), and holding rallies, boycotts, die-ins, and read-ins across the country, fostering youths' media literacy is more vital than ever. Education needs to heighten students' critical consciousness, challenging racism disguised as entertainment (Yosso, 2002); understanding that messages in the media have historical, social, political, and economic contexts (Kellner & Share, 2007); and recognizing that only part of the story is provided by the media (Horn, 2003). Centering Black girls' lived experience through critical media literacy can teach critical thinking and questioning and enables Black girls to negotiate visibility by counternarrating racist, sexist, and classist media narratives with authentic stories of Black girlhood (Muhammad & McArthur, 2015). As Kellner and Share (2005) emphasize, "coming to voice is important for people who have seldom been allowed to speak for themselves, but without critical analysis it is not enough" (p. 371). Students—particularly Black girls—are often disconnected from the curriculum (Evans-Winters, 2005). As an educator, I believe that it is our responsibility to connect students' histories, stories, and lived experiences in classroom settings so they can identify, deconstruct, and problematize the complexity of power relations operating in society, specifically through media. The goals of critical media literacy practices are to upset the dominant discourse about individuals and groups of people who contribute to oppressive relationships (Kellner & Share, 2007; Luke, 2000), emphasizing the questioning of social norms. When engaged in critical media literacy, students are taught to interrogate texts, question myriad oppressive social structures, and unpack and analyze how stereotypes and prejudices are communicated through media (Scharrer, 2015; Yosso, 2002).

Media includes such mediums as radio, television, magazines, newspapers, print ads, popular culture, and new technologies, to name a few, and represents a site of education situated outside of the traditional context of formal educational institutions (McArthur, 2016). Kellner and Share (2007) assert that it is irresponsible for educators to ignore the educative nature of the media, especially in the media-saturated environment of the twenty-first century. Educators concerned with bringing media into the classroom space should recognize that their students are already bringing media into schools with them. They come in listening to media and watching media on their phones. They are reading comics and novels and discussing video games. Because youth are being socialized and conditioned through their engagement with media, what teachers choose to do with media pedagogically becomes significant. There is a strong need to define critical media literacy in a pedagogical context for practice in classrooms (Alvermann, 2006; Alvermann & Hagood, 2000; Morrell, 2014). Critical media literacy is the ability to critique and analyze, as well as create, media. Therefore, I emphasize the use of critical media literacy to teach youth about their agentic power. Once children and youth recognize the dominant messages prevalent in the media they engage, it enhances their ability to read the world as text and recreate the world as text. This incites what Giroux (2013) calls a "radical democracy," which he defines as a "political, social, and ethical referent for rethinking how citizens can be educated to deal with a world made up of different, multiple, and fractured public cultures" (p. 53). A radical democracy requires a commitment to equity in education (Alsup & Miller, 2014). Schools can serve as a site to cultivate an understanding of the world—how to read it and navigate it to "help students develop the language to counter the sophisticated politics of public portrayal that target them every day" (Morrell & Duncan-Andrade, 2006, p. 279).

Students can be taught to use media to create new and innovative ways to engage in social justice as twenty-first-century citizens (Haddix & Sealey-Ruiz, 2012). In our market-driven information society, media promotes various political and cultural values (Horn, 2003), and this promotion is possible because entire industries are under control of a few corporate conglomerates (Compaine & Gomery, 2000). Because 90% of American media are operated by six companies, the values, perspectives, and viewpoints of the controllers of those six companies permeate mass media and thus have authority over what knowledge is disseminated (Lutz, 2012). Educators must constantly engage in critique of media representations, for themselves and to develop curriculum for students, for the purpose of disrupting the stereotypical way that Black girls and other marginalized populations are represented in the media. In effort to disrupt stereotypes in the media and engage in socially just curriculum, teachers could ask: *Why is sex used to sell everything from hamburgers to cars? What type of women are chosen to represent those images? What body sizes are represented in commercial and print ads? What skin tones? What hair textures?* The ability to comprehend and stave off the barrage of information is as important as the ability to read; McBrien (1999) asserts reading is only one part of traditional literacy, while comprehension is the other. If our students can read but cannot understand the print they read, we are failing them within instructional practices. Similarly, if our students can read media through their engagement with them, but do not know how to interpret and understand the messages they are receiving, we are once again failing them. The key components of media literacy (Hobbs, 1997) proffer that all messages have social, political, and commercial implications, that is, media are usually endeavoring to make a profit or a point. Because of how media are used as indoctrination, teachers can utilize critical media literacy to disrupt normative discourses and encourage civic engagement, democratic practice, and social activism.

## Critical Media Literacy in Action

In the spring of 2014, I co-created and co-facilitated the critical media literacy collective Beyond Your Perception (BYP) in Atlanta, Georgia. This collective worked with high school Black girls to critique and analyze the media they engage and to empower them to disrupt the dominant narrative presented by the media with their own voices. Before beginning instruction in BYP, the co-facilitator (another Black woman) and I worked to get to know the girls. BYP contextualized, listened to, and learned from their experiences as Black girls. Based on the experiences they shared, when we moved into our lessons, our goal was to deconstruct the media they engaged and provided them space and place (McArthur, 2018)[1] to create counternarratives and push back against the hegemonic discourse around Black woman- and girlhood. Our first unit of study was to provide historical understandings of the stereotypes for Black women—Jezebel, Mammy, Matriarch, Welfare Mother, and Sapphire (Harris-Perry, 2011; Stephens & Few, 2007; Stephens & Phillips, 2003). For contemporary young Black women, the imagery presented of who they are or can become—their "media role models"—resemble the stereotypes of old. The program provided a space and place for Black girls to use counter-storytelling to speak back to hegemonic narratives.

## Fostering Activism: Lessons From *Beyond Your Perception*

BYP's lessons on historical understandings utilized the Black Girls' Literacies Framework. In our first unit of study, I discussed the cruel and inhumane roots and justifications of these restrictive tropes for Black women. One activity that stemmed from this unit was a chalk-walk and writing activity to provide depth and character to these women. After posting a piece of chart paper for each label, I asked the participants to walk around and begin to write on the chart paper a backstory for each woman. The questions they answered were: *Why might the Welfare Mother need governmental assistance?* And, *Why might Sapphire be angry?* After each participant was satisfied with her contribution, we discussed the reasons they provided. In a follow-up activity, I asked the girls to write counterstories to provide a reimagined representation of Jezebel, Mammy, Matriarch, Welfare Mother, and Sapphire. Each participant chose who she wanted to write about, named her, and composed a narrative that was counterhegemonic. The excerpt below written by Dakota (all girls' names are pseudonyms) was composed for Sapphire, who is the foundational stereotype of the "Angry Black Woman" trope.

> If the color of my skin is just too much for you, then I'm sorry. If the way I am is just too pushy for you, then I'm sorry. If the way I stand with this deep arch in my back, this head held high, this smile painted on my face, this strut I take with each step . . . I mean if that's too much for you, then I'm sorry. . . . Because of the color of my skin, I won't be burdened with the stress of life. Just because of the way I push, I know I won't fail in life. . . . The days get longer and the nights get shorter, but I'm done fighting by myself.

This excerpt from Dakota's counterstory, articulating why she might be perceived as angry "because of the color of my skin" and "because of the way I push," is just one example that demonstrates the girls' ability to understand and uncover the stories of Black people, broadly, and Black women and girls, specifically, and to speak against the hegemony within the metanarrative.

The following counterhegemonic narrative, written by Audrey, exposes structural inequalities for the trope Welfare Mother.

> I am the ratchet baby momma. And so was my momma. I love my hood and so do my brothers. I never had the chance to love anything else. How can you love what you don't know? . . . I can't want what's not in reach, or better yet, I can't want what doesn't exist to me.

In her analysis of the piece, Audrey shared, "She is a product of her environment. No one stops to think about why she thinks that life is suitable and it's because that's all she knows. . . . She can't want better for herself if she doesn't think it gets any better." This narrative allowed BYP to analyze media and discuss economic disparities and their impact on neighborhood composition, schools, and the meaning of success. For the girls, as articulated by Audrey, success "has a different meaning in every neighborhood." Where girls live and attend schools makes a great impact on their lives. Historical discrimination in housing policies has had lasting effects on neighborhoods, their schools, and the students who live in and attend them. Cashin (2004) claims that "housing was the last plank in the civil rights revolution, and it is the realm in which we have experienced the fewest integration gains" (p. 3). Current housing policies—gentrification, zoning, and redistricting, and those that provide housing assistance—continue to maintain segregated neighborhoods and schools. BYP's dialogue about stereotypes that impact the image of Black women led our collective into discussions about wealth and class disparities, school segregation, equity, and opportunities.

## Learning From *Beyond Your Perception*

Maria W. Stewart encouraged Black women to know themselves and to act on that knowledge of self to produce social change. In BYP, we studied the history of ourselves in effort to engage in knowing and acting. We gained sociohistorical understandings by analyzing foundational stereotypes of Black women/womanhood to better understand the origins of gendered racism and sexism. We analyzed media, viewing and listening to music videos and clips from television shows and films in effort to address blind consumerism and to critically examine media and the music, television, and film industries. We also moved to action by composing counternarratives. I introduced the girls to a variety of mediums to express themselves and encouraged them to write personal counterstories. By doing so, they were better able to understand the dangers of a single story and the importance of self-definition. These lessons and activities allowed the girls to understand the power of their own voice, to be literate social practitioners, and underscored the importance of deconstructing the dominant narrative.

## Critical Media and the Black Girls' Literacies Framework

The work illustrated earlier with the girls in Beyond Your Perception reflect all six of BGL framework and serve as a practical example of how to utilize the framework, which is critical and humanizing, within curriculum and instruction, while the work of BYP illuminates how centering Black girls' lived experiences in critical media literacy teaches critical thinking and interrogation. This assignment builds on multiple literacies by espousing critical literacy (uncovering underlying messages), media literacy (analyzing media representations and creating media), historical literacy (historically conceptual reasoning), and economic literacy (funding and resource availability). The literacy practices we engaged in BYP were layered. Further, BYP's lessons were tied to the girls' identities and collaboration. We shared our knowledge on the topics presented and co-constructed meaning and understanding. We problematized our thoughts on the topics. We did not instantly arrive at critical consciousness, but through deliberate dialogue and collective musing, we advanced our thinking on our communities and ourselves. Our teaching and learning were co-constructed, and we were in a constant state of selfhood. We used an historical lens to examine the phenomenon of current stereotypes that are overlaid onto the bodies of Black girls that come from old tropes of Black women, and we situated our conversations in an historical analysis on the oppressive structures that marginalize Black women, like housing policies and wealth distribution. These discussions were intellectual, political, and critical, building on the knowledge and experiences the girls brought to the conversation and expanded that knowledge through the curriculum and instruction of BYP. Not only did we discuss power and oppression, we also talked about possible solutions for marginalized populations, specifically Black women.

By highlighting the Black Girls' Literacies Framework in practice, I have demonstrated the feasibility of employing a framework that aids in creating socially empowered critical thinkers. Classroom teachers could use the BYP activity of creating counternarratives by asking their students to rewrite characters as different identities (e.g., race, ethnicity, class, gender, language, sexuality, gender identity, and/or religion) and discuss how the change in identity shifts the story and changes the reader's perception of their character's position in the text. Grouping students together based on the character they chose would also provide rich discussion, as students may have chosen to rewrite the same character as various identities. Chapters of texts, or whole texts, could be rewritten, with characters taking on new identities, and as a class discussing the way the changes in identity transform the storyline, specifically focusing on how historical, racialized, gendered, classed, or other structural changes to the life and livelihood of the characters becomes based on the change in identity. Engaging students in the practice of considering how a story, fictional or nonfictional, changes based on identity fosters critical autonomy so that students will want to critically question media when they are not with their teacher (Masterman, 1990). In this way, curriculum and instruction use multiple literacies, are tied to students' identities, and are historical, collaborative, intellectual, political/critical; all students are able to advance through deep interrogation of the world as text and discover, or cultivate, their agentic power to be conduits of social change.

## Moving *Beyond* Sanctioned Curriculum

The members of Beyond Your Perception recognized social stigmas and issues surrounding marginalized populations, as a whole, and Black women specifically. They became empowered to take their grounding in multiple literacies and act on them in ways to help others. For example, Sy, a BYP sister, created healing circles on her college campus in an effort to address the void of space for female students of color on her predominantly white campus. Other BYP sisters took up the arms of activism in other ways on their campuses and in their neighborhoods. Teaching them how to read media and the world as text BYP, the girls, in turn, read that world and found ways to make it better. They continued in the Black women's social activism tradition. From early activists, such as Harriet Tubman, Anna Murray Douglass, Mary Ann Shadd Cary, and Sojourner Truth to their successors, such as Angela Davis, Kathleen Cleaver, Clara Muhammad, and Coretta Scott King, to today, through Alicia Garza, Patrisse Cullors and Opal Tometi, Bree Newsome, and Johnetta Elzie, these women's lives are evidence that traditions of striving for social change are continuing and still necessary. Black girls and women are a part of an ongoing movement that calls for radical change. As testament to this history, the Black Lives Matter movement was an ideological intervention spearheaded by three women—Alicia Garza, Patrisse Cullors, and Opal Tometi—after the not-guilty verdict for George Zimmerman in the killing of Trayvon Martin. Their efforts helped to propel the movement forward. There are other recent examples of this activist lineage. "The Millions March," which began in New York City (NYC) after the November 24, 2014, decision not to indict officer Darren Wilson in the killing of Michael Brown in Ferguson, was organized by Synead Nichols and Umaara Elliot through Facebook; and Carmen Perez, co-founder of Justice League NYC, initiated the "die-in" movement. The Millennial Activist United organization was started by three queer Black women—Ashley Yates, Alexis Templeton, and Brittney Ferrell—in Ferguson, Missouri. However, when people mention the Black Lives Matter movement, the way that the media have characterized the "radical" nature of the movement has led many to believe that the protests in Ferguson to the "Millions March" across the country are in fact "leaderless." To the contrary: These movements have deep and sustained leadership. Often, women's contributions and leadership are, however, left invisible and minimized in the broader conversations and historical records.

Black girls need more spaces and places in which they can critique the world they live in and where they can be taught social activism practices that challenge the dominant narrative. This means moving beyond the sanctioned curriculum in schools and classrooms. Youth need opportunities to develop their narrative voice to relate racialized, gendered, and classed experiences to expose bias in the worlds in which they live and learn to express arguments against injustice. Utilizing the Black Girls' Literacies Framework, the work of Beyond Your Perception advanced the criticality, intellectual development, and the girls' understanding of, and their proficiency in, their multiple literacies and the role of media in influencing their construction of self and others. The roles of Black women throughout history have helped to make society better for all people, and through critical inter-rogation for deeper understanding of multiple oppressions and counternarrating racist, sexist, and classist media narratives with stories of multidimensionality of Black girlhood, Black girls can continue the fight.

## Note

1. A previous version of this article appeared as:
   McArthur, S. A. (2016). Black girls and critical media literacy for social activism. *English Education, 48*(4), 462–479.

## References

Alsup, J., & Miller, S. J. (2014). Reclaiming English education: Rooting social justice in dispositions. *English Education, 46*(3), 195–215.

Alvermann, D. E. (2006). Pointers for introducing critical media literacy to your students. *The Journal of Media Literacy, 53*(2), 12–15.

Alvermann, D. E., & Hagood, M. C. (2000). Critical media literacy: Research, theory, and practice in "New Times." *Journal of Educational Research, 93*, 193–205.

Barnett, B. M. N. (1993). Invisible southern Black women leaders in the civil rights movement: The triple constraints of gender, race and class. *Gender & Society, 7*(2), 162–182.

Brown, M. (2017). #SayHerName: A case study of intersectional social media activism. *Ethnic and Racial Studies, 40*(11), 1831–1846.

Cashin, S. (2004). *The failures of integration: How race and class are undermining the American dream.* New York City, NY: PublicAffairs Publishers.

Compaine, B. M., & Gomery, D. (2000). *Who owns the media?: Competition and concentration in the mass media.* Mahwah, NJ: Routledge.

Evans-Winters, V. (2005). *Teaching Black girls: Resiliency in urban classrooms.* New York: Peter Lang.

Giroux, H. (2013). Is there a place for cultural studies in colleges of education? In H. Giroux, C. Lankshear, & M. Peters (Eds.), *Counternarratives: Cultural studies and critical pedagogies in postmodern spaces* (pp. 47–58). Florence, KY: Routledge.

Haddix, M., & Sealey-Ruiz, Y. (2012). Cultivating digital and popular literacies as empowering and emancipatory acts among urban youth. *Journal of Adolescent & Adult Literacy, 56*(3), 189–192.

Harris, Fredrick C. 1999. *Something within: Religion in African-American political activism.* New York: Oxford University Press.

Harris-Perry, M. (2011). *Sister citizen: Shame, stereotypes, and Black women in America.* New Haven: Yale University Press.

Hinchey, P. H. (2003). Introduction: Teaching media literacy: Not if, but why and how. *The Clearing House,* (6), 268.

Hobbs, R. (1997). Literacy for the information age. In J. Flood, S. B. Heath, & D. Lapp (Eds.), *Handbook of research on teaching literacy through the communicative and visual arts* (pp. 7–14). New York: Simon & Schuster.

hooks, b. (1994). *Teaching to transgress: Education as the practice of freedom.* New York: Routledge.

Horn, R. A. (2003). Developing a critical awareness of the hidden curriculum through media literacy. *The Clearing House,* (6), 298.

Jackson, S. J. (2016). (Re)Imagining intersectional democracy from Black feminism to hashtag activism. *Women's Studies in Communication, 39*(4), 375–379.

Kellner, D., & Share, J. (2005). Toward critical media literacy: Core concepts, debates, organizations, and policy. *Discourse: Studies in the Cultural Politics of Education, 26*(3), 369. doi:10.1080/01596300500200169

Kellner, D., & Share, J. (2007). Critical media literacy is not an option. *Learning Inquiry, 1*(1), 59–69.

Lemieux, J. (2014, March). Black feminism goes viral. *Ebony, 69*(5), 126–131.

Luke, C. (2000). Cyber-schooling and technological change: Multiliteracies for new times. In B. Cope, & M. Kalantzis (Eds.), *Multiliteracies: Literacy, learning & the design of social futures* (pp. 69–105). Melbourne, Australia: Macmillan.

Lutz, A. (2012, June). These 6 companies control 90% of the media in America. *Business Insider.*

Masterman, L. (1990). *Teaching the media.* London: Routledge.

McArthur, S. A. (2016). Black girls and critical media literacy for social activism. *English Education, 48*(4), 462–479.

McArthur, S. A. (2018). 'My Sister, Myself': Why the miseducation of Black girls requires spaces and places for their healing. In M. B. Sankofa Waters, V. E. Evans-Winters, and B. L. Love (Eds.), *Celebrating twenty years of Black girlhood: Lauryn Hill Reader* (pp. 101–111). New York, NY: Peter Lang Publishing.

McArthur, S. A. (2019). Centering student identities in critical media literacy instruction. *Journal of Adolescent and Adult Literacy, 62*(6), 686–689.

McBrien, J. L. (1999). New texts, new tools: An argument for media literacy. *Educational Leadership, 57*(2), 76–79.

Morrell, E. (2014). Popular culture 2.0: Teaching critical media literacy in the language arts classroom. *New England Reading Association Journal, 50*(1), 5–7.

Morrell, E., & Duncan-Andrade, J. (2006). Popular culture and critical media pedagogy in secondary literacy classrooms. *International Journal of Learning, 12*(9), 273–280.

Muhammad, G. E., & Haddix, M. (2016). Centering Black girls' literacies: A review of literature on the multiple ways of knowing of Black girls. *English Education, 48*(4), 299–336.

Muhammad, G. E., & McArthur, S. A. (2015). "Styled by their perceptions": Adolescent girls' interpretations of Black girlhood in the media. *Multicultural Perspectives, 17*(3), 1–8.

Paugh, P. (2014). Introduction. In P. Paugh, T. Kress, & R. Lake (Eds.), *Teaching towards democracy with postmodern and popular culture texts.* New York: Sense Publishers.

Richardson, M. (1987). *Maria W. Stewart, America's first Black woman political writer: Essays and speeches.* Bloomington: Indiana University Press.

Scharrer, E. S. (2015). Intervening in the media's influence on stereotypes of race and ethnicity: The role of media literacy education. *Journal of Social Issues, 71*(1), 171–185.

Stephens, D., & Few, A. (2007). Hip hop honey or video ho: African American preadolescents understanding of female sexual scripts in hip hop culture. *Sexuality & Culture, 11*(4), 48–69.

Stephens, D. P., & Phillips, L. D. (2003). Freaks, gold diggers, divas, and dykes: The sociohistorical development of adolescent African American women's sexual scripts. *Sexuality & Culture, 7*(1), 3–49.

Tisdell, E. J. (2008). Critical media literacy and transformative learning. *Journal of Transformative Education, 6*(1), 48–67.

Wheeler, M. S. (1993). *New women of the new South: The leaders of the women suffrage movement in the southern states.* New York: Oxford University Press.

Williams, S. (2015). Digital defense: Black feminists resist violence with hashtag activism. *Feminist Media Studies, 15*(2), 341–344.

Yosso, T. J. (2002). Critical race media literacy: Challenging deficit discourse about Chicanas/os. *Journal of Popular Film and Television, 30*(1), 52–62.

# KITCHEN TABLE TALKS

## Creating Spaces for Black Girls' Literacies

*Bettina Love in Conversation with Sherell McArthur,*
*Erica Womack, and Gholdy Muhammad*

The authors in this section gathered around a virtual kitchen table, using the online platform Zoom, to engage in conversation around shared ideas and guiding questions about Black girls' literacies practices. They participated in a conversation where they talked across their respective work as literacy educators and scholars who foreground Black feminist/womanist epistemologies in their personal, social, and professional lives. This kitchen table talk is organized around these sub questions:

- Why is it critical that educators acknowledge Black girls' literacies in their work?
- Why is it important to create spaces for Black girls' literacies both in and out of schools?
- How are Black girls' literacies honored in your work?
- When you think about spaces for Black girls, what are important considerations for the field of literacy education?
- What practical recommendations would you offer educators working with Black girls?

In the sections that follow, we highlight our dialogic exchanges in response to these questions and conclude with final words of wisdom. To recreate our kitchen table talk, we video-recorded our Zoom chat and transcribed the video. Each section that follows captures key points that were made to address the guiding questions.

## Acknowledging Black Girls' Literacies

### *Why Is It Critical That Educators Acknowledge Black Girls' Literacies in Their Work?*

ERICA: For me, if Black girl literacies are not acknowledged then they can be rendered mute, unacknowledgeable, and worse yet, invisible. I feel like if Black girls are in high poverty or low poverty schools we have to be seen and heard. Have to be challenged with the type of work that we are given. If not, what I see and I'm already seeing it a little bit with my daughter, who is 12 years old and in the 7th grade, is a lack of confidence in your voice, identity, appearance, and the list goes on. So, we have to be able to work with teachers to build those types of character traits up and that's what led me to this work in the first place. Going into an English Language Arts classroom and seeing Black girls ignored by their white teachers. That's why I feel like the work is important and why Black girl literacies need to be acknowledged.

SHERELL: I agree. I think that Black girls continue to remain hyper-visible particularly as it relates to what schools deem problematic behaviors but invisible as it relates to Black girls' needs. In the work I have done with Black girls in the variety of spaces and cities particularly in the Northeast and Southeast—they don't feel seen or heard. Whatever it is that they do that draws attention to them in any way, it's never in a way that makes them feel like they get the attention they want or need. They're put out of classrooms, they're yelled at, they're labeled, they're put in different groupings, right? But until they come into the different groups and programs in my spaces, do they feel seen and heard for the problems that are going in their social groups, with romantic partners, with their friends, with their family members, with parents, right? They're hyper-visible for laughing in school for what teachers call disrespectful and disobedient behavior but rarely do they ever feel seen in those spaces. So, it's really significant for educators to understand Black girls' way of being, ways of knowing, their first practices so that they can be honored in those spaces fully.

GHOLDY: I'll just add that I've read so many books about girls and their educational practices. There are a lot of books that use the title "girls" but then don't include the experiences, the racialized, gendered experiences of Black girls at all. And there are so many intersections of Black girlhood that really if you center them, this begins to be a roadmap to get to right with all different youth. Because Black girls uniquely can be oppressed or marginalized based on race, class, gender, sexuality, religion, and other categories. That's unique compared to a lot of other groups.

SHERELL: And where do Black girls get to see themselves, right? It's also important that educators acknowledge Black girl literacies in schools because where do Black girls get to see themselves? In schools, they get to see themselves in a Rosa Parks maybe a Coretta Scott King. But, where else? Where else in 13 years do Black girls get to see themselves? Why don't educators think that's not problematic? That they can sit in a school space from math, to science, to social studies, to music—Black girls don't get to be represented in those spaces. It's very important that Black girls understand who they are and how they are because that level of representation matters as well.

BETTINA:  I think for the four Black women who are on the phone right now, we all are successful not because of the system but despite the system. And each and every time you talk to Black girls and you talk to Black women, you hear these stories of always triumphing, always finding a way out of no way and making a way out of no way. What we know is that the system is not sustainable. So, the system asks Black girls to do the labor of this country all the time, even as little girls. So, you hear about little girls in the classroom doing the work of the teacher, being the teacher's assistant, being emotionally there for everybody. What this school system and what this country asks Black girls, who then become Black women to do is unsustainable, it's not healthy and we know what happens to us when we can't keep this thing up and death is one of those options.

And so, we know why it is important to do this type of work and to try to get a teaching force who understands that this work is for the mental well-being of Black girls, for the health, the physical health of Black girls and we know that this is also soul work. This is spiritual work. It's all wrapped up for me. It's all wrapped up in Black girl joy. It's all wrapped up in Black girl magic. I think we have to help people understand that when we say Black girl joy or Black girl magic, we are not just talking about us living these whimsical lives where everything is perfect. We are constantly trying to reinvent ourselves. We are constantly trying to make something out of nothing because we are constantly given the shit of this country. I think that's "supposed" to be right because we have so much joy and so much love. So, for me, you know, Black women are the soul of not only Black folks but this country. As Sherell said, we are hyper-visible but invisible at the exact same time and that has always been our relationship to this country, and it is our relationship to schooling.

## Importance of Creating Spaces for Black Girls

### Why Is It Important to Create Spaces for Black Girls' Literacies Both In and Out of Schools?

BETTINA:  I think the one thing we have in this group that is important to highlight is being a black girl is not monolithic. We have four different Black girls on this call right now. For me, it's always making sure that we find a space for Black girls. Queer Black girls, as well, All the representations of what we say

Black girls are. That they feel loved, they feel cherished, they feel beautiful, they feel special and as bell hooks talk about in her work, that we give Black girls a "homeplace". A place to replenish. A place to get your soul nurtured. A place that nurtures your spirit, your mind, and body so you can go back out there and fight and deal with the racism. Creating a space for black girls for me is like creating a home space. That we do the work of helping provide and maybe thrive in these spaces.

SHERELL: I think we created those spaces because there is a lack of racial literacy that's prevalent within them. We know that because we recognize that, like Tina is saying, we have to make space that allows them and gives them room to breathe because those spaces are confining, they're constraining for us.

ERICA: Kind of pigging backing off that, just again a space without apology or question. Bettina already mentioned like a place where we can resist, to be able to combat the daily assaults on Black girlhood. Girls need spaces to be able to do that on a daily basis.

GHOLDY: And when the schools don't offer that, you know . . . I think Black girls have always created something out of nothing but especially when the curriculum and the schools don't. These spaces become extra necessary. When the schools or the curriculum don't offer it.

## Honoring Black Girl Literacies

### How Are Black Girls' Literacies Honored in Your Work?

SHERELL: I center Black girls in my work. That for me is the complete homage by centering their history, their literacies, their cultural practices, their language practices, the games they play, the music they listen to. And anybody who comes into spaces that I have created who aren't Black girls are more than welcomed as long as they know Black girls are going to be centered. So, you know, I've been a part of different organizations and different institutions. And they say, "does it have to say Black? What if somebody who is not Black wants to come?" And I say, "they are more than welcome to come, as long as they know that I'm going to center Black girls". I have had white girls in my spaces, I have had Latino boys in my spaces. They enjoy it just as much! Southeast Asian girls have been in my spaces and they enjoy it just as much, but I am going to continue to center Black girls because that's who I do it for.

GHOLDY: It's funny how when you put "Black girls" people think they can't learn from it. You know like people ask me all the time, "these implications you have from your research with Black girls, is it just for Black girls?" I always say, "why would we just keep excellence for Black girls?" We have never been selfish people as Black people. If it's good for us and it's good for you, then you can use these practices. You can use these implications.

It's something interesting when people think that when they see something for girls that has nothing to do with Black girls, they think it's for all girls. If you flip that, right, they think they can't learn from the practices of Black girls' spaces.

SHERELL: And, also when there's void of any level of diversity, right? Racial, ethnic, cultural, gender diversity. When it's void of that, there's no problem there, right? It's like they walk with blinders. You actually have to have point out the problem with that. Everybody should be able to learn when there's a complete lack of any level of diversity. But when you say, well it's Black, well wait a minute. Can anybody else learn? Well, how is it possible that the rest of us have been able to function in these schools the way they are situated with whatever functionality looks like? We need to question what functionality looks like because that's problematic. But when we attach, like you're saying, "Black" now it's a problem. That is the problem.

BETTINA: I think for me it's everything Sherell and Gholdy have said. I would just add for me and my work when I think about Black girls is the idea that they inherently always have something important to say. I've learned that. I've seen that. I've been part of that. I am that. When Black girls and Black women speak, they inherently have something to say that makes us better as human beings. I don't know what that is or why we have that. I don't know what that is about us but when you listen to Black girls, they are not only going to tell you about what's going on with them but what's going on with society. How to make things better for everybody else. How this world can be different if we would understand this. I'm always ready to be in awe of what Black girls have to share. Ready to learn from them. Ready to listen to them. It's not like Black girls haven't been listened to so you have to listen to them. No, they just have something to say that's profound about the situations that they are living in. And I think when you live at so many intersections you just have a really deep understanding of what makes this world better. I think when you live at all of these intersections and you experience all these intersections there's a way in which you see the world that is valuable for everybody.

## Important Consideration When Creating Spaces for Black Girls

### When You Think About Spaces for Black Girls, What Are Important Considerations for the Field of Literacy Education?

GHOLDY: I think like Sherell said you center their voices, listen to them, and be prudent in responsibility even with the data if you are a researcher because everything doesn't need to be shared in publication. Or, like if you're presenting stories seeped in pain, what kind of joy-giving stories can you include? You know, we can't get caught up in that narrative as well. Somebody told me, "how do I teach these novels that are really great African American literature but seeped in pain?" I said, contextually you can go to the context of that story and pull out examples of Black love, Black joy, Black innovation during the time context of the story. You can balance the joy. I feel like that's the responsibility that researchers should have when working with Black girls. There are some responsibilities there in knowing the types of ways they've [Black girls] been misrepresented, invisible, hyper-visible, and stereotyped.

ERICA: Yeah, I was just reading recently that's called "trauma porn". So, I was careful about that in my work having a balance between showing pain and then also progress or resistance. Some of the girls did share stories of being sexually assaulted or abandoned by one or more of their parents but then also, showing ways through the literacy engagements we had that they resisted through visual representation, writing, so on and so forth. That was important to me, so you know it wasn't just focused on pain all of the time.

## Implications for Teachers of Black Girls

### What Practical Recommendations Would You Give Educators Working With Black Girls?

BETTINA: I would say the very first thing is give Black girls a space, a loving space, an affirming space to be heard. To speak their truths. Not feel like there is going to be any retaliation. Not feel like they're going to be reprimanded but to speak their truths. The most powerful thing you have as a person of color in this country is your voice. And Black girls have something to say. You have to create a space where these Black, young girls know that they can speak their truths and that they will be heard. And then after they have spoken their truths, it's up to the teacher to find space and make space for what they have said to be taken seriously. So, to make an opportunity for them to speak and then for them to see what they said has made a change— has made a difference in that classroom. I think that it's important that they be heard, be affirmed, and then you do something with that is what I think one of the most important things you can do for Black girls in the classroom. For them to see their voice as a literacy practice, that's important. For them and the classroom.

ERICA: Also, for them [educators] to seek their input on what these spaces could look like and encourage them to create counter-narratives in terms of some of the public ideologies that are out there, ways that they can resist those of Black girls being loud, un-ladylike, or deviant.

SHERELL: And also, give them room to be. When they're not being poetic, or prophetic, or resisting. Just give them room to be sometimes. Black women and Black girls are in constant critique. They are constantly being critiqued. What they say, how they dress, what they look like, or how they move. Just let them be. How they're speaking at the time is not significant to the academics. If it's not about the writing at the time, let them be. Let them come to the space as themselves. And too often in any classroom, teachers don't let children and youth—particularly of color—just be. Just let them show up and when it's time to be academic then teach them how to be academic. But otherwise, just let them be. Let them show up as themselves.

GHOLDY: Yeah, it's not just all academics. We privilege it in schools. We honor, we hold up academic success but what about personal development, identity development? What about a consciousness to navigate this world? What about anti-oppressive education? Black girls have to have intellectual spaces too. But they need room to make sense of who they are.

We concluded this discussion by declaring that Black girls and their literacies matter. For those interested in working with Black girls, they must do the self-reflective work necessary to seriously and authentically engage with Black girls. We conclude with these final words of wisdom.

SHERELL: I just think that people doing work, educators doing work with Black girls must know that it takes self-reflection. We have to ask "why label her with that? Where does that come from?" I think that requires self-reflection. I think it requires thought in order to do this work so that they [Black girls] don't get cast with our own fears and doubts, negative perceptions of what we think about Black women. What we've been taught to believe about Black women from media representation, or society, or our experiences, or what have you. Black girls tend to get that short end of the stick.

# SECTION 2
# Black Girls' Language and Literacy Practices

# 4

# ROOTED RELATIONS

## Toward Black Girl Placemaking

*Tamara T. Butler*

### Not Strangers

We ascended quickly—3, 4, 5,000 feet above the city of San Diego and then out over the Pacific Ocean. I caught a glance of a glowing horizon over the left wing of the plane—orange growing between black, cerulean, and indigo. We turned east and climbed another 5 or 20,000 feet. I wasn't too sure. As some passengers settled in for the 3-hour flight, I turned to Howard's reminder in *Black Nature*:

> At some point, the terms *urban* and *black* became interchangeable. Such terminology would have us believe that our history began in cities and that we are a people of concrete and bricks, far removed from the oaks, rivers, and low country.
>
> *(Howard, 2005, p. 37)*

As I re-read "began in cities . . . we are a people of concrete and bricks", I kept sky and ocean in my peripheral. Much pull-and-pull—migration fueled by unemployment, property taxes, industrialization, resort development, schooling—made us concrete, brick, and mortar people, who also knew dirt, grass, and trees. I inhaled a fleeting vision of California cliffs and rocky shores, then remembered Carolina sand dunes and cattails. As a child of the South Carolina Sea Islands, also called the Lowcountry, I understood being a people of "oaks, rivers, and low country." Tunnels of Spanish moss and Grand oak tree encapsulate the two-lane roads that weave through Johns Island. When the tunnels open, there are fields of pine trees or crisping sunflowers, marshland or farmland, scattered mailboxes and "land for sale" signs. The emerging BlackGirlLand project started when I first came to understand how property taxes, changing racial and class demographics and Heirs' property impacted my family and other Black families who lived on the island for generations (Jones-Jackson, 1987). The project, and it multiple components, is deeply informed by Black Girls' Literacies (Muhammad & Haddix, 2016) in that it is a critical, personal, political, and intellectual venture. Black women's placemaking practices generate spaces to learn and help families like mine, who still live in the same community where my maternal great-grandmother raised three sons, five daughters, and several grandchildren. Learning, listening, and documenting are placemaking practices connected to fortifying Black families' ties to land and one another.

I developed the BlackGirlLand Project with the intention of documenting stories of Black women living on Johns Island. Having internalized Morrison's (1993) assertion that "narrative is radical" (p. 203), I believed that the stories of those who lived on the island were powerful tools that could be used in fights for property rights. For months, I listened to elders in the community—Black women who shared their stories of working in the fields, attending school and church on the Island, learning how to share with and care for one another. I spoke with, listened to, and video-recorded each woman with the belief that if I could document what the community means to them, then maybe this would stop distant relatives from selling their family's property and stop resort developers from buying said property. If I could not intervene in this capitalistic destruction of family lands, then at least I would have stories to help future generations imagine what Johns Island was like for our parents, grandparents, great-grandparents, and other ancestors.

As I continue to interview community elders, I am interested in how educators can be involved in the process of preserving Black land, documenting community narratives, and remembering community histories. For local K-12 educators, such a project opens up possibilities for social studies and language arts classrooms. Students and educators can begin to foster relationships with community members that begin to transform the way we think about local history, narrative writing, and primary sources. In this chapter, I turn to my own classroom, where I began to think about other stakeholders who are connected to land and communities like the South Carolina Sea Islands.

One group of stakeholders key to this project are the individuals who do not live in rural southern Black communities. Howard (2005) asserts that the conflation of *black* with *urban* "would have us believe that our history began in cities and that we are a people of concrete and bricks" (p. 37). Through the work of Wilkerson (2011), Boehm (2010), Chatelain (2015), and others, we come to recognize that some of the stakeholders are individuals who moved north and west through the Great Migration of the 1920s or the 1940s. As they emigrated out of southern Black communities, future generations did not develop a clear understanding of how land, property, and labor informed their families' practices, ways of knowing and being. As an educator at a Midwestern university that prided itself on being a "pioneer land grant" institution, I often thought about how students and their families come to a place, where their histories begin, and what their stories are. As a graduate of and an educator at a "land grant" institution, I was constantly thinking about who granted Indigenous lands to whom.

In Spring 2017, I launched an African American & African Studies special topics course entitled The BlackGirlLand Project, which borrows its name from my larger research project, described previously. It was an opportunity to have students think about what it means to be from, of, and in a place. As students attending the "pioneer land grant" institution, they were encouraged to think about what it meant to be visitors on the lands of the Ojibwe, Odawa, and Potawatomi peoples. Through various readings and activities, we began to question our relationship not only to the land on which the university was built, but the places where our families live and have lived. I envisioned the course as a space where students would begin to ask questions about their families' migration stories and possibly reach a place where they would return home to ask about rural southern roots, family land, or their responsibilities as descendants of land-owning/land-working/(seemingly) landless peoples. What types of practices might emerge from such a space? What types of stories would we need to listen for, share or not share? Over the course of 16 weeks, I came to know 15 students who each came from Midwest metropolises and suburbs (Indiana, Michigan, and Illinois). Through 28 class sessions and a one-day retreat, they shared stories and reflections that taught me about disruption, connections, and memory. Collectively, the students showed me that the course was a space for young people to engage in the practices of mapping and placemaking.

## Grounding Interstitial Frames

Black women scholars across geography, ecology, and African American & African Studies push us to think about the legacy of Black women's connections to land and the various fields of study. If we are to study place, space, race, and gender, we must consider the ways in which women, Black women, and Women of Color have shaped and continue to shape landscapes. Also, we must consider the ways in which land, space, and place have shaped and continue to shape women, Black women, and Women of Color. Therefore, the title of the project and the course pay homage to the work of Mistinguette Smith, Eve Tuck, Alison Guess and the Black/Land Project, while bringing specific attention to the ways that women, specifically Black women, are redefining our connections to land (e.g., property ownership, community protection, environmental justice). In *Demonic Grounds*, McKittrick (2006) asserts that the study of Black women's connections to land is not new; therefore, our work must be grounded in the practice of imagining, uncovering, and rearticulating those connections. Such work moves us toward more "humanly workable geographies" (p. xii) that can begin to describe and study various, multifaceted relationships to land, space, nature, place, and one another.

In an effort to explore how my students and I imagined and navigated those multifaceted relationships, I turn to the generative interstitial space between the frameworks from Black feminist (Collins, 2000; Dotson, 2014), decolonial (Figueroa, 2015; Lugones, 2010; Mendez, 2015), Indigenous (Styres, 2011; Simpson, 2014; Tuck, McKenzie, & McCoy, 2014), and Black Girls' Literacies scholars (Muhammad & Haddix, 2016). In previous research, I engaged in a "plurilogue" (Roshanravan, 2014) between Women of Color feminist philosophies and English education in order to center Black women's voices and lived experiences in K-12 and teacher education classrooms (Butler, 2017). In this chapter, I invite more perspectives to the plurilogue, including the writings of Indigenous scholars who offer responsible conceptualizations of land that focus on listening, respect, and reciprocity. Black feminist, decolonial, and Indigenous frameworks inform my conceptualization of the course and the larger project. Black Girls' Literacies shape my understanding of the practices that are enacted in the larger project and emerged out of the course.

### Indigenous Relations: Land as Pedagogy and First Teacher

In starting with the notion that Land (Styres, Haig-Brown, & Blimkie, 2013) is a living relative and teacher, we must start with the work of Indigenous scholars. Land (with a capital L) focuses on relationships, knowledge, and people as well as environment (e.g., animals, plants, air, water). Therefore, who we are and what we know are linked to our relationship with where we are and other people. Simpson (2014) echoes this in "Land as pedagogy", where she opens with a story of *how* the Kwenzen learned to access maple sugar. Through the story, we come to see that Kwenzen "comes to know maple sugar in the context of love", in a place where discovery is encouraged and she is recognized, seen, and appreciated.

Styres (2011) writes that when we recognize "Land as first teacher", we are able to discuss "the interconnectedness and interdependency of relationships, cultural positioning and subjectivities that extend beyond the borderlands of traditional mainstream conceptualizations of pedagogy" (p. 722). We learn about who we are and where we are through listening, observing, sharing, and respect—practices are reinforced through visiting with elders. Simpson (2014) and Styres (2011) in conversation with their communities emphasize visiting and being in conversation with elders as central practices for learning histories and developing ways of being and knowing that can only be learned through intricate connections.

### Black and Decolonial Feminisms: Black Women's Knowledge

Similarly, practices of listening and visiting inform how and what Black women know as well as how we share what we know. Since Black women's epistemologies are essential to Black feminist theoretical, intellectual, and political projects, the central course is informed by Black and decolonial feminist conceptions of knowledge. Therefore, our ways of knowing inform the methodologies that we use to access, make sense of, and represent knowledge. For example, in spaces where Black women often tell stories that emerge from their experiences as racial-gendered bodies, the research methodologies must focus on listening and storytelling. When paired with Indigenous land education and decolonial feminisms, methodologies not only begin to focus on women's stories and interconnected knowledge, but also call into question where else research practices might still uphold legacies of colonialism.

The larger research project and course are informed by epistemologies rooted in Black and decolonial feminisms and Indigenous land education. Black and decolonial feminisms bring to the forefront the intellectual work of Black women and Women of Color as deeply personal and political. Black and decolonial feminists (Figueroa, 2015; Dotson, 2014; Lugones, 2010; Mendez, 2015) articulate how race, gender, sexuality, and class became identity markers that, when intersected and mapped onto bodies in colonial contexts, became markers for dehumanization, exploitation, and erasure. Similarly, they explicitly bring attention to how Women of Color have transformed the "interstitial" spaces where race, class, gender, and sexuality overlap to develop theories of survival, agency, resistance, and social transformation. Indigenous land education centers the practices and conversations that we have about our relationship to one another, physical environment, and spiritual knowledge.

## Geographies of Black Girls' Literacies

The practices of mapping and remembering that emerge from the course embody tenets of Black Girls' Literacies. Muhammad and Haddix (2016) reviewed 46 studies that focus on Black girls' reading, speaking, and writing practices and ways of being. Through their research, they conclude that Black Girls' Literacies are: multiple, tied to identities, historical, collaborative, intellectual, and political/critical (Muhammad & Haddix, 2016, p. 325). Black women and girls can begin to (re)inscribe one another to space, place, and land that they/we may have been written out of through the practice of remembering. By engaging in Black and decolonial feminist mapping practices, we place Black women and girls' knowledge and ways of knowing at the center of placemaking practices.

Savoy (2015) reminds us of the ways that mapping has served (and continues to serve) as a colonial practice. Naming and renaming of place often relied upon the erasure of people and histories (Tuck, Guess, & Sultan, 2014; Morgan, 2004) and ignoring land as a living relative and teacher (Styres, 2011). In "What's in a Name", she writes, "it may be commonplace to consider place-names or toponyms as givens, distinguishing one piece of terrain from another. To think this, though, is to see a reflecting surface and not what lies beneath" (Savoy, 2015, p. 71). Throughout the text, she brings attention to European "explorers" (colonizers) and politicians misnaming Indigenous communities, waterways, and landscapes. For example, she offers an extensive discussion of how *Kitchigame* became known as Lake Superior (pp. 50–52) and how the name *Wyoming* was dislodged from its origins in the eastern United States and attached to a state west of the Mississippi River (pp. 78–79). Alongside my students, I was interested in learning more about the "what lies beneath" the cities and places that we call home. Through our conversations, we approached the questions: *What stories are we overlooking? Who do we not see? Who are we not listening to?* Most importantly: *why?* Over the course of the semester, we began to develop our own practices of mapping that began to tear away at the plundering, deception, and erasure that is embedded in colonial naming and categorizing practices.

Contemporary works in Black Geographies, Women's & Gender Studies, and Critical Ethnic Studies highlight the ways that Black women's knowledge shape places, socially, culturally, politically, and geographically. In her work on aging Black women in Brazil, Henery (2011) walks with 34 women to learn how their labor and lived experiences shape the landscape of Belo Horizonte. The women's stories challenge dominant narratives of favelas as "low-income neighborhoods which are now visually characterized by their densely packed homes" located in "precarious or peripheral spaces of cities" (p. 98). Instead, the women share that the favelas are shaped by women's movement in and out of homes and through the streets as domestic workers. Henery positions the women's stories as narratives that begin to complicate our understanding of space, place, land, and memory. In the changing climate, the women express concern about "unfurling of the ethics of honest labor and collective investment" they have cultivated among one another and sought to pass on to future generations (p. 95). Perry (2013) documents how women in Gamboa de Baixo, Salvador, defended their communities against corporations' and individuals' exploitative efforts to remove them from their homes and land. She highlights how women served as social justice foot soldiers who often placed their bodies on the line in order to protect their homes (p. 3) and to demand safer neighborhoods for their families (pp. 55–59). Collectively, the studies highlight how geography develops as a physical, intellectual, and metaphorical project.

With these lenses, mapping, when guided by Black women's remembering and memory work, becomes a Black and decolonial feminist practice. In this way, we recognize our interdependence and reengage land (physical location) as Land—spiritual, interconnected spaces that are living and filled with memories and stories. Such work also challenges our understanding of home, place, and land. According to Savoy (2015), "we may find that home lies in the *re-membering*—in piecing together the fragments left—and in reconciling what it means to inhabit terrains of memory, and to be one" (p. 2). Such ways of knowing create spaces within and beyond the academy to imagine women's roles in transforming communities. Using the frameworks set forth by current studies that focus on Black women's geographies, my students and I work through theories in an African American & African Studies course to think about their own map-making, knowledges and memories.

## Placemaking in Practice: The BlackGirlLand Project

In Spring 2017, I launched an African American & African Studies special topics course entitled The BlackGirlLand Project. In this section, I focus on three elements of this course to theoretical frameworks in action. First, I discuss co-constructed elements of the course (i.e., objectives and assignments) to highlight how the course took up the emphasis of Black Girls' Literacies on multiple and collaborative elements. Second, I turn to a conversation on how the course was curated as a space that focused on developing students' criticality and literacies using Black women's stories, research, and productions as central texts. I conclude the section with a discussion of intergenerational dialogues that reflects how the students made sense of and shared the course materials and experiences through their own lenses.

### Multiple and Collaborative: Syllabus as a Co-Constructed Text

On the first day of class, I provided each student with the first page of the syllabus, which contained information about my office location and email address, the date, time, and location of the course, and the course goals/description.

> The goal of [the course] is to study several forms of writing, including academic and nonacademic texts, fiction and nonfiction, poetry, and music in order to learn about Black women's land practices and theories connected to land. In this course, you will contribute to classroom discussions, develop well-crafted writing assignments, and share your writings as you engage with communities of writers–activists–advocates both within and beyond the classroom. By the end of the semester, you will have interdisciplinary, justice-centered theories that explore the connections Black women had (and continue to have) with land, nature, and spaces.

Since I wanted to hear from students of why they came to the course and what ideas or questions they brought with them, I asked them to complete a section of the syllabus. Under **"Our Collective Strivings: Course Objectives and Potential Outcomes"**, students offered the following responses to three prompts (bold-print headings).

## I. Students enrolled in this course seek to develop a critical understanding of:

- The goal of the BlackGirlLand project (explore Black women's connections with land, nature, and spaces)
- How Black women have created change and impact in society (past, present, and future)

- The motive for Black women's drive to successfully push themselves for justice and land
- Who the Black woman is and not who is portrayed to be
- The struggles Black Africans have faced and continue to face
- How African American women shaped land and writings

## II. Students enrolled in this course seek to examine strategies for:

- Exploring new ideas of Black women as writers
- Community among various ethnicities and religions, and recreating the once thriving and unified Black community
- Coping as a Black woman in a world against them
- Raising awareness of Black injustices and communicating this to people of privilege
- Being a helping hand to assisting Black women in their transition
- Understanding and mastering new ideologies of Black women and landscape
- Teaching male and white women how their appearance is and can be helpful in life-changing situations
- Art that has displayed Black feminism and the many layers of it
- The way Black women navigate this world

## III. Students enrolled in this course seek to construct a final project that illustrates their emerging understanding of:

- Black women's creative writings
- The history of Black women, the places in history Black women have held for themselves or been forced into
- Themselves as Black women and what they hope to gain
- Black women's growth over a course of four months (hopes, dreams, where they are successful, mood during the time, etc.)
- Africana's relationship with land, her struggles, and the societal climate she lives in today
- Effect land, nature, and spaces had on Black women
- The complexities of Black feminism with land, nature, and space in today's time

"Our collective strivings" served as the starting point in that these lists take into account the students' personal, political, and intellectual identities. With 13 Black women in the course, the course goals focused on understanding their relationship to history, land, women, men, and one another. The student goals also reflected an interest in building coalitions ("being a helping hand", "teaching male and white women . . . can be helpful in life-changing situations") and imagining justice ("recreating the once thriving and unified black community"). I reminded students that—aside from the readings—this course, starting with the course goals, is co-constructed. In recognizing that a white woman student and Black man student were enrolled, the syllabus was still an opportunity for them to bring their multiple identities into the construction and facilitation of the course.

To uphold African American & African Studies as an interdisciplinary field, I selected texts from various fields, disciplines and areas of study based upon colleagues' suggestions that aligned with the concept of Black women and land. As I thought about central texts, Literary Studies colleagues suggested *Mama Day* (Naylor, 1988), while an interdisciplinary scholar who works across History, Women's & Gender Studies, American Indian Studies, and African American Studies suggested *Trace* (Savoy, 2015). Black and Decolonial Feminists suggested writings from members of the Crunk Feminist Collective (Cooper, 2015; Morris, 2013) and poets (see Dungy, 2005). Colleagues in History pointed me to a text on Black environmental history (Glave & Stoll, 2006) and films about (Welsh & Vibert, 2017) and by Black women (Dash, 1992).

The emerging syllabus contained the work of scholars, writers, artists, poets, musicians, and filmmakers. In thinking about classroom texts that promote Black girls' literacies, Muhammad and Haddix (2016, p. 327) put forth the following criteria for English educators. They assert that texts must have the potential to advance youths': "skills and proficiencies in multiple literacies", "sense making of their multiple identities", "intellectual development", and "criticality" (p. 327). The syllabus was designed to ensure that students thought about how the theories connected to practice *and* to who they are. Over the course of 16 weeks, 15 undergraduate students from various academic majors forged connections between their major areas of study, the readings, their lived experiences, and current events. The final syllabus, which was revised throughout the semester to make space for students to attend on-campus events (i.e., art exhibits, visiting scholars, invited lecturers, town halls) that were relevant to the course, stood as a collaborative document that had the potential to advance students' literacies, intellectual development, sensemaking, and criticality.

## Curated Space: Criticality in Conversations

Before entering conversations about Black women's relationship to land, we read the work of Indigenous women scholars who informed our understanding of Land as: first teacher (Simpson, 2014; Styres, 2011), relative (Styres, Haig-Brown, & Blimkie, 2013), and contested site of settler colonial practices (Tuck, Guess, & Sultan, 2014). This step was crucial to students' development of an intellectual framework for Land that starts with what is often overlooked or erased, Indigenous knowledges. We used literature, music, film, and poetry to think through complex notions of migration and displacement. For example, unpack

McKittrick's (2006) argument that the "socioeconomic mapping of blackness . . . shows the material base of race/racism" (p. 13), we discussed Perry's work (2013) about women in Brazil alongside Nikki Giovanni's "The Yellow Jackets" and Audre Lorde's "The Bees". Students also drew connections between the aforementioned texts and Simpson's (2014) "Land as Pedagogy", in which we could learn from one another and the environment. Through this conversation, we started to imagine how our relationship with bees and yellow jackets may parallel society's relationship with people of color, poor and working class, multilingual communities, immigrant communities, and those who are situated outside of white heteropatriarchal identities. By focusing on texts created by Black and Indigenous women, we engaged in conversations about coalition building within and across communities.

Readings in conjunction with conversations with Black women also helped students develop their abilities to make sense of their multiple identities. Our conversation with Shakara Tyler, who is a mother and was a doctoral candidate in the Department of Agriculture, started with her asking us to think about the connections between Black, womyn, and land. In preparation for the conversation, students read Tyler's current (Tyler & Fraser, 2016) and (at the time) forthcoming (Baxter, Cooper, Fraser, & Tyler, 2017) publications. Some students offered selections from the readings, while others responded with personal stories about being outdoors, learning to embrace their natural hair, and memories of relatives' homes filled with potted plants. Through this conversation, each student began to articulate what it meant to be racialized and gendered bodies in relationship to land.

As students had to think across texts and experiences, they forged "skills and proficiencies in multiple literacies" and developed more complex notions of criticality (Muhammad & Haddix, 2016). When asked to incorporate course readings into mini-workshops for an audience that was not familiar with the topic, students moved the theories into practice. For some of the students, the workshops were their first times presenting to an audience made up of people that they did not know. By encouraging students to speak in such spaces, they are invited to own their learning and represent their understandings in ways that speak to who they are.

## Emerging Educators and Intergenerational Dialogues

Course midterm and final projects offered students opportunities to engage in intergenerational conversations—real and imagined. Originally, I asked students to work in groups to design a 45-minute interactive workshop that they would facilitate at the one-day intellectual retreat, which would be held on Earth Day at another university. Although the project, as presented on the syllabus, was met with some optimism, the groans, silence, and furrowed brows also illustrated that there was an air of skepticism and resistance among the class. While students were accustomed to the practices of reading, writing, and speaking, teaching this semester's range of theories to a new audience was an act of literacy that students did not get to enact often and were leery of.

In designing and facilitating their mini-workshops, students thought about audience—who would they like to speak with and why? What do they want their participants to walk away knowing and thinking? Through a partnership with faculty in the Department of Afro-American Studies at the University of Michigan, the retreat was originally envisioned as a one-day event where middle school, high school, undergraduate, and graduate students would come together to converse, theorize, and write. As the semester progressed, the logistics and demographics for the retreat, and consequently the mini-workshop assignment, shifted. Instead of developing workshops for potential students at the retreat, students and I discussed the possibilities of facilitating the workshops for audiences on our campus. While one group developed their workshop for college-aged peers, three groups developed their workshops for high school students who would visit the campus later in the semester. The option to present to high school girls was made possible through the work of a student who was new to the African American & African Studies course, Miran.

Miran, a sophomore with interest in math education, joined the class two weeks after the semester started. As a student from the Honors College, we met often to discuss what her Honors project would be for this course. During our conversations, I would learn of her work as the co-founder of the organization Crowning Young Queens (CYQ). Through the organization, she, a co-founder, and fellow college women mentored Black girls attending the high school from which she graduated. In one meeting, she shared that her team was in the process of organizing a three-day campus visit for the 15 CYQ mentees. We decided that her Honors project would involve co-developing a workshop and coordinating her students' visit to our class. One week later, we pitched the idea to her classmates. In class, she described her program, the group of students, and the goals of the campus visit. During our meetings, we discussed whether or not the proposals would meet the goals for the day.

Students enrolled in the African American & African Studies course were required to submit workshop proposals as their **midterm assignment**:

You will be responsible for developing a 45-minute workshop that you will facilitate before the end of the semester. You are invited to work in a group of 3-4 students. Your group must provide a proposal (double-spaced, 5-page minimum) for a session that you will facilitate at the Black Women's Leadership Conference, a session with "Crowning Young Queens" or a session for another group of learners. The proposal must contain:

**Abstract:** 50-word description that is engaging. Imagine it as a 20-second commercial about your workshop.

**Overview:** 500-word description of what activities you will do/what participants will gain from attending your workshop.

**Rationale:** This section should focus on: Why are *you* focusing on this particular aspect? Why should retreat participants think about this issue now?

**Researchers:** Which scholars or authors are you building upon? Why? (Section must contain at least 5 references. This could include poetry, scholarly articles, or books.)

**Materials:** Will your group need arts and crafts supplies? (If so, what kind? How many?) Will your group need an LCD projector, costume jewelry, A/V equipment, yoga mats, etc.?

**Evaluation:** Create an evaluation sheet so participants could provide feedback on your session.

I developed this assignment as an opportunity for students to create projects for audiences beyond the class. By asking students to make sense of the course materials and share with others, the mini-workshop assignment speaks to Muhammad and Haddix's notion (2016) that Black Girls' Literacies must be intellectual, political, *and* critical practices.

Three months later, the students enrolled in the course used an 80-minute class session to facilitate three workshops: Self-Care as Resistance, Health and Wellness, and Music Rehabilitation. The "Self-Care as Resistance" group focused on natural hair care products, which included making body butters and hair conditioners. After learning about the beneficial qualities of each ingredient, each CYQ girl received a small sample to take home. In the "Health and Wellness" session, Miran and her partner emphasized the importance of healthy eating and physical activity. CYQ girls who attended the session made seedbombs, or small balls of clay filled with soil and sunflower seeds, to encourage young women to grow their own flowers and food. Members of the "Music Rehabilitation" group asked CYQ girls to track how hip-hop artists connected women and land. The CYQ participants then used the remaining time to co-write their own lyrics to student-generated beats. Collectively, the three workshops illustrated how students filtered the course content through their own ways of knowing and being. Through this work, students were able to develop responsible and sustaining learning spaces for not only themselves, but also the girls of CYQ.

In addition to the workshops, students reached into their own communities to reflect on their learnings. Two Black women students, Darye and Varis, wrote about their grandmothers. Varis rarely spoke during class. For a while, I often misread her silence—as educators often do with students—as somewhere between shy, anxious (stemming from failure to complete the readings or an assignment), feigned interest, or genuine confusion (stemming from the teacher's poorly framed question or series of questions). Before class started, she would engage in small talk and smirk at classmates' jokes or comments. Sitting in the front cluster of desks, she occasionally glanced up from her phone to look at some of the diagrams, concepts, or names that I etched across the chalkboard. Occasionally, she would pose a question that sounded as if she had been ruminating on it for days at time, questions that challenged classmates to work beyond their surface observations, questions that made me realize that she had been listening and processing. For her final project, Varis wrote a letter to her grandmother where she shared what she gained from the class.

Another student, Darye would offer comments during class discussions and post extensive comments on the course site for her weekly reading reflections. She and I spoke after class about how she was discussing the course with her former high school teacher. In neither the digital nor the physical classroom spaces did she mention her grandmother until mid-semester, when her grandmother passed away. In an effort to grieve and remember, Darye included connections to her grandmother and her grandmother's connections to land in more conversations and assignments. At the one-day retreat, she talked about how her grandmother would do her hair as a child and use Blue Magic hair grease, which was still being used on her niece's hair. Since she was in the "Self-Care as Resistance" group, she spoke about wanting to teach her niece about more natural ways to care for her skin and hair (such as avocado, shea butter, olive and coconut oils). During our retreat conversation with author Lauret Savoy, she asked the author to elaborate more on her notion of ecological footprint (Savoy, 2015, p. 42). After Savoy answered, Darye shared that she had thought of ecological footprints as connections to land. Since her grandmother once harvested cotton, Darye conceptualized her grandmother's footprints as larger than her parents' footprints since they did yard work and significantly larger than her own because she loathed being outdoors. In her final project, she shared that the course helped her see her and her grandmother's contentious relationship with land. Both Darye and Varis's projects illustrate how Black women/girls use remembering in their efforts to move toward placemaking.

## Literacies of Becoming

> Yes, I am palimpsest too a place made over but trying to trace back.
>
> (Savoy, 2015, p. 86)

Through the BlackGirlLand Project course, Varis and Darye began to engage the practices of remembering and mapping. When rooted in Black and decolonial feminisms, such practices allow us to see that not only are we living on maps that are influx, but we too are palimpsests of maps-in-the-making; thinking about what we know, where we've been, and who we are becoming. Therefore, I want to end this chapter where I began my class: our collected strivings. This course emerged from a deep interest in me understanding my family's connections to a Sea Island community that is lodged in a web of Heirs property and resort development. It is through collective remembering that we are able to do the work of filling in incomplete, erased, or missing maps with stories. Through the course, my students and I swapped stories, reconsidered our relationships to one another and the land on which live, teach and learn.

I cannot say whether or not students were fully invested in the goals they jotted down in this section of our co-constructed syllabus. However, I do want to reflect on three that speak directly to how this first iteration of the BlackGirlLand Project course made room for literacies of becoming. By engaging with poetry, film and interdisciplinary scholarship, students developed a "critical understanding of how African American women shaped land and writings." We learned to see poets such as those featured in *Black Nature* as the theorists who inform, translate, and complicate our understandings of Black Geographies. When placed in conversation with Indigenous land education scholars, our lenses sharpen to see land as "Land", or a deeply interconnected and spiritual location and way of being. In our conversations with Black women writers and scholars, and their classmates, students were able to "examine strategies for the way Black women navigate this world." Black and decolonial feminist works offered us more languages for articulating how we traverse, disrupt and subvert colonial mappings. Finally, I am consistently drawn to two goals that read more like premonitions or commitments: "Construct a final project that illustrates their emerging understanding of themselves as Black women" and "Black women's growth over a course of four months." Since the goals were submitted anonymously and compiled on the final syllabus without students' names, I am unsure who penned these two desires to develop final projects that showcased personal growth and knowledge of self. Regardless, these two students knew that this new African American & African Studies course was going to offer them space for growing and introspection—or in other words, space to develop literacies of becoming.

Collectively, these "goals" highlight that interdisciplinary studies are not egocentric navel-gazing; instead, such studies are critical triangulations—especially for Black girls and women—between self, community knowledge, and academic theories. Poetry, books, films, articles and conversations offer us more languages to speak about our lived realities, movements, and imaginations of our ancestors. Students and educators learn to trust our instincts, value one another and respect each other's lived experiences. Although I close this chapter with students' goals, it is my hope that they will serve as springboards for future work with Black girls and women. How can we begin to acknowledge and forge ties with one another in ways that allow us to reclaim our stories, journeys, and humanity?

## References

Baxter, K., Cooper, D., Fraser, A., & Tyler, S. (2017). Womanism as agrarianism: Black women healing through innate agrarian artistry. In J. Williams & E. Holt-Gimenez (Eds). *Land justice: Re-imagining land, food and the commons in the United States*. Oakland: Food First Books.

Boehm, L. K. (2010). *Making a way out of no way: African American women and the second great migration*. Jackson, MS: University Press of Mississippi.

Butler, T. (2017). #Say[ing]HerName as critical demand: English education in the age of erasure. *English Education, 49*(2), 153–178.

Chatelain, M. (2015). *South side girls: Growing up in the great migration.* Durham, NC: Duke University Press.

Collins, P. H. (2000). *Black feminist thought: Knowledge, consciousness and the politics of identity.* New Brunswick, NJ: Rutgers University Press.

Cooper, B. (2015). Love no limit: Towards a Black feminist future (in theory). *The Black Scholar, 45*(4), 7–21.

Dash, J. (Producer & Director) (1992). *Daughters of the dust* [motion picture]. Berlin, Germany: Kino International.

Dotson, K. (2014). "Thinking familiar with the interstitial": An introduction. *Hypatia, 29*(1), 1–17.

Dungy, C. (Ed.) (2005). *Black nature: Four centuries of African American nature poetry.* Athens, GA: University of Georgia Press.

Figueroa, Y. (2015). Faithful witnessing as practice: Decolonial readings of *Shadows of your Black memory* and *The brief wondrous life of Oscar Wao. Hypatia, 30*(4), 641–656.

Glave, D. D., & Stoll, M. (2006). *"To love the wind and the rain": African Americans and environmental history.* Pittsburgh: University of Pittsburgh Press.

Henery, C. S. (2011). Where they walk: What aging Black women's geographies tell of race, gender, space, and social transformation in Brazil. *Cultural Dynamics, 23*(2), 85–106.

Howard, R. (2005). We are not strangers here. In C. Dungy (Ed.), *Black nature: Four centuries of African American nature poetry* (pp. 37–38). Athens, GA: University of Georgia Press.

Jones-Jackson, P. (1987). *When roots die: Endangered traditions on the Sea Islands.* Athens, GA: University of Georgia Press.

Lugones, M. (2010). Toward a decolonial feminism. *Hypatia, 25*(4), 742–759.

McKittrick, K. (2006). *Demonic grounds: Black women and the cartographies of struggle.* Minneapolis: University of Minnesota Press.

Mendez, X. (2015). Notes toward a decolonial feminist methodology: Revisiting the race/gender matrix. *Trans-Scripts,* 5, 41–59.

Morgan, J. (2004). *Laboring women: Reproduction and gender in new world slavery.* Philadelphia: University of Pennsylvania Press.

Morris, S. M. (2013). Black girls are from the future: Afrofuturist feminism in Octavia E. Butler's *fledgling. WSQ: Women's Studies Quarterly, 40*(3), 146–166.

Morrison, T. (1993, December 7). The Nobel lecture in literature. In S. Allén (Ed.), *Nobel lectures, literature, 1991–1995* (pp. 198–207). Singapore: World Scientific Publishing Company.

Muhammad, G., & Haddix, M. (2016). Centering Black girls' literacies: A review of literature on the multiple ways of knowing of Black girls. *English Education, 48*(4), 299–336.

Naylor, G. (1988). *Mama day.* New York: Vintage Books.

Perry, K. K. (2013). *Black women against the land grab: The fight for racial justice in Brazil.* Minneapolis: University of Minnesota Press.

Roshanravan, S. (2014). Motivating coalition: Women of color and epistemic disobedience. *Hypatia, 29*(1), 41–58.

Savoy, L. (2015). *Trace: Memory, history, race and American landscape.* Berkeley, CA: Counterpoint Press.

Simpson, L. (2014). Land as pedagogy: Nishnaabeg intelligence and rebellious transformation. *Decolonization: Indigeneity, Education & Society, 3*(3), 1–25.

Styres, S. (2011). Land as first teacher: A philosophical journeying, *Reflective Practice, 12*(6), 717–731.

Styres, S., Haig-Brown, C., & Blimkie, M. (2013). Toward a pedagogy of land: The urban context, *Canadian Journal of Education, 36*(2), 188–221.

Tuck, E., Guess, A., & Sultan, H. (2014, June 26). Not nowhere: Collaborating on self-same land. *Decolonization: Indigeneity, Education & Society.* https://decolonization.word press.com/2014/06/26/not-nowhere-collaborating-on-selfsame-land/

Tuck, E., McKenzie, M., & McCoy, K. (2014). Land education: Indigenous, post-colonial, and decolonizing perspectives on place and environmental education research. *Environmental Education and Research, 20*(1), 1–23.

Tyler, S., & Fraser, A. (2016). Womanism and agroecology: An intersectional praxis seed keeping as acts of political warfare. In P. Godfrey, & D. Torres (Eds.), *Emergent possibilities for global sustainability: Intersections of race, class and gender* (pp. 19–30). London: Routledge.

Welsh, C. (Producer & Director), & Vibert, E. (Producer) (2017). *The thinking garden* [documentary]. Vancouver, BC: Moving Images.

Wilkerson, I. (2011). *The warmth of other suns: The epic story of America's great migration.* New York: Vintage.

# 5

# BLACK GIRL TO BLACK GIRL

## Gratitude Journaling as an Emancipatory Practice

*Damaris C. Dunn*

### Black Girls "Write It Out!"

When asked at the Schomburg Center for Research and Black Culture, by my former education coordinator, to write out what I needed when I was my scholars' age, I wrote out and shared that I needed "a tall Black woman." To this, my sister friend, Subha, replied, "you needed yourself, Dee?" I immediately responded with a slow head nod and a sense of comfort: "Yes, I needed myself." Confident and one year into therapy sessions, I was actively practicing telling people what I needed. Though my sixth-grade self-needed a "tall Black woman," I could not have articulated then the importance of having a Black educator, let alone a Black woman educator. As an instructor of poetry and archival research at the Schomburg, I had cultivated meaningful relationships with an all-Black team of educators who cared deeply about the wholeness and well-being of Black children. In sharing my longing for a tall Black woman educator, I was not afraid to speak my truth because I knew that my peers would understand. I needed not only "a tall black woman," but also a Black sculptor, a Black comic book lover, a Black television producer, a Black actor, a Black dancer, and a Black poet, each of whom would have equally made my K–12 experience one to remember. It was at the Schomburg, where I served Black children and taught with an all-Black staff, that I had recognized how important it was for Black children to see Black educators.

As I reflect, my elementary school principal was a tall Black woman who made us recite "I am somebody" in our monthly assemblies from kindergarten through fifth grade. I also had Ms. Mason and Ms. Becton in first and third grade, both Black teachers who were taller than me at the time. By the time I had reached middle school, I did not have any Black teachers, which is probably why I was looking for a tall Black woman. Though my mom will always be my first teacher, by then, I was taller than her, too. In my own reflection, I began to wonder what this might mean for my own scholars; in the United States, 18 percent of teachers are teachers of color, and 7 percent of those teachers are Black (Griffin & Tackie, 2016), meaning that the likelihood of meeting another Ms. Dee would be slim to none. While it did not matter to me growing up, research shows that representation matters in schools. As a former community school director, youth developer, and social studies teacher, I have connected with most of the Black girls that I have served; it is our likeness and our ability to see one another that links us.

Remembering the Black women educators that I have cultivated relationships with over the years has allowed me to reflect on two gratitude journals that I received from two of my former scholars. Before departing New York to pursue my PhD at the University of Georgia, Nova and Charlee sent me off with well wishes and their own reflections on what our relationships meant to them. Their ability to "write out" their thoughts and express gratitude have helped me to understand the importance of Black girls having spaces to write their lives, and also reaffirms the importance of having educators who look like them. I was Nova and Charlee's youth developer and community school director at their high school in the South Bronx. My commitment to the wholeness of all my scholars often included: food, space to be, warm hugs, and laughter. My relationships with Nova and Charlee are a microcosm of the legacy I hope to leave, their expressions of gratitude, by way of writing, are not only expressions of love, but also an example of how Black girls "write it out" (Muhammad, 2012). "It" can be many things, but historically writing has been a tool for the liberation of Black women and girls.

Education researchers and teacher educators who take up this work have examined Black girls and their relationship to multiliteracies (McArthur, 2016; Muhammad & Womack, 2016). This body of scholarship is committed to examining the ways in which Black girls "know" and "be" (Muhammad & Haddix, 2016). By understanding Black girls' epistemological and ontological nature, we can develop and provide spaces for them to thrive. Education researchers who produce research in partnership with Black girls have used critical literacy as a tool to provide these spaces, furthering our understanding of how Black girls read the world and their responses of how the world reads them (Muhammad & Haddix, 2016). When Black girls "write it out" (Muhammad, 2012), they write themselves and those they deem valuable into history. According to Griffin and Tackie (2016), educators of color are an asset beyond that of content and pedagogy; we are also role models, parental figures, and advocates who contribute to the experiences of students of color in schools. In this particular case, I believe that my scholars' gratitude journaling is attributed not only to how I show up for them as Black girls but also to how I show up as a Black woman.

In this chapter, I will "write it out": first, by examining the importance of seeing Black girls, and then, following this, I will discuss gratitude and gratitude journaling as a writing intervention that has a positive impact on well-being. I will then analyze Nova and Charlee's gratitude journals, which I have defined as an emancipatory writing practice. In closing, I will address what it means to move toward a Black girl magic for the wholeness and well-being of Black girls. This chapter highlights implications for writing and journaling for self-expression in and out of school.

## Theorizing *Seeing* Black Girls

As I began to think about what made my relationship to Nova and Charlee so special, I kept coming back to this notion of seeing. Nova and Charlee could see me and I them. To further complicate this notion of seeing, I started to think about how Black girls are generally seen in society. The hypervisibility of Black girls, in their "acting out" and "being grown," is the adultification of Black girls and serves as a means to control their bodies. Furthermore, the invisibility of Black girls in the classroom and school (Evans-Winters, 2005) says something more about how society is reading and writing us. I started to think deeply about this and how those ways of seeing Black girls were incomplete and innocuous, but very much a part of how educators are socialized to see Black girls. Media tells us stories about Black girls that are not necessarily steeped in truth. Do Black girls have attitudes? Yes, most girls do. Do Black girls get to act out? No, but girls who are not Black girls do. I started to think about how my responses to attitudes and acting out might differ from my colleagues', and I kept coming back to this notion of seeing. I had also learned over the years to ask questions like "having a bad day?" or "would you like to check in?" or "come talk to me when you have a moment?" Further, I believe that, as an educator, it is both my role and my responsibility to see and inquire, which I believe has much to do with how Black girls read and write one another. What makes Nova and Charlee's experience of me different is our ability to see one another. There were times when I was having a bad day and both Charlee and Nova saw and inquired. Education researchers who work in partnership and in service of Black girls have also taken up this notion of seeing by using theories such as the politicized ethic of care (Lane, 2018), which Lane argues is specific to the ways of model Black female teachers; homegirling (Brown, 2013), as described by Brown, is attentive to black girlhood and "exists out of time and order" (p. 50); and creating space and place for healing (McArthur, 2019) with Black girls in order to humanize and honor them. Seeing Black girls in schools means that we acknowledge their humanity outside of the hypervisibility that often stifles Black girl magic. Nova and Charlee's ability to see me led to relationship building and practicing of gratitude through gratitude journaling. hooks (2013) reminds us that "our right to read and write as black folks is a legacy of liberation struggle" (p. 161). This struggle for liberation is all too common for Black girls in and outside of schools and is the reason why seeing and practicing gratitude toward one another are so important.

## Gratitude and Gratitude Journaling

According to McCullough, Tsang, and Emmons (2004), gratitude is often associated with positive emotions, life satisfaction, vitality, and optimism. In order for Black girls to be able to express gratitude, we have to create spaces that reflect Black girls' ways of knowing and being (Muhammad & Haddix, 2016). Expressing gratitude is important because it humanizes and makes Black girls visible, rather than invisible. The notion of hypervisibility can be attributed to how people are conditioned to see Black girls, mostly as things needing to be controlled and less as human beings needing to be understood. Black girls do gratitude differently; they see and read the people around them. Most scholars I know can see whether or not an educator wants to be present; they play on this and react based on whether the adult is genuine. As discussed earlier, Nova and Charlee's intuitiveness with who I am and how I show up are characteristics of seeing. Black girl gratitude comes in the form of "you cute miss" or "miss I like that outfit" or "miss why do you work here?" Black girls' gratitude practice is seeing. Black girls are observant, and their quietness is usually attributed to their reading of others. I know this well because I am a Black woman and I serve Black girls. Spaces constructed for Black girls by Black girls center their ways of being, providing room for them to be their whole selves. In the cases of Nova and Charlee, seeing and gratitude practices often took place in my office. Gratitude looked like hugs, felt like warmth, and sounded like "hey mama, how are you feeling?" or "how did you do today?" Gratitude and relationship building are inseparable. Further, educators in the spaces I have served in often asked, "how did you get this scholar to do this?" Building relationships, extending grace, and expressing gratitude for the littlest things can go a long way. When I showed up unapologetically, it allowed my scholars to return the favor.

If it were not for relationships built with Nova and Charlee, I am not sure that I could write about the importance of gratitude journaling. Gratitude journaling is a literacy practice that can be defined as individuals regularly recognizing specific life experiences that they are thankful for (Emmons & McCullough, 2003; Watkins et al., 2003). In a study at the University of Kansas, researchers examined student well-being with writing interventions that include stress management and gratitude journaling (Flinchbaugh et al., 2012). Researchers found students had improved levels of meaningfulness and engagement in the classroom (Flinchbaugh et al., 2012). Furthermore, gratitude journaling for my scholars in the Bronx is used to express how they read me as an educator and the memories that we have made over the years. Black girl gratitude is seen and felt: it is the way Black women show up for one another; it is making time (Brown, 2013) for Black girls and recognizing their humanity. Nova and Charlee's gratitude journals are merely a reflection of time spent, being seen, and memories made.

## Scholars and Their Writings

Nova's letter and Charlee's journal entry in this section can be read as gratitude journals. The gratitude journals are a reflection of the connectedness that exists between a Black woman educator and Black girls who choose to see her. Nova and Charlee's gratitude journals are also an example of why representation matters in schools. As discussed earlier, Nova and Charlee are my former scholars, hailing from the Bronx. I met both girls at their high school; however, they attended the same middle school. Nova is younger than Charlee. Nova will graduate in June of 2020; Charlee graduated in June of 2019. Nova identifies as Afro-Latina. She is kind, soft spoken, and the true definition of a scholar activist. She is committed to becoming an ER physician, and she never lets me forget it. She has been diligent in her efforts to become a physician as she has sought out programs outside of school to learn and understand the field of medicine. Charlee identifies as a Black girl. She is strong, sensitive, and often tells me "I am the child you don't have." Charlee's relationship with school has not been the best; the hypervisibility that I discussed earlier in the chapter contributes to why Charlee struggled in school. She acted out in response to the world around her. Most times, instead of inquiring about how to support Charlee, people grew tired of laboring with the young woman, who just wanted to be seen. She was a handful, no doubt, but she was so worth it. In Charlee's case, attending the same school from sixth grade through high school did not necessarily benefit her. Every scholar is different, and occasionally we all need a change of scenery. While I value and understand the benefits of having a six through twelve school, they are not for everybody. I am proud to say that Charlee completed her eleventh and twelfth grade years at another school, but she has remained in touch and did tremendously well in a smaller school setting that could attend to her needs. Charlee continues to fight and prove people wrong; I am proud and excited for her future.

I have different relationships with Nova and Charlee, because they are different girls. Educators must be attentive to the fact that all Black girls are not the same and should be attended to as individuals. Both Nova and Charlee's gratitude journals are saved in my phone as a reminder that Black educators matter not only to their families and friends, but also to the young people they meet and serve. Black girls read the world to tell their truths (Freire, 1985); they also write it out (Muhammad, 2012). Both Nova and Charlee lifted me up so that I, too, could write. Nova and Charlee's ability to see me gives me permission to speak truth to power.

## *Nova*

6/25/19

Dear Ms. Damaris,

Since you are leaving in pursuit of greater things, I decided to write you a letter thanking you for everything. You are such a powerful and intelligent woman and I thank you for sharing your wisdom in some topics I didn't know much about, along with what to do in certain situations in life. You and your speeches taught me that it's okay to be uncomfortable and if I'm not, I'm not really developing as a person. Believe it or not, many of your motivational and blunt talks motivated me to search and pursue the things that truly interested me, but I was too afraid to go after. I also thank you and appreciate you for talking to me about being a woman of color with the huge dreams/goals that I have in mind. You served as an outlet, mentor, and a guide for me during the time I spent with you. If I wrote everything I wanted to say we would be here for ages, but I just want you to know that you are greatly appreciated. Although I will miss you, I'm so happy that you are chasing your goals and I have no doubt that you'll accomplish them all. Don't stress, you got this!

*Nova*

(Sorry I know it's kind of a lot)

Since you are leaving in pursuit of greater things, I decided to write you a letter thanking you for everything.

—*Nova*

The first line of Nova's letter negates the notion that Black girls are impartial and all of the other negative wraps we receive. When I see how Black girls are portrayed in the media and within education, I am always critical and trying to piece together the rest of the story. My transparency with my scholars has always served me well. My entire village, including my scholars, knew that I was in "pursuit of greater things." Many of them should know that receiving an education was the greatest thing I was afforded because it led me to them. In my role as a community school director and in my former role as a youth developer, one of my primary goals was to make sure that our scholars had access to college trips. At this point, Nova has visited well over eight or nine colleges. She will likely visit more in her senior year. As a first-generation college student, I have grown to understand the importance of exposure, and that is why I shared my journey to a doctoral program with Nova and other students. I was taught early on that seeing is the first step to moving forward. It is important that Black girls get to see us as Black women and also see what we are capable of.

I also thank you and appreciate you for talking to me about being a woman of color with the huge dreams goals that I have in mind.

—*Nova*

From the time I met Hilary, she has expressed that she wants to be in the medical field, used to want to be a pediatrician, and has shifted her aspirations more recently to an ER physician. When I asked her why, she would explain the importance of children having doctors who look like them. As a peer group coordinator, Nova has always been a leader in her own right. Nova has taken it upon herself to find internships and opportunities that would advance her understanding of the field and move her to her dream of becoming an ER physician. About a year ago, Nova came to my office up in arms about a consistently absent teacher and her lack of access to math and science classes beyond the ones she had already acquired as a junior in high school. I recall her saying, "Ms. Damaris, why don't the good teachers want to teach in the Bronx?" Both taken back and overwhelmed by the question, I took a deep breath and chose my words wisely. I explained that systemic racism often gets in the way of our being great, but we are not to stop at what they give us—they, in this case, is white supremacist capitalist patriarchy. With the South Bronx, the poorest congressional district in the country, many of my colleagues and I tried to make our scholars feel seen and heard, but there were obvious disparities that our scholars could see both in and out of school. In short, Nova knew some of the answer to her own question, but our daily conversations often focused on the ways in which people of color are marginalized in our communities and that it was often left up to us to be agents of change.

Further, Nova's assessment of not having access to teachers in the Bronx is how she has begun to read her world, and she expresses this in her letter to me. As an advocate for young people, particularly Black girls, and a true youth developer at heart, I often tried to model advocacy in ways that my students could see and make use of in their own spaces. Nova's ability to inquire about the hard questions is her thinking critically about what she has come to know about her school and community. Nova's inquiry and persistence not only led her to question administrators but also helped me to understand how she sees and navigates the world to better support her.

Though Nova's letter was a production of her gratitude, her letter helped me to reflect deeply on how Black girls use writing to tell their truths. Her letter serves as both a reminder and signifier that Black girls are taking notes and critically thinking about how their educators are showing up for them. More importantly, Nova recognizes her position as a woman of color and the importance of having access. In a study done by Muhammad and Womack (2016), they found that Black girls wrote across representations, displaying knowledge of girlhood and public perceptions of what it means to be a Black girl. Nova uses her gratitude letter not only to write her world, but also to acknowledge her appreciation for our talks of what it means to be a woman of color in the world we live in. In our conversations, Nova always speaks candidly about race and is aware of how race, class, and gender permeate various spaces, particularly in school and outside of school. Nova is incredibly observant and always ready to engage in conversation.

> You served as an outlet, mentor, and guide for me during the time I spent with you. . .
>
> —*Nova*

Nova could always read me. She knew better than anyone if I was having a bad day. Nova, like many of my other students, also knew my schedule. She was very keen on which days contained which meetings, and as I think about it, she would approach me differently each day depending on what meeting would ensue. This is to say, that Black girls see one another and that they are paying attention to detail. Thus, the relationship and bonds that we form with our scholars is good for them and their educators. Nova always remembers and sees. In many ways, Nova showed up for me as a homegirl (Brown, 2013) would. There were many days that I was guided by Nova and her peers. Her energy along with the other Black and brown girls and educators in the space often kept me going. Furthermore, in relationships between homegirls, roles are often reversed and interchangeable. As a result of this relationship, my office became the site for lunch conversations and a space where scholars felt comfortable being vulnerable about both in school and out of school experiences. My "blunt talks," as Nova described in her letter, often happened during these lunch conversations as I encouraged Nova and her peers to show up and be responsible for their own education. If there was not enough of a window to continue our lunch conversations, we would continue to talk after school. This homegirl made time, as did Nova and her peers. These "blunt talks" were my way of telling scholars that there is a world outside that may not fully value or show up for them and I needed them to be prepared.

> Although I will miss you, I'm so happy that you are chasing your goals and I have no doubt that you'll accomplish them all. Don't stress, you got this!
>
> —*Nova*

As I reflect on my experience at my former school, I am reminded that Nova's gratitude practice is her own but was also true of our school's culture. Every year, our school has a harvest festival where scholars are asked to make thank you cards for their fellow peers or educators in the building that they love and respect. Our school's core goals of centering scholar activism and gratitude was very much a part of our harvest feast every year. Hilary's eighth grade teacher, Genevieve DeBose, a Black woman educator, also encouraged her scholars in middle school to practice gratitude. While Nova's letter was affirming and thoughtful, I am moved by the ways in which she has come to be, mainly because of her own ability to access gratitude, but also because of the teachers and her school culture. Nova is a scholar activist in her own right, and there is no doubt in my mind that she will accomplish all of her goals. Her gratitude journal is a marker that Black girls are reading the world and writing out what they know to be true to them. Nova's letter was formally written but was not even close to a writing assignment in the context of school. Black girls are reading and writing all the time.

## Charlee

7/15/19

*Charlee J.*

**Journal Entry #3**

Someone I truly admire would be Damaris Dunn. She works at my first high school. She wasn't necessarily a teacher but someone who worked for an organization called Global Kids. Me and her grew a bond that I would never have with anyone else. Whenever I'm going through something she is my go-to even if there's no issue I always enjoy her company. She cares deeply about her students, especially the ones she close to. She is someone I want to be like. She may not feel like she's successful yet but in my eyes she's successful. She motivates me to keep going with everything I pursue in. When Im slacking she gets on me and tells me about myself and makes sure I get back on track immediately. I grew to love her and will always keep in contact with her even after Im done with school. Many adventures I had in the past 2–3 years wouldn't have happened if it wasn't for her.

Black girls are complex and always trying to make sense of the world around us. In a lot of cases, Black girls are "defined more by what they do not do than what they do" (Edwards, 2017, p. 6). Enter Charlee! Charlee attended our school from sixth grade up until eleventh grade. I knew of Charlee because my former supervisor told me about her. It is likely in many school spaces that if you know a young person before you meet them, that this young person has a reputation. Charlee showed up to my office in the month of October, ready to discuss life. For some reason or another, she felt comfortable with me. From the time I met Charlee, she's always been candid, real, and kind. Though the world might read her as "grown" because of her forthrightness and ability to call out educators who she deemed to be inauthentic, she has always had an innocence about her that made me think of her as my own child. Early on, I became an advocate for Charlee—hence, "she wasn't necessarily a teacher, but she worked for Global Kids."

Charlee and I weathered the storm that is school for some Black girls. I stuck with her and she stuck with me. My approach to Charlee is much like that of a child I never had. As described earlier, Black teachers are an asset to schools beyond content knowledge; in some instances, for certain young people, we are much more (Griffin & Tackie, 2016). In Charlee's case, my supervisor and

I negotiated lunch incentives for showing up to school and often advocated for Charlee on days that she was not in the mood to deal with school administration. For every time Charlee had an issue, she would exclaim, "I'm not speaking to anyone except Ms. Damaris," with other choice words. Further, what myself and some of my peers began to recognize was that Charlee wanted out of the space, and that in order to thrive, she probably needed a change of scenery. Though we all knew this, Charlee fought hard to try and graduate from the school she had known since the sixth grade. In our time together at her first high school, Charlee went through drastic changes in changing her hair, as did I. I was a homegirl (Brown, 2013) to Charlee in every sense of the word, making time to meet her needs. Once she had recognized that she was over the space, she grew annoyed by her teachers' approaches to teaching and learning. She also found herself in various altercations, which led to suspension. "She cares deeply about her students, especially the ones she's close to," was a true statement. Furthermore, the alarming statistics that are associated with Black girls leading behind Black boys in suspensions had happened right in front of my face as my advocacy for her grew to be unaccepted by my colleagues.

Charlee's behavior and her recognition of the unsupportive adults in the space made her weary of school. Daily morning text messages and encouragement began to go unheeded as she grew less and less interested with what school had to offer her. She writes:

> Whenever Im going through something she is my go-to even if there's no issue I always enjoy her company.
>
> *—Charlee*

Not only was I Charlee's go-to in times of navigating the space, I showed up, in conversations with mom and grandma about how to best serve her. When other staff members grew tired, somehow, I would find the courage to try and try again. This effort to try and try again is a part of a long history of Black women educators whose radical love permeated their teaching and learning practices. Charlee and I had many talks about her work in Midtown Manhattan, at the supermarket and Gregory's coffee shop. She enjoyed YA author Elizabeth Acevedo. She often shared her starting and ending point in the texts. Charlee probably enjoyed my company because I spent a lot of time pushing her off to class, and when she did come to school, she would only turn in her phone to me. Now that I think about it, Charlee needed someone to cultivate a space for her in which she was comfortable and able to show up as herself. Myself and my supervisor, Moriah, did our best to try and make Charlee feel seen and heard without coddling her to the point that she would not take us seriously. We provided a space of love and a space that also said, "take your butt to class."

In this case, this Black girl needed something more. In our conversations, Charlee and I often discussed whether or not college was something she wanted to do. The first college trip that she was actually able to go on with my organization, she was not able to attend because of an altercation between her and another Black girl. Though I argued that Charlee's going on the trip would help her see something outside of the Bronx, my idea was immediately shut down by school administration. Initially, Charlee had the perspective that I did not fight for her, but later on we were able to come to an agreement that our actions have consequences. Though at that time she probably believed I was not sticking up for her, I fought on her behalf. I also knew that by allowing her on the trip, I was enabling fighting, and that did not sit well with me. Further, in Charlee's case, we talked about the consequences and came to an agreement using restorative practices. Black girls in schools throughout the country are not necessarily provided spaces to talk things out, because oftentimes schools do not acknowledge their humanities. Schools are often sites for spirit murdering (Love, 2016). Though Charlee probably knew what it meant to experience spirit murdering in her previous encounters with school administration, it was my hope that we might find ways to support rather than to punish. Though sometimes hard, love was always my approach with Charlee. As she states:

> She may not feel like she's successful yet but in my eyes she's successful. . . .
> She motivates me to keep going in everything I pursue in.
>
> —*Charlee*

Charlee, like Nova, has always read me. She always asked me if I would stay at her school or would I go on to do something else. "You too good for this miss" is how she would often describe me and Moriah in comparison to our colleagues, almost as if she and her peers were not deserving. Charlee read me in more ways than one; her vulnerability to construct, write, and send this journal entry was sent with, "don't cry."

> When Im slacking she gets on me and tells me about myself and makes sure
> I get back on track immediately. I grew to love her and will always keep in
> contact with her even after Im done with school.
>
> —*Charlee*

There are no truer words than these. When she slacked, I was on her; when she was off track, I was on her—but never because I pitied her. I knew what it was like not to feel seen and heard. I was the opposite of Charlee growing up, but I probably wanted to say all the things that she was able to articulate at her age. We grew to love one another because we could see and read one another in more ways than one. Though she did not finish at her first school, she did graduate from an alternative high school. She was the first in her family to get a high school diploma, and she will attend college in the future. She will keep in contact with me even after school, because we have cultivated a student–mentor relationship that says, "you have no choice but to communicate with Ms. Damaris." Charlee's journal is yet another display of how vulnerable young people will and can be if we cultivate spaces for them that allow them to be. Gratitude journaling helped Charlee to express love.

## Toward a Black Girl Magic

McArthur and Lane (2019) remind us that Black women's philosophy of teaching is deeply political and emotional. Traveling to the Bronx every morning from Queens was a labor of love, with the hope that I could touch, move, and inspire my scholars, especially my Black girls. Historically, Black women educators have committed to teaching and learning as a labor of love; their leadership, activism, and theorization transformed education as we know it (Muhammad et al., 2020). Countless Black women scholars within education have been attentive to the fact that youth need spaces where they can gain an understanding of Black genius and the historical contributions of Black women and girls beyond enslavement (Muhammad, 2020; Love & Duncan, 2017). When I return to my experiences as an educator, I am bogged down by all of the ways in which Black girls' intersectional identities are markers of oppression, rather than a celebration of their rich and dynamic complex histories. Over the years, I have met all different types of Black girls, and I am hyperaware of their needing and wanting to be seen and heard, as do all children across racial and socio-economic backgrounds. Furthermore, as I read the literature on Black girls in language and literacy, the commitment to critically contend with how we make Black girls feel seen and heard is largely covered by Black women scholars. This work is to be appreciated because it does not center whiteness and Black girls' proximity to whiteness; this work is in partnership with and in service of Black girls.

Charlee and Nova's gratitude journals are their own. Their journals open up a larger conversation on what Black girls need in schools. This does not take away from any other race of teachers, but we are different. Identity matters, how we show up in the spaces we teach matters, and so for Black girls to see Black women in school spaces that care for them matters. Gratitude journaling for Black girls in this case gives us room to reimagine: what if Black girls had various representations of Black women in school? What would this mean for their personal growth and humanity? This is not to say that all Black teachers see Black girls; taking a closer look at how we partake in our own hegemony is a hard pill to swallow. Sealey-Ruiz (2020) suggests that in order to be racially literate and to attend to the needs of young people in schools, as educators we must first tend to ourselves; thus, archaeology of the self is the way we begin to name ourselves for ourselves and our students. Further, all educators have not fully committed to developing relationships with Black girls. If we did, then Black girls would not have the second highest expulsion rate in schools behind Black boys. In this very particular case, gratitude journaling for Black girls allows them to reflect on what is true for them and how they experienced me, their educator. They "write it out" (Muhammad, 2016); they share their truths; and they do it vulnerably.

When I think back to the question of what I needed by the time I was my scholars' age, I thought about how important it is for me to be seen and heard. I thought about hypervisibility and the ways that Black girls are seen and often misunderstood. I thought about how important it must have been for me to have a principal that was a Black woman who was 6 feet tall. It was the things that I remembered to help me make sense of how we cultivate a Black girl magic, a Black girl joy, a Black girl pleasure that exists in and out of schools. Further, as I reflect on and think about the ways in which Nova and Charlee used their writing to be vulnerable and express gratitude, I cannot pinpoint a Black woman at their age that made me feel seen and heard, besides my mother. When I think about what this means on a macro level, only 18 percent of teachers are teachers of color in the US, and only 7 percent of teachers are Black teachers (Griffin & Tackie, 2016). This means that the likelihood of a young person seeing themselves in their teacher is unlikely. When we are attentive and are diligent in seeing Black girls, we contribute to them being well. When we think about teacher pipelines and preparing educators, we have to be more attentive for developing educators who see Black girls.

Moreover, there are a number of things to consider as we think about ways to provide spaces for Black girls to be vulnerable and whole. While providing space to "write it out" is extremely important, we must continuously reflect on what it means for Black girls to be well. What it means for all of us to be well. We learn how to treat people well by including them in the conversation. When Black girls write, we reclaim our time and our stories. We write ourselves back into a history that has deemed us unworthy of being written about, unworthy of being human. Our stories and ways of being matter. They have always mattered. The world has found ways to box Black girls in, and so writing is a way for us to say, "we are here" and we exist too, on our own terms. If we as educators can gain a full picture of what Black girls value and deem worthy of gratitude, we can learn a great deal about how to better serve them. This notion is particularly helpful in our reading of Black girls. Black girls are not a monolithic group to which we can apply a one-size-fits all solution; in fact, Black girls are not the problem. If educators are truly committed to the wholeness of Black girls, we should inquire before we assume. I cannot stress enough how different Nova and Charlee are, yet they both partook in seeing, reading, and writing me. There is magic in seeing, reading, and writing. There is magic in writing despite understanding how the world sees you. There is magic in gratitude and acknowledging someone else. Black girl magic lies in every Black girl; it is our responsibility to see it and to create the spaces for it to flourish. The role of the educator is to touch, move, and inspire. There is no better way to do this work than partaking in and witnessing Black girl magic.

## References

Brown, R. N. (2013). *Hear our truths: The creative potential of Black girlhood.* Baltimore: University of Illinois Press.

Edwards, Erica B. (2017). (Bad) girls: Black girls' and school administrators' perceptions of re-entry after exclusionary discipline through a womanist approach to narrative inquiry. Thesis, Georgia State University. https://scholarworks.gsu.edu/eps_diss/180

Emmons, R. A., & McCullough, M. E. (2003). Counting blessings versus burdens: An experimental investigation of gratitude and subjective well-being in daily life. *American Psychological Association, 84,* 377–389.

Evans-Winters, V. E. (2005). *Teaching black girls: Resiliency in urban classrooms* (vol. 279). New York: Peter Lang.

Flinchbaugh, C. L., Moore, E. W. G., Chang, Y. K., & May, D. R. (2012). Student well-being interventions: The effects of stress management techniques and gratitude journaling in the management education classroom. *Journal of Management Education, 36*(2), 191–119. https://doi.org/10.1177/1052562911430062

Freire, P. (1985). Reading the world and reading the word: An interview with Paulo Freire. *Language Arts, 62*(1), 15–21. www.jstor.org/stable/41405241

Griffin, A., & Tackie, H. (2016). *Through our eyes: Perspectives and reflections from Black teachers.* Washington, DC: The Education Trust, 3.

hooks, b. (2013). *Writing beyond race: Living theory and practice.* New York: Routledge.

Lane, M. (2018). "For real love": How Black girls benefit from a politicized ethic of care. *International Journal of Educational Reform, 27*(3), 269–290.

Love, B. L. (2016). Anti-Black state violence, classroom edition: The spirit murdering of Black children. *Journal of Curriculum and Pedagogy, 13*(1), 22–25.

Love, B. L., & Duncan, K. E. (2017). Put some respect on our name: Why every Black & Brown girl needs to learn about radical feminist leadership. *Occasional Paper Series, 2017*(38).

McArthur, S. A. (2016). Black girls and critical media literacy for social activism. *English Education, 48*(4), 362.

McArthur, S. A., & Lane, M. (2019). Schoolin' Black girls: Politicized caring and healing as pedagogical love. *The Urban Review, 51*(1), 65–80.

McCullough, M. E., Tsang, J. A., & Emmons, R. A. (2004). Gratitude in intermediate affective terrain: links of grateful moods to individual differences and daily emotional experience. *Journal of Personality and Social Psychology, 86*(2), 295.

Muhammad, G. (2020). *Cultivating genius: An equity framework for culturally and historically responsive literacy.* New York: Scholastic.

Muhammad, G. E. (2012). Creating spaces for Black adolescent girls to "Write It Out!" *Journal of Adolescent & Adult Literacy, 56*(3), 203–211. doi:10.1002/jaal.00129

Muhammad, G. E., Dunmeyer, A., Starks, F. D., & Sealey-Ruiz, Y. (2020). Historical voices for contemporary times: Learning from Black women educational theorists to redesign teaching and teacher education. *Theory into Practice, 59*(4), 419–428.

Muhammad, G. E., & Haddix, M. (2016). Centering Black girls' literacies: A review of literature on the multiple ways of knowing of Black girls. *English Education, 48*(4), 299–336.

Muhammad, G. E., & Womack, E. (2016). From pen to pin: The multimodality of Black girls (re)writing their lives. *Ubiquity: The Journal of Literature, Literacy, and the Art, 2*(2), 6–45.

Sealey-Ruiz. (2020, August 13). *Archaeology of self.* www.yolandasealeyruiz.com/archaeology-of-self

Watkins, P. C., Woodward, K., Stone, T., & Kolts, R. L. (2003). Gratitude and happiness: Development of a measure of gratitude and relationships with subjective well-being. *Social Behavior and Personality: An International Journal, 31*, 431–452.

# 6

# "THERE'S MORE THAN ONE WAY TO BE BLACK"

## The Literacy Experiences of Black African Immigrant Girls in the United States

*Maima Chea Simmons*

### I Am a Black Liberian-American Woman

I am the proud daughter of Liberian immigrants and a 2nd generation Liberian American, which means I was born in the United States to immigrant parents. I was born in the American South but raised in a traditional Liberian home. Before kindergarten began, I did not know that I was different from the other kids in my neighborhood. The cultural differences in my home life were made clear to me as I entered public school. My earliest school memories involve me being bullied by my peers, some who looked like me and some who didn't, because of my chocolate brown skin, big lips, and different sounding name. I remember being taunted because of my African heritage with the ethnic slur "African booty scratcher", which is a commonly used derogatory term directed at U.S. and foreign-born African immigrants (Adjepong, 2018). Instead of calling me Maima (pronounced My-ma), my peers would call me "Mama" or make references to Aunt Jemima. Kids would make fun of my last name (Chea) by singing the popular commercial jingle for Chia pet plants. "Ch-Ch-Ch-Chia!" I distinctly remember begging my parents not to wear traditional West African garb to my 5th grade graduation because I did not want them to stick out and look "weird". In my 10-year-old head, I believed I could hide my Africanness if I tried hard enough.

Well, I never could hide my Africanness, and thankfully, I learned to love and be proud of my heritage despite the bullying and negative experiences. My parents and older sisters also experienced discrimination because of their identity as African immigrants in the early 1990s. The tamer insults included people asking if my family lived in trees before they moved to America and if they lived in close quarters with lions, tigers, and giraffes. I will not share the nastier insults because words have power and those types of words don't belong in this book.

I grew up in a predominately Black community, but my family's lived experiences and culture differed greatly from many of my peers. My family talked differently, ate different foods, and stood out as different from the other Black families in the neighborhood. Throughout my K–12 schooling, I tried my best to assimilate into Black American culture by removing Liberian English words from my vocabulary.

Although I attended majority-Black K–12 schools, our texts and curricula were not culturally relevant to our identities as Black youth growing up in the deep South. As I reflect upon my English Language Arts classes throughout those years, I do not recall ever reading any African American literature, besides *Their Eyes Were Watching God*, nor did I ever learn anything about Africa or African literature within my formal academic schooling. My parents provided my sisters and I with cultural knowledge by sharing traditional African fables, Liberian history, and other texts with us at home. My teachers never addressed my identity as a Black African immigrant girl; however, I excelled academically throughout my K–12 years.

It was not until I began my undergraduate schooling (at a predominately white institution ironically) that I was exposed to a variety of African diasporic literature in a formal academic setting. I immersed myself in African American literature courses, African studies courses, and comparative literature courses focused on diasporic texts. These texts helped me to explore and develop my identity as a Black African immigrant woman who was born and raised in the American South. I have encountered (and continue to encounter) racial microaggressions and blatant racism due to my identity as a Black woman with a "weird" name, which serves as a marker of my ethnic identity. My perceived youth only compounds the tacit microaggressions and sometimes-overt racism that I have experienced within academia. Oftentimes, people of various races will ask me "What are you?" in an attempt to decipher my ethnicity based upon my name or refer to Africa as a country. Africa is made up of 54 different countries, all with distinct languages, cultures, and customs. So, it's disheartening how often people learn that I am Liberian and proceed to ask me if I know their Nigerian friend, John, in Texas.

Because my lived experiences were often left out of school-sanctioned texts as a Black African immigrant girl, I am most interested in understanding how girls who share similarities to my ethnic and racial background make sense of their identities when their identities are constantly omitted from English Language Arts curricula selected by teachers and districts. As stated by James Banks (1998), my biographical journey as a researcher "greatly influences my values, research questions, and the knowledge I construct" (p. 4). My lived experiences as a 2nd generation, Black Liberian-American woman who was born and raised in the American South, shape my worldviews, wonderings, and experiences within the various communities I traverse.

## African Immigrants in the United States

According to the Migration Policy Institute's 2017 report, "Sub-Saharan African Immigrants in the United States" of the 2015 census, there are 1.7 million sub-Saharan African immigrants in the United States. West African immigrants comprise the largest group of African immigrants (766,000) and include people from countries such as Nigeria, Ghana, Liberia, and Sierra Leone, among other countries. Sub-Saharan African immigrants have moved to large metropolitan areas such as New York City, the Washington, D.C./DMV area, Atlanta, Minneapolis, Houston, Dallas, Boston, Los Angeles, and Chicago. There are approximately 3.3 million members of the sub-Saharan African diaspora living in the United States, which includes people born in sub-Saharan Africa and those with ancestral ties (1.5, 2nd, and 2.5 generation sub-Saharan Africans). These statistics illustrate the rapid growth of sub-Saharan African immigrants in the United States, as this population has "doubled every decade between 1980 and 2010" (Zong & Batalova, 2017). For clarification, 1.5 generation immigrants are those who moved to the United States before the age of 12, 2nd generation immigrants were born in the United States but their parents were born outside of the United States, and 2.5 generation immigrants were born in the United States and only one of their parents was born in the U.S. Members of the sub-Saharan African diaspora differ in terms of origin, ethnic identity, religious affiliation, generational status in the United States, and cultural practices (Awokoya & Clark, 2008). Although African immigrants are one of the fastest growing immigrant populations in the United States, there is little attention paid to the educational experiences and challenges of Black African immigrant youth within U.S. schools (Adjepong, 2018; Awokoya, 2012; George Mwangi, 2014; George Mwangi & Fries-Britt, 2015; Rong & Preissle, 2009).

## The Invisibility of Black African Immigrants

Black African immigrants' experiences are often subsumed under the larger racial category of Black, which completely ignores the nuanced differences of culture, language, migration, acculturation, and transition for Black African immigrants in the United States. Researching Black people in America as a monolithic group overlooks the ways in which interracial and intraracial relationships impact identity development and fails to acknowledge the diversity of Blackness within the diaspora (Adjepong, 2018; Awokoya & Clark, 2008; Smith, 2019). Black Africans' experiences are often ignored within immigrant discourse research and political arenas, as these areas tend to focus on immigrants of Asian and/or Latino descent (Knight & Watson, 2014). Furthermore, anti-immigrant discourse permeates American culture, which further marginalizes and distorts the experiences and concerns of Black African immigrant populations in the United States. Minoritized immigrants, regardless of race, are depicted as hazardous to national and financial security within anti-immigrant discourse (Allen, Jackson, & Knight, 2012).

## Identity Borderlands

Exploring the experiences of Black African immigrant youth, particularly Black African immigrant girls, is important because of the multiple borderlands these youth traverse. Black African immigrant girls' experiences are heavily shaped by their race, *ethnicity*, and gender, among other factors such as socioeconomic status and skin color. Black African immigrant girls constantly navigate their multilayered identities of what it means to be a woman who is Black and African in the United States. To be clear, Black African immigrant girls must push back against falsehoods and stereotypes about Africanness, Blackness (in America), Black African womanhood, and Black American womanhood in addition to other facets of their identities such as language, religion, sexual orientation, and socioeconomic status (Showers, 2015; Traoré, 2004, 2006).

Black African immigrant youth often face negative, primitive stereotypes and limited portrayals of Africanness in popular culture and academic curriculum. These limited portrayals of Africa promote deficit narratives of Africans as victimized, primal, and impoverished (Dokotum, 2020; Imoagene, 2015; Showers; 2015; Watson & Knight-Manuel, 2017). Black African immigrant women and girls are often stratified on the lowest rungs of the social hierarchy due to their race, class, and gender. Exoticized and hypersexualized media portrayals of topless African women and desolate African communities diminish the cultural and intellectual accomplishments of Black African women.

Many Americans are uninformed and uneducated about Black American history, and even more so are unfamiliar with Africa's rich cultures, histories, and geographical boundaries. Identity markers such as language, accents, and/or non-American names have served as obstacles for some Black African immigrants, as these differences are used to characterize Black African immigrants as deficit and inferior. Traoré (2004) draws strong connections between the systemic underrepresentation and misrepresentation of African culture to the long-standing, adverse effects of colonialism. The systemic erasure of African history and Black history prior to slavery has contributed to gross cultural misunderstandings and missed opportunities to critically engage Black African immigrant girls.

Black African immigrant girls must also push back against deficit perspectives of what it means to be Black in the United States. Systemic and institutionalized racism in the U.S. continues to negatively impact the lived experiences of Black people, and Black African immigrants are not exempt from anti-Black racism (Adjepong, 2018). Furthermore, Black African immigrant girls must also contend with negative myths about Black womanhood that attempt to characterize the group as loud, aggressive, sexually promiscuous, and economically dependent (Brown, 2013; Stephens & Phillips, 2003). These myths about Black womanhood are perpetuated by the media and affect the ways in which Black girls are educated within the U.S. school system (Muhammad & McArthur, 2015).

## Situating Purpose

Examining the ways in which nationality, ethnicity, and language add dimension to the identity of Black African immigrant girls helps to elucidate their experiences within U.S. classrooms while also providing them space to make meaning of their intersecting identities for themselves (Berry, 1997; Kim, 2014). There is a dire need for more research that explores how Black African immigrant girls understand their literacy experiences by negotiating their "complex set of status variables, such as gender, social class, age, political affiliation, religion, and region" (Banks, 1998, p. 5). The identity formation of Black African immigrant youth in the United States is nuanced and complex (Knight & Watson, 2014). Black African immigrant girls navigate their home, school, and social communities in the midst of racism, xenophobia, sexism, classism, and patriarchy. Although there is a glaring gap in research surrounding the literacy experiences of Black African immigrant girls, this chapter seeks to provide analysis of selected studies that focus on the literacy practices of U.S. and foreign-born immigrant youth in order to highlight the ways in which educators can better support Black African immigrant girls in using literacy to make sense of their gendered, bicultural identities.

## Reviewing Literature and Inclusion Criteria

I engaged in several searches using the EBSCO database to locate empirical studies related to Black West African immigrant girls' literacies. I searched for several terms, including: African girls' literacies, immigrant girls' literacies, immigrant youth literacies, Black girl literacies, African girls writing, and Black West African immigrant girl literacies. When I searched the term, "Black West African immigrant girl literacies", I was rerouted to studies that focused on Black (American) girls. Because of the dearth of research surrounding Black West African girls, I broadened my searches to include "immigrant girls" and "immigrant youth". These searches populated approximately 30 studies that I then used to read the references and select more related studies and research scholars who were heavily cited. I reviewed 40 studies total and focused on approximately 7 studies that were most relevant to my research inquiry on the literacy practices of Black African immigrant girls.

## Black Girls' Literacies Framework

This literature review is directly connected to the Black Girls' Literacies Framework developed by Muhammad and Haddix (2016). The authors posit that Black girls' literacies are "multiple, tied to identities, historical, collaborative, intellectual, political and critical" (p. 325). Within this review, I draw strong connections to each facet of this framework. The literacies of Black African girls in the United States are multiple, tied to identities historical, collaborative, political and critical. As children of African immigrants, Black West African girls engage in various modes of literacy to make meaning of the texts around them. The studies included in this chapter explore the experiences of immigrant youth in United States literacy spaces through the lens of the Black Girls' Literacies Framework. The foci of these studies vary due to the dearth of research surrounding the experiences of Black African immigrant girls. The studies discussed include participants of various ethnic and racial backgrounds who identify as immigrants or the child(ren) of immigrants in the United States. Only one of these studies focuses exclusively on the literacy experiences of Black African immigrant girls; however, several of the included studies include Black African participants. All of the reviewed studies make connections to the pressing issues surrounding the literacy experiences of Black African immigrant girls.

## Literacies Are Multiple and Tied to Identities

The identities of Black African girls are salient and multilayered, as these girls must develop and negotiate bicultural identity formation within the context of life in the United States as a Black girl of foreign descent (Showers, 2015). Dávila's (2015) study focused on the experiences of two Black African immigrant girls (from Somalia and Congo respectively) who were newcomers to the United States. Within the study, the researcher explored how these students developed their multiliteracies and remained connected to their home cultures. Dávila (2015) employs a sociocultural and diasporic literacy framework to uncover how these Black African immigrant girls constructed and understood texts from "indigenous and multilingual perspectives" that involve social practices to make sense of how readers see the world (p. 642).

The study's findings highlighted the participants' multilayered uses of literacy, such as school-sanctioned academic literacy within the ESL classroom, literacy as a gatekeeper to mobility (written driving tests), and literacy as a tool to connect with relatives and friends in their home nation. Most importantly, this study reinforces the significant nature of how gender impacted the girls' identities dually as immigrants and as literate beings. Dávila (2015) posits,

> diaspora literacies must be understood from a gendered lens because of the different spaces men and women occupy in society, and because gender is directly linked to reading practices through the mediation of social systems, cultural values, ideologies, and power relations.
>
> *(p. 642)*

An important implication of this study is the need for Black African immigrant girls to be given space and autonomy to select texts that reflect, challenge, and connect their identities to diaspora literacies and language practices in transnational spaces.

Ghiso and Low's (2012) study examined the ways that immigrant students in the United States use multimodal literacies to share their immigration narratives and develop their nationalistic identities. The authors foreground the deficit perceptions and difficulties that immigrant students face in U.S. schools because immigrant students must constantly "negotiate their identities along a preconceived model of what it means to be American, including the message that success requires shedding their ethnic identities and smoothing over their struggles" (Ghiso & Low, 2012, p. 26). The participants in this study were mixed gender and hailed from Latin American, West African, Caribbean, Asian, and Middle Eastern countries. The study was hosted through a five-week English Language Learning summer program. The students' language proficiencies varied greatly, and the study included Spanish, Bengali, Vietnamese, Punjabi, Chinese, Urdu, Arabic, and French speakers. The researchers facilitated a literacy program that focused on how students developed their multimodal literacies in an environment that valued their cultural and linguistic funds of knowledge. The first author utilized her own immigration narrative as a strategy to demonstrate the power of creating agency through narratives. The study's data included visual representatives of immigration narratives in the form of comic panels. Students visually represented their literal and metaphorical immigration narratives through drawings and graphic novels, which were shared with other participants and the research facilitators.

The findings suggest that the struggles that immigrant students face as they navigate varied cultural spaces "give them privileged insights about the world we share" (Ghiso & Low, 2012, p. 31). The implications of this study are salient for Black African immigrant girls because the authors suggest literacy educators must create curricular spaces that welcome multiple perspectives, encourage multimodal literacies, and support divergent expressions of national identity.

### Literacies Are Historical and Collaborative

The histories of Black African girls are powerful, and familial stories of migration and acculturation impact their educative experiences in U.S. schools (Imoagene, 2015). The collaborative nature of Black African girls' literacy development is shaped by their social and lived experiences within U.S. schools. Black African girls engage in "co-construction of knowledge with the world and with other Black girls" as they negotiate how their race, class, gender, and ethnicity shape their schooling experiences (Muhammad & Haddix, 2016).

Bigelow and King's (2015) study focused on youth aged 14–21 who were newcomer Somali students in an ESL classroom. The study's participants were mixed gender and had limited schooling experiences in Somalia. Within the ESL class, there were various immigrant students, and the languages spoken in the classroom included Somali, Oromo, Amharic, Vietnamese, Lao, French, Hmong, and Nepalese. The site of study, Franken International, was a Minnesota school that catered to newly immigrated adolescents and young adults. The findings of this print literacy study indicated that although the Somali students were fluent in spoken Somali, they were not formally educated on how to write in Somali. This gap in knowledge led to more intricate and complicated ESL instruction, as the students "had an unresolved and evolving relationship within their ethnic heritage and language", particularly because they "may not have had the opportunity to become literate in their home language" (Bigelow & King, 2015, p. 5). Transnationalism was a pervasive theme within this study, as the Somali youth presented a dialect diversity through their intense contact with non-Somali speakers. This contact led to new forms of Somali-English being born within this Minnesota community.

Bigelow and King's (2015) study is most important to Black African immigrant girls' literacy education experiences because it emphasizes the importance of recognizing and honoring students' home languages, as their languages are tied to "national history and identity, processes of resettlement and how individuals relate with their co-ethnic community" (p. 5). The implications of this study suggest that there are power hierarchies within every classroom, even those portrayed as a "safe space", because of their perceived racial and/or ethnic homogenization. These power hierarchies can reproduce national patterns of marginalization for Black African immigrant girls inside literacy classrooms.

## *Literacies Are Political and Critical*

Black African girls' literacies are undoubtedly political and critical, as they are often forced to interrogate issues of power, stereotypes, and social justice issues in the wake of negative depictions of what it means to be a woman who is both African and Black in America (Ojo-Ade, 2001).

Stewart's (2013) study focused on how one immigrant girl's literacy education experiences were shaped by her status as a new immigrant in the United States. Valeria, the study's sole participant, was of El Salvadoran descent. Her experiences reflect and connect to those of Black African immigrant girls because she grappled with issues of language, economic status, agency, and national identity, similar to the experiences of Black African immigrant girls.

This study is similar to Dávila's (2015) study in that Valeria maintained a digital presence using multimodal literacies to stay connected with people from her home country. Stewart (2013) highlighted the themes of L1 literacy (Spanish, survival), L2 literacy (English), digital escape, and aspirations. The most important implications to this study surround the concerns of "language, economic circumstances, and legal status, which leads some immigrant students to lose their sense of agency" (Stewart, 2013, p. 48). The implications of this study suggest that literacy educators must make a targeted approach to increase immigrant students' agency by making space for students to read and write about their lived experiences. Stewart (2013) suggests, "immigrant students who read literature that mirrors their experiences become more engaged readers, gain cultural confidence as they identify with literary events, and learn to negotiate their transnational identities" (p. 48). This suggestion directly connects with the Black Girls' Literacies Framework because it encourages educators to provide multiple opportunities for girls to speak back in political and critical ways that increase their own agency in educational spaces.

Park's (2016) study focuses on the experiences of six immigrant and refugee girls who were new arrivals to the United States. The girls participated in an after-school ESL literacy program designed to use graphic novels to make sense of how these girls understood critical multicultural citizenship. The study's participants were from various countries, including China, Dominican Republic, Ghana, Nigeria, Mali, and Jordan. Graphic novels were selected as the primary text genre for the after-school literacy program because it provided opportunities for students to engage with multimodal texts (reading images and print). Park (2016) posits, "immigrant youth need opportunities to engage in dialogue where they grapple with what it means to belong to, and lead powerful lives in, their new country" (p. 127). Park and her female co-facilitator, an ESL teacher, designed this program because of their "own gender identity and observations that immigrant girls were often positioned as silent in the school" (Park, 2016, p. 129). The participants were grappling with what it meant to be American, and how their gender identity as girls influenced their educative experiences. The findings of this study suggest that the girls utilized the graphic novels as a tool to incorporate their own personal beliefs about critical multicultural citizenship. The salient themes that emerged from the interview and focus group data focused on challenging government structures, analyzing the United States' entanglement within the world, and discussing their struggles in the United States. The implications of this study directly connect to the experiences of Black African immigrant girls' literacy education experiences because it suggests that literacy educators should include more multimodal texts to diversify school-sanctioned curricula that present deficit or incomplete viewpoints. Literacy educators should strive to develop classroom environments where students can collaborate and discuss issues from diverse worldviews.

Enciso's (2011) study focused on analyzing the storytelling practices and cultural funds of knowledge of immigrant and nonimmigrant youth within one middle-grade classroom. This study utilized critical literacy pedagogy to make sense of how students "name what matters to them, to speculate about what is possible in their lives, and to unravel contradictions" (Enciso, 2011, p. 21). Storytelling is emphasized as a powerful literacy education activity because it provides space for students to expound upon their lived experiences, emotions, and understandings of their cultural and historical background. The researcher gathered data from audiotaping classroom dialogue and analyzed the data using discourse analysis methodology.

The classroom was heterogeneous and mixed gender, and included immigrant and nonimmigrant youth. This factor was important because many of the immigrant youth felt threatened by anti-immigrant discourse, in the form of ethnic slurs from their nonimmigrant classmates "who challenged their right to belong in the school, their neighborhood, and nation" (Enciso, 2011, p. 22). These two groups of students were rarely given space within academic settings to discuss or learn about the other groups' lived experiences. An important implication of this study is the need for more dialogue between nonimmigrant and immigrant youth to learn more about similar and different lived experiences. Black African immigrant girls would benefit from this practice because dialogue with nonimmigrant and immigrant students alike can help these girls to make sense of their identities and the identities of others around them (who may or may not identify as the same race) and learn how their relationships can strengthen the learning environment. Fostering dialogue where youth can compare and contrast their experiences will lead to increased cultural understandings and unity. Although students may share racial similarities, students with ethnic, linguistic, and cultural differences are often structurally divided or segregated within school environments (Enciso, 2011). Educators play an important role in this dialogue and must come to their own cultural understanding by exploring personal prejudices and biases and doing the internal work to push back against systemic racism. This internal awareness will help educators to be intentionally antiracist and to become more effective in making space for Black African immigrant girls' stories to be told *and* heard.

## Black Girls' Literacies Framework Embodied

In summation, the studies reviewed draw strong connections to the Black Girls' Literacies Frameworks in four key ways. Educators must present and make space for multiple perspectives that promote intercultural, intracultural, interracial, and intraracial dialogue.

The ideologies and pedagogies enacted by educators must reflect culturally aware and antiracist beliefs to best support Black African girls in literacy spaces. When educators are culturally aware and actively antiracist, their day-to-day practices and decision making can positively shift the literacy experiences of Black African immigrant girls. By carefully selecting and curating learning experiences that provide multiple opportunities to read, write, and speak in diverse ways, educators can promote positive identity development, intellectual growth, skill development, and criticality with their Black African girl students (Muhammad, 2020).

## Limitations of the Review

The studies discussed provided valuable insight into the literacy education experiences of some immigrant youth in United States classrooms. The limitations to the studies presented in this chapter are representative of the dearth of research surrounding the experiences of Black African immigrant girls in literacy classrooms. Most of the studies reviewed focused on newcomer immigrants within English Language Learning classrooms or after-school settings formed within ESL environments. This characteristic is important to interrogate because it generalizes all immigrant youth into the category of developing English learners. Furthermore, the body of existing research does not tend to focus on immigrant youth, especially Black African immigrant girls who may have immigrated to the United States as children, those born in the United States to immigrant parents, or youth who have one foreign-born parent.

Most of the research surrounding adolescent immigrant youth literacy experiences ignores the experiences of Black African immigrant youth and silences the experiences of Black African immigrant girls even further. Dávila's (2015) study was the lone study analyzed that focused solely on the literacy experiences of two Black African immigrant newcomer girls. The other studies focused on diverse immigrant experiences or mixed gender participants (such as Bigelow and King's Somali print literacy study). While these latter studies add to the conversation about the experiences of immigrant youth in general, there is a dire lack of research concerning the nuanced experiences of adolescent Black African immigrant girls. It is therefore important to expand the research base beyond simply studying immigrant newcomers, as there are varied experiences within Black African immigrant groups, whether they are born inside or outside of the U.S. (Knight, Roegman, & Edstrom, 2016).

Existing research on the literacy experiences of immigrant youth often ignores issues of race and gender and focuses mainly on immigrant and linguistic status. This is a detriment to Black African immigrant girls because Black African immigrant girls are identified as Black and woman alongside their status as African/immigrant. Immigrant youth are not a monolithic group (Davies, 2008). Identities are complex, and for Black youth, their experiences are always shaped by their race, gender, perceived socioeconomic status, and ethnicity. In some environments, specific factors are more apparent than others, but they all are constantly present. Research that interrogates how Black African immigrant girls experience literacy education should strive to engage all facets of these girls' identities. To ignore how race or gender impacts their experiences as immigrants or children of immigrants would be to ignore their lived realities and multiple literacies (Muhammad & Haddix, 2016).

## Future Directions for Education

In what follows, I provide suggestions and future directions for literacy education for Black African immigrant girls. These directions will support literacy and language practices that advance the education of girls.

## Text Selection

Literacy research encompassing the experiences of Black African immigrant girls must focus on exploring their identities alongside the textual choices that the girls make while reading, writing, and discussing their lives. Stewart's (2012) article focuses on textual representations that appeal to adolescent immigrant girls. Stewart suggests that texts selected for use with adolescent immigrant girls should incorporate an "adolescent protagonist who is a 1st, 1.5, or 2nd generation immigrant girl", develop as a bildungsroman story, take place in a contemporary setting, and be written by a female author who also identifies as a 1st, 1.5, or 2nd generation immigrant (p. 18). Representations of immigrant girls in curricular texts must move past stereotypical representations and strive to provide and promote whole images of immigrant girls.

Muhammad's (2015) work strengthens this suggestion by emphasizing the historical nature of literacy for Black women. It is not enough to expose Black African immigrant girls to the writing of female immigrant writers; there must also be a concentrated effort to present Black African immigrant girls with multiple opportunities to "draw upon the writings of other Black women" to shape their writings and dialogue (Muhammad, 2015, p. 6). Traditional academic curriculum and canonical texts ignore the experiences of marginalized groups such as Black American and Black African immigrant girls. Drawing upon the Black Girls' Literacies Framework, it is important to keep the identities of Black African immigrant girls at the forefront of text selections. Selecting texts that highlight the experiences, strengths, and struggles of Black African immigrant girls provides space to further learn about this special group of students. When reading these texts, Black African immigrant girls can be critical of messages about power and representation throughout the text.

## Literacy Collaboratives

Black girls' literacies are collaborative in nature, whether they are drawing upon the writings of Black women literary mentors or working alongside other girls to construct their worldview (Muhammad & Haddix, 2016). Literacy collaboratives provide space for Black African immigrant girls to interrogate and resist stereotypes and misrepresentations of their identity, an opportunity that is often invisible in typical, mainstream English Language Arts classrooms (Carter, 2007). Literacy collaboratives are historical in nature. Literary societies and social clubs were spaces that helped African Americans to educate themselves, strengthen community bonds, fight social injustices, and develop plans of action to combat oppression (McHenry, 2002). African American literary societies did not always carry this title and were sometimes referred to as social clubs or book clubs. These collaborative literacy spaces were often gender-based and separated by socioeconomic status.

Contemporary literacy collaboratives for Black girls, such as the one detailed in Muhammad's 2015 study, provide space for Black girls of various ethnic, religious, and socioeconomic backgrounds to come together in intellectual and political pursuit. The Sister Authors (Black girls) created a space that was "culturally responsive and focused on advancing their sensemaking of their histories in ways that were connected to their lives and the social conditions of our times" (Muhammad, 2015, p. 5). Examining and critiquing the social conditions of our times requires an astute look at structures of power, privilege, and perspective. Creating spaces for Black African immigrant girls from various backgrounds and migration histories is important because there is not an African immigrant monolithic experience. Black African immigrant girls' worldviews are vastly shaped by their familial migration stories, linguistic differences, religious identities, socioeconomic status, and skin color, among other factors. Making space for Black African immigrant girls to come together within a literacy collaborative space will allow girls to reflect upon their shared and varied life experiences. These spaces can help to illuminate how Black African immigrant girls develop their bicultural identity in relation to the texts, people, and structures around them.

## Developing Spaces for Black African Immigrant Girls' Literacy Practices

Developing more spaces for Black African immigrant girls to engage in literacy practices with other Black African immigrant girls as well as Black American girls will prove to be powerful in these young ladies' literacy development. While Black African immigrant girls and Black American girls may hold different experiences with familial migration stories, it is important these girls have multiple opportunities to come together (Muhammad, 2012). Although their ethnic origins and national identities may differ, Black African immigrant girls and Black American girls face many of the same obstacles as Black girls in the United States. Issues of racism, sexism, colorism, and classism impact these girls in many ways, and there is a dearth of research regarding how Black African immigrant girls and Black American girls develop their identities in relation to each other. The relationships that I have cultivated with Black women and girls of African and American descent along my journey have supported my personal, academic, and professional growth, even in situations when I felt marginalized, invisible, or hypervisible.

I have experienced the feeling of not being *fully* seen by some educators throughout my academic career, from kindergarten through my doctoral program, despite my status as a "high-achiever". These educators have ignored my perspectives, reinforced stereotypical myths, and/or asked me to act as a spokeswoman for the monolithic Black experience. In contrast, the educators who have had the *greatest* impact on me recognized my personhood by actively developing a relationship with me, challenging racism, sexism, and xenophobia, and valuing multiple perspectives within their classroom. Developing spaces, structures, and practices to support Black African girls' literacy practices will be a catalyst in developing the next generation of leaders who will continue this work.

## References

Adjepong, A. (2018). Afropolitan projects: African immigrant identities and solidarities in the United States. *Ethnic and Racial Studies, 41*(2), 248–266.

Allen, K. M., Jackson, I., & Knight, M. G. (2012). Complicating culturally relevant pedagogy: Unpacking African immigrants' cultural identities. *International Journal of Multicultural Education, 14*(2), 1–28.

Awokoya, J. T. (2012). Identity constructions and negotiations among 1.5- and second-generation Nigerians: The impact of family, school, and peer contexts. *Harvard Educational Review, 82*(2), 255–281.

Awokoya, J. T., & Clark, C. (2008). Demystifying cultural theories and practices: Locating Black immigrant experiences in teacher education research. *Multicultural Education, 16*(2), 49–58.

Banks, J. A. (1998). The lives and values of researchers: Implications for educating citizens in a multicultural society. *Educational Researcher, 27*(7), 4–17.

Berry, K. A. (1997). Projecting the voices of others: Issues of representation in teaching race and ethnicity. *Journal of Geography in Higher Education, 21*(2), 283–289.

Bigelow, M., & King, K. A. (2015). Somali immigrant youths and the power of print literacy. *Writing Systems Research, 7*(1), 4–19.

Brown, R. N. (2013). *Hear our truths: The creative potential of Black girlhood.* Champaign: University of Illinois Press.

Carter, S. P. (2007). "Reading all that White crazy stuff": Black young women unpacking whiteness in a high school British literature classroom. *The Journal of Classroom Interaction, 42*–54.

Davies, A. Z. (2008). Characteristics of adolescent Sierra Leonean refugees in public schools in New York City. *Education and Urban Society, 40*(3), 361–376.

Dávila, L. T. (2015). Diaspora literacies. *Journal of Adolescent & Adult Literacy, 58*(8), 641–649.

Dokotum, O. O. (2020). *Hollywood and Africa: Recycling the "Dark Continent" myth from 1908–2020.* Makhanda: NISC (Pty) Ltd.

Enciso, P. (2011). Storytelling in critical literacy pedagogy: Removing the walls between immigrant and non-immigrant youth. *English Teaching: Practice and Critique, 10*(1), 21–40.

George Mwangi, C. A. (2014). Complicating blackness: Black immigrants and racial positioning in U.S. higher education. *Journal of Critical Thought and Praxis, 3*(2), 1–27.

George Mwangi, C. A., & Fries-Britt, S. (2015). Black within Black: The perceptions of Black immigrant collegians and their U.S. college experience. *About Campus, 20*(2), 16–23.

Ghiso, M. P., & Low, D. E. (2012). Students using multimodal literacies to surface micronarratives of United States immigration. *Literacy, 47*(1), 26–34.

Imoagene, O. (2015). Broken bridges: An exchange of slurs between African Americans and second generation Nigerians and the impact on identity formation among the second generation. *Language Sciences, 52*, 176–186.

Kim, E. (2014). Bicultural socialization experiences of Black immigrant students at a predominantly White institution. *The Journal of Negro Education, 83*(4), 580–594.

Knight, M. G., & Watson, V. W. M. (2014). Toward participatory communal citizenship: Rendering visible the civic teaching, learning, and actions of African immigrant youth and young adults. *American Educational Research Journal, 51*(3), 539–566.

McHenry, E. (2002). *Forgotten readers: Recovering the lost history of African American literary societies.* Durham, NC: Duke University Press.

Muhammad, G. E. (2012). Creating spaces for Black adolescent girls to "write it out!" *Journal of Adolescent & Adult Literacy, 56*(3), 203–211.

Muhammad, G. E. (2015). The role of literary mentors in writing development: How African American women's literature supported the writings of adolescent girls. *Journal of Education, 195*(2), 5–14.

Muhammad, G. E. (2020). *Cultivating genius: An equity framework for culturally and historically responsive literacy.* New York, NY: Scholastic.

Muhammad, G. E., & Haddix, M. (2016). Centering Black girls' literacies: A review of literature on the multiple ways of knowing of Black girls. *English Education, 48*(4), 299–336.

Muhammad, G. E., & McArthur, S. A. (2015). Styled by their perceptions: Black adolescent girls interpret representations of Black females in popular culture. *Multicultural Perspectives, 17*(3), 133–140.

Ojo-Ade, F. (2001). Africans and racism in the new millennium. *Journal of Black Studies, 32*, 184–211.

Park, J. Y. (2016). Going global and getting graphic: Critical multicultural citizenship education in an afterschool program for immigrant and refugee girls. *International Journal of Multicultural Education, 18*(1), 126–141.

Rong, X. L., & Preissle, J. (2009). *Educating immigrant students in the 21st century: What educators need to know.* Thousand Oaks, CA: Corwin Press.

Showers, F. (2015). Being Black, foreign and woman: African immigrant identities in the United States. *Ethnic and Racial Studies, 38*(10), 1815–1830.

Smith, P. (2019). (Re)positioning in the Englishes and (English) literacies of a Black immigrant youth: Towards a transraciolinguistic approach. *Theory into Practice,* 1–12.

Stephens, D. P., & Phillips, L. (2003). Freaks, gold diggers, divas, and dykes: The sociohistorical development of adolescent African American women's sexual scripts. *Sexuality and Culture, 7*, 3–49.

Stewart, M. A. (2013). Giving voice to Valeria's story: Support, value, and agency for immigrant adolescents. *Journal of Adolescent and Adult Literacy, 57*(1), 42–50.

Traoré, R. (2004). Colonialism continued: African students in an urban high school in America. *Journal of Black Studies, 34*(3), 348–369.

Traoré, R. (2006). Voices of African students in America: "We're not from the jungle". *Multicultural Perspectives, 8*(2), 29–34.

Watson, V. W., & Knight-Manuel, M. G. (2017). Challenging popularized narratives of immigrant youth from West Africa: Examining social processes of navigating identities and engaging civically. *Review of Research in Education, 41*(1), 279–310.

Zong, J., & Batalova, J. (2017). Sub-Saharan African immigrants in the United States. *Migration Information Source.* www.migrationpolicy.org/article/sub-saharan-african-immigrants-united-states

# KITCHEN TABLE TALKS

## Black Girls' Language and Literacy Practices

*Valerie Kinloch in Conversation with Tamara Butler, Maima Chea Simmons, Damaris Dunn and Gholdy Muhammad*

The authors in this section gathered around a virtual kitchen table, using the online platform Zoom, to engage in conversation around shared ideas and guiding questions about Black girls' literacy practices. They participated in a conversation where they talked across their respective work as literacy educators and scholars who foreground Black feminist/womanist epistemologies in their personal, social, and professional lives. This kitchen table talk is organized around these sub questions:

- Why is it critical that all educators acknowledge Black girls' literacies in their work?
- How are Black girls' literacies honored in your work?
- What considerations should researchers forefront when studying with Black girls and their literacy and language practices?
- What practical recommendations would you offer educators working with Black girls?

In the sections that follow, we highlight our dialogic exchanges in response to these questions and conclude with final words of wisdom. To recreate our kitchen table talk, we video-recorded our Zoom chat and transcribed the video. Each section that follows captures key points that were made to address the guiding questions.

## Acknowledging Black girls' Literacies

### *Why Is It Critical That All Educators Acknowledge Black Girl Literacies in Their Work?*

MAIMA: When I thought about that question, I thought about the importance of acknowledging Black girls' literacies because oftentimes Black people are left out of the canonical texts that are presented in classrooms related to English Language Arts throughout school in general. So then, when we compound that with saying not only do our texts that students read sometimes provide a limited or very deficit perspective of what it means to be Black, you erase a lot of their identities by not acknowledging their culture, their ethnicity. That further leaves people out of the conversation. And we are a part of the conversation, if we are a part of the classroom.

DAMARIS: I think, simply when we see Black girls, we see everyone. When I was writing my chapter, a lot of the theory is around seeing and the importance of seeing Black girls. I think we see them in a hyper-visible way. I think there's often this mold where we try to control their bodies, but I think just being seen. Seeing a Black professor on campus means so much, right? And being able to connect with them one-on-one means a lot. In the space that I'm in as a first semester doctoral student, it was so important for me to write about the Black girls that I see on a regular basis.

TAMARA: I agree with what's been said. This idea that if you see . . . I really like what Damaris just said in terms of when you see Black girls, you see everybody. I think to center Black girls goes back to the thinking of the Combahee River Collective. If you think about the liberation of Black women and in this case of Black girls, we think about the liberation and freedom of everyone else. So, for me, I think centering Black girls in your classroom and really thinking about their ways of being and our ways of knowing is really important and key to thinking about what literacies are and what literacies are for.

VALERIE: I agree with everything that already been said. You know, Black is brilliant and beautiful. Why not focus on Black and Blackness? It's rooted in everything that we do. It is rooted in the history of this entire country and the world. And so, Blackness often times gets constructed as this negative and dangerous and violent site. When it became constructed in that way, I think that's purposeful and intentional in order to try to convince people that Blackness as a construct is something that is just too violent to even embrace. And if we don't embrace it, and if we don't honor and recognize it and love it—and then hence, talk and teach about it. Then we fall into that deficit narrative. We fall into that particular way of pervasively describing the pathological insanity that some people have of Blackness.

Why is it critical that we acknowledge Black girls' literacies? Because we made the world. I think that's it. You know being a dean in a predominantly white institution, where I was the only Black girl here. I'm the first Black woman to be dean of any school on this campus. You get to a point where you don't hide it, you embrace it, and you don't have to teach it to other people that have to learn it for themselves. You walk in that grace.

## Honoring Black Girls' Literacies

### How Are Black Girls' Literacies Honored in Your Work?

TAMARA: Black girl literacies are honored in my work as I'm really thinking about placemaking. In some of my work, I've been thinking a lot around notions of geography and cartography and really trying to take serious what does it mean for Black girls to take up space and to make place. For me, it's really saying there's a knowledge that Black girls have and that if we're going to take up and really understand what Black girls are doing then we really have to pay attention to the space that they are in. I think so often, in a piece I have written before, so often we go to the same pockets of a place to find Black girls. We're like "Oh they're in the inner city. Oh they're in this after-school program". But it's like, Black girls are in class. They're in classes, they're everywhere. I think they're on the bus, they're walking on the streets. They're everywhere. I think if educational research is going to take Black girl literacies seriously. We can't keep relegating Black girls to the same pocket when it comes to research. So for me, here are all the places that we can look at and go to if we really want to figure out what it means to be a Black girl.

MAIMA: When I think about my work as a doctoral student, I think the idea of being seen is important, as Damaris said, in the study that I am working on because it is about creating a space for understanding how Black girls interpret and understand their Blackness, their girlhood, and for my particular participants, their African identity in the midst of the messages that they receive and seek out from popular culture. I think that idea of being seen and then also making space for Black girls to speak for themselves and to develop their own identities in the midst of what we talked about like hypervisibility, negative identity, or the pervasiveness of stereotypes. In my professional work, like Dr. Kinloch mentioned, I work in a very, very white space. A really important part in my work is having the tough conversations with teachers and school leaders about how are we holding ourselves accountable for the things that we say and do as it relates to our Black students and I isolate race a lot in my work because of this importance of honoring Black girl literacies and holding educators accountable in the work that we do with students.

DAMARIS: This is new work for me, on this end of it. I've kind of been on the ground for the past couple of years as a community school director and as teacher. So, stepping into this role my goal was to really center us—I'm not interested in what white folk got to say about us. I'm not interested in centering whiteness, by any means. As I was writing my personal statement applying to graduate school, I was very clear about that. I was very clear about who I wanted to work with and so I think that starting off in this work, I just want to center our experiences and not make them unnormal. We are people, we are human beings, we move throughout the space. We own spaces, we take up space. That's really important for me. To not center whiteness in the work that I hope to do. I'm always thinking about the Black girls that I worked in partnership with when I was in school. I'm always going to try to keep that in mind or have people hold me accountable for keeping that in mind.

VALERIE: I guess the reality is that you all have said everything. To echo what you said, it's honoring Black girls and Black women in our work. How can we not? My mother is a Black woman and she was a Black girl at one time. I have so many Black girls and women who are cousins, and friends, and nieces, and aunts. I'm named after a Black woman, my grandmother. And some of those folks in my family have been told, those Black girls and women, have been told somewhere along the way that they were not enough. Inside of schools and also inside of relationships and other people's communities. And sometimes, we get too internalized in that stuff and that's dangerous. When we internalize it and accept that and in order to not do that, how do we have the type of scholarship but also unity, engagement, and humanity to see beyond those types of perspectives that other people might have? Even some of us might have those perspectives of Black girls and Black women. You have to write against that. We have to walk and work against those perspectives. That is what I hear in all of your responses and I think that's what we have to do. That's a way of honoring not just a Black girl but the history of all Black girls and Black women and our future. Just being able to center all of that and to use these theoretical frameworks and methodological approaches that are grounded in Blackness. How do we take a moment to understand the history of our literacies in this country? I think that if we do that, which is what you do really well, Gholdy, in your work. Then, we begin to reimagine what it means to be Black and girl, and Black and woman in this country and in this world. That's a beautiful thing.

## Important Consideration for Researchers Working With Black Girls

### What Considerations SHOULD Researchers Forefront When Studying With Black Girls and Their Literacies and Language Practices?

DAMARIS: Read Toni Morrison! Read, just read. Read before you start writing. There's so much stuff, so much research on Black girls in proximity to whiteness. I am always encouraged to center us. I can't say that enough because I think that everything is always in comparison to somebody in education research unless Black women are taking it up and doing that work. So, read. Read about us. Read our stories. Read who writes about us. Read the fictional work, the real stuff. The Octavia Butlers. Read the work to really understand Black girls before writing or thinking you have a handle on who we are.

TAMARA: I think there's something about nuance. So, recently I went to a talk with Elaine Castillo, who's the author of "America's Not the Heart". She's a Filipina writer. One of the things that she really drove home for me was the idea that people read white authors for like a universal experience and then they read Black authors, and they're like "oh, this is exactly what Black communities go through". I think there's something about nuance. The idea that Black girls are very unique. They are trailblazers. They are cultural setters. So, I think when you're looking at research there's this kind of "don't write off the things that Black girls do as the thing that all Black girls do". So, if you're working with a Black girl, that doesn't stand in for all Black girls. As well as this idea that there's a level of creativity that some Black girls are aware of and they're like "oh, I didn't know that this person does this. I didn't know that was like a creative thing". That was one of the things I would piggyback on. It's like keep talking. Talk me through, walk me through, show me this, and keep asking questions. I think sometimes, we find that researchers may go work with Black girls and they're just like "oh, okay, this is what I read, this is how I read the situation, this is what she said. The end". But there's a little bit more nuance than that. I think that Black girls are way more witty than we give ourselves credit for. There's more nuance than what they say. So they said it the first time, okay? Can you tell me a little bit more, can you expand on that? Or we're also the kind of people to be like, "I said what I said". Right, but it's really getting to that point where we recognize when doing research, you have to have a much more critical eye in doing the work with Black girls and it takes time because there's a level of trust. You may get a reading the first day and then a couple weeks later, actually that things that I said last week I said it because I didn't trust you. Or didn't say it because I didn't trust you. Recognizing we are multilayered, multifaceted group of folks.

MAIMA: I agree, and I would add to read "The Black Girl Literacies Framework" developed by Dr. Muhammad and Dr. Haddix, which really helped me to center myself in the work that I was trying to do. Black girl literacies are multiple, tied to identities, historical, collaborative, political, intellectual, and critical. As I was thinking through my work, thinking through those different lenses, I think it really helped me to center myself and reflect a lot on my own literacies. That helped me to enter the work and to the place I needed to be.

## Implications for Teachers of Black Girls

### What Practical Recommendations Would You Give Educators Working With Black Girls?

GHOLDY: When you are preparing to be a teacher you have your teacher preparation classes. I remember learning about Maslow, Vygotsky, Piaget, and Dewey. But we didn't learn about Black educational theorists in education. We certainly didn't learn about Black women theorists who have done incredible work in terms of education—Mary McCleod Bethune and Anna Julia Cooper. . .

VALERIE: Septima Clark.

GHOLDY: So, now we have teachers who may have had one diversity class on how to teach Black and Brown students. You're supposed to learn that all in that one class.

TAMARA: There's a special issue out on Black women curriculum theorizing in *Gender and Education*. I love that issue because it tries to center all the folks that people usually leave out. One of the articles in particular, Belinda Morton's "Southern Womanism", she was talking to her aunt and she was talking to her mom. She was like "I'm in this place. I've overenrolled in this class. Should I let these students in?" They were just like, "yeah". The university said "no, don't do it because if you do that's your fault". But talking to her family, they're like "that's not who we are, that's not how we handle this. These students are here. They want to be in your class. Let them in". Think about that. Your educational theorists. If we are going to talk about future teachers, you should also be talking about Black women in the community. Not just administrators, not just teachers, but grandmothers, aunties, the lady down the street who is selling candy out of her house. All of those people really inform who your students are.

VALERIE: You're talking about Ms. Grant. Don't be playing with me, Tamara. You talking about Ms. Grant from my community who I told you about who was selling candy, hot sausage and pickles, and now-and-laters. Don't try to drop that in there.

TAMARA: I forgot her name. I also think about the lunch ladies in the cafeteria. Most of the time, those are the only spaces, at least for me when I think about my education, where I saw Black women. They weren't my teachers. I probably can say I had like three Black women teachers in my whole K–12 experience. But the Black women who I interacted with the most was the lunch lady, the bus driver, the janitor, and the people who worked in the office. So, as a future teacher, it's like how did we get here? How do we get to a place where most students only encounter Black women in schools but outside the classroom? So, really having real conversations with the Black women there and inviting them into your class.

Dr. KINLOCH:  I think that connects to this idea that education is transformative and transgressive. Education is not just about being in a classroom. Education happens everywhere. Just thinking expansively about what learning means inside of schools and communities. Learning happens everywhere and Black girls have always been learning and we have always been learners even if schools, the institution have tried to name us as other. How do we build on that, and how do we, in terms of what you're saying, connecting with our communities that are really paying close attention to our Black women warriors who have always been there? Who will always be there, and who actually made a way for us to really enter into these spaces that they probably weren't able to enter into at times themselves? I think that's what people need to realize and to study deeply. You know I heard someone say, "read us" and thinking about the levels of Black girls and women's creativity. Keep asking questions. Become more nuanced by thinking about that Black girl literacy framework and thinking about how we are multi-layered and multi-faceted. I think all of those things contribute to what people need to do when working with Black girls inside of schools or outside of schools. But that community piece you just mentioned, that's fundamental. If we are talking about Black people in isolation of talking about Black histories, legacies, and traditions, then we're really not talking about Black people. So, I appreciate hearing that.

DAMARIS:  Lead your classroom with love.

GHOLDY:  Love is always the answer, isn't it?

DAMARIS:  Just straight love.

VALERIE:  I love you. This is the first time we are meeting, you and I are meeting, but yes!

DAMARIS:  I love you too!

TAMARA:  I'm just thinking about how do we talk about Black girls, in a way that includes a wide array of girls across age spectrum.

VALERIE:  People need to see us and even if they don't, we have to see ourselves. I can't rely on what other people are going to do and not do. We have to take responsibility and be responsive to seeing us and to seeing each other. To embracing ourselves with each other and for each other if we're going to have any kind of change happen in this world. Because the reality is, it's not about other people, it's about us. And if you can't see and love and care for ourselves with each other then why are we doing this work?

GHOLDY:  A sista told me we need to have some entitlement about our brilliance and our excellence.

# SECTION 3

# Reading Black Girlhood in Literature

# 7

# BLACK GIRLS LIVING BETWEEN

## A Critical Examination of Liminality in *The Hate U Give*

*Melanie A. Kirkwood-Marshall*

The call to more carefully consider the writings of Black women about Black girls and women is not new to fields such as women's studies and English literature. Indeed, it is a task that requires great care and depth, considering not only the texts themselves but also the uniqueness of this doubly marginalized existence. As literacy researchers and educators, we are attuned to the importance of engaging various lenses and approaches in the consideration of texts (Appleman, 2014), but we must continually seek new ways to read, teach, and understand the specific lived and written experiences of Black girls and women as they manifest in literature.

This chapter attempts to take on that charge. With an increasingly diverse body of YA literature available to young people, we are now privy to the stories and realities that far surpass the all-white world of children's literature described by pioneering African-American librarians such as Charlamae Rollins and Augusta Baker in the mid-twentieth century. Using Angie Thomas' (2017) novel *The Hate U Give* (hereafter *THUG*) as the focal text, this chapter considers Black women authors' relationships with their Black girl protagonists and how an attunement to this relationship can deepen our consideration and understanding of Black girls' literacies as readers, teachers, and literacy researchers. Guiding this study is the following question: What can we as literacy researchers and practitioners learn from the relationship between Black women authors and their Black girl protagonists? To address this question, I begin with a brief overview of Black girls' representation in YA literature. From there, I introduce the theories undergirding this study and share an analysis of examples that answer my questions and embody the theoretical tenets. I conclude with a discussion of implications for literacy researchers and practitioners.

## Championing Black Girl Realism in Young Adult Literature

The development and evolution of African-American literature created specifically with children in mind has been ongoing since the turn of the twentieth century (Harris, 1990). The subject matter, style, and thematic patterns that have emerged within and across this body of literature since then have grown to be markers of the times—documenting the lives, experiences, issues, and trends of African-American youth. As these texts have emerged, so too have tools and systems by which we as literacy scholars and educators can critically engage them (Harris, 1992; Sims, 1982; Bishop, 1990, 1992). However, as the passage of time ushers in new voices of Black youth, so too must our scholarship grow and shift to meet the needs of these voices. African American YA literature of the 2010s (and perhaps also the 2020s) is heavily concerned with coping with issues of social injustice, survival of urban life, body image, and the multiplicity of lived experiences that Black youth have. Concerning Black girls more specifically, research shows that these texts, whether all or in part, work to legitimize their lived experiences and offer entry points for meaningful engagement in English Language Arts curricula (Gibson, 2010).

Given this knowledge, there is an emergent body of research attempting to critically consider representations of Black girlhood in YA literature. Rountree (2008), in her book *Just Us Girls*, considered 11 contemporary YA novels written by Black women and featuring Black girl protagonists. She found that regardless of the intended audience, adults or young adults, the authors addressed similar issues of racism, sexism, and classism. She asserted that YA literature serves the purpose of teaching young African-American students "so that racism and sexism do not hinder their lives irrevocably" (p. 2). Brooks et al. (2010) explored the heterogeneity of Black girl protagonists in school-sanctioned YA literature. Using Black Feminist Theory and identity-focused cultural ecological theory (ICE), they were able to examine works of award-winning authors through both a critical perspective and a perspective of adolescent development. They found that the variations in protagonists fit into four distinct categories or enactments of identity: intellectual, physical, kinship, and sexual.

Most recently, Cueto (2018) explored the trajectory of research in African-American children's literature as it pertains specifically to Black girls. In their article, it is noted that while there has been an increase in the recognition of the complexity and multiplicity of experiences of Black girlhood, current research lacks in-depth treatment of the texts themselves. Instead, the present body of scholarship relies heavily on either the presence (or absence) of relevant titles or children's responses to particular representations. In response to this, across the past two years there has been an uptick in scholarship that focuses on the literary evaluation of contemporary YA featuring Black girls. Perhaps a result of publishing trends, this research has had a thematic focus on titles that fit into the sci-fi and Afrofuturism genres. These categories, once believed to be reserved for white men, offer potential for the creative reimagining, existence, and genius of Black girls.

Thomas (2019) offers her book, *The Dark Fantastic*, in which she explores the role of race in popular youth and young adult speculative fiction. In the book, she considers Black girl characters from four of the most acclaimed titles of the early twenty-first century and analyzes them for the mirror images of violence against Black girls in our present day. From her analyses, she asserts the power that lies within speculative fiction and counter-storytelling. As a result of these stories and of this genre, Black and brown girls are afforded the space to re-envision their own realities. Likewise, Toliver (2019) offers an analysis of Nnedi Okorafor's YA literature, in which she asserts that through Afrofuturism and speculative fiction, notions of respectability politics can be challenged. Using the conceptual framework Black Ratchet Imagination, she challenges the notion of respectability politics as understood in traditional Black literary cultural production. Her study concluded with a call for the breaking of preconceived binaries and for embracing ratchetness as a "celebratory space of agency and Black Girl Magic."

Despite these developments in research, there remains a gap in the consideration of realistic fiction that this chapter attempts to address. *THUG*, specifically the book's protagonist Starr, signals a shift in contemporary realistic YA fiction—one that makes room for the complex negotiation of life and racialized as experienced as a Black girl. To briefly summarize, *THUG* follows the life of 16-year-old Black girl Starr, who straddles life between her Black, inner-city neighborhood of Garden Heights and her experience as a Black girl at the white, suburban Williamson Prep School. Already struggling with the balancing act of her home and school selves, Starr is present when her childhood best friend Khalil is wrongfully killed at the hands of a white police officer. The news of the shooting quickly becomes a national story, placing Starr at the center of the investigation and causing turmoil within her community, personal life, and understanding of herself as a Black girl in America. In the midst of the case that will determine whether Khalil, his family, and his community will receive the justice they deserve, Starr grapples with questions of racism, friendship, and self-awareness that many would consider far beyond what is expected of a 16-year-old.

This chapter seeks to meet this shift in literature with an approach by which to read and understand these complexities. By not only emphasizing *THUG* and protagonist Starr but also considering the liminal experience of author Angie Thomas, readers are afforded a more in-depth lens through which to read and reveal Black girls' literacies in young adult literature in the English Language Arts context. Speaking to the necessity of literary analysis, Appleman (2014) reminds us that, "when taught explicitly literary theory can provide a repertoire of critical lenses through which to view literary texts" (p. 4), but without explicit knowledge and understanding of the people for which the critical lens was created to study, the lens is meaningless. By studying deeply not only *The Hate U Give* but also the life, experiences, and process of the book's author, I bring to the forefront the ways that Black girls' and women's literacies are inextricably woven into the texts that they read and create and the liberatory effects of writing. Guiding this study is the research question: What can we as literacy researchers and practitioners learn from the relationship between Black women authors and their Black girl protagonists?

## Undergirding Ourselves, Centering Black Girls' Knowledge

### Black Girls' Literacies Framework

Though still under-researched, the body of knowledge on Black girls' literacies that has emerged within the past decade is indeed something to be celebrated. Scholars are addressing the heterogeneity of Black girlhood, highlighting their genius ways of knowing and coming to know, and perhaps most importantly, exploring how we can bring these same humanizing efforts to the pedagogical and curricular levels of the field of education (Brown, 2009, 2013). Muhammad and Haddix (2016) synthesize this body of literature on Black girls' literacies, subsequently offering a framework for subsequent research.

This framework builds on the central tenets that Black girls are "generators and producers of knowledge," that Black girls' epistemological stances vary greatly from those of others, and that the doubly marginalized position of both Black and female critically distinguishes their way of being and experiencing the world around them (Muhammad & Haddix, 2016, p. 325). Those assumptions stated, the Black Girls' Literacies Framework operates from six interlocking and continually related components. Black girls' literacies are *multiple*; they are layered and collectively work to make meaning of the world around them. They are also *tied to identities*, meaning that when these multiple literacies are employed, they result in a deeper consideration of self for Black girls. Black girls' literacies are *historical* and *collaborative*, derived from practices of African-American people (Black women specifically) before them and co-constructed with other Black girls. Finally, Black girls' literacies are *intellectual* and *political/critical*. They consider deeply and with great criticality social issues that affect their lives and the lives of those around them. These considerations are often tied to issues of power, representation, and a strong desire for social change and uplift.

### Black Women Writers, Liminal Existences

In the early twentieth century, the term liminality was first used to describe the second stage in "transition rituals" (p. 71), rites of passage such as adolescence that marked one's growth and establishment within a society. Liminality, derived from the Latin term *limen*, marks a point of reaching but not yet completing the rite and therefore crossing the threshold. This crossing, as first offered by Arnold van Gennep (1909), marks one as having an evolved role in society, and subsequently reaggregating into society.

Extending van Gennep's conceptualization of liminality, Turner (1990) and Daly (1990) suggested that the purpose of these rituals was to establish *communitas*—"a sense of comradeship among equals to which liminality is supposed to lead and from which identification of self with communal culture derives" (p. 78). Those identified as being in liminal positions crave to be in communitas—among those with whom are shared a communal culture. But this definition left in the air just *how* equals are defined and by what standard communal culture is defined.

This grey area made way for subsequent research extending beyond the boundaries of anthropology. Turner himself contributed to this boundary crossing, bringing liminality, communitas, and the status of in-between to the realm of English literature (Gauthier, 2002). He asserted that literature expanded liminality to world building (L'Engle's *A Wrinkle in Time* or C.S. Lewis' *Narnia*) and, naturally, characters. But beyond that, Turner believed that writers "were often liminal individuals because writing is a liminal activity" (Gauthier, 2002, p. 71). Writing fiction requires an author to take their understanding of the world as it is, and how they envision it, and share it with a broad audience, who in turn engage and bring further meaning to the text. However, the engagement of an audience does not inherently necessitate communitas for the author.

As far as elements of race and gender are concerned, the isolation and experience of the liminal state and the transition ritual as a whole seems to fluctuate, particularly for Black women authors. Acknowledging the role that dominant and "traditional" society plays in the creation of knowledge and epistemological truths, Mascia-Lees et al. (1987) push back by extending the boundaries of how liminal experience is defined. While the authors are not Black women, they assert the potential of Black women authors' doubly marginalized stance as a catalyst for alternative world building—whether through myth, fantasy, or realism. Analyzing the work of author Toni Morrison, they offer a literary analysis of *Sula*, employing what they coin "double liminality." Double liminality, as experienced by the Black woman writer, is defined as existing "betwixt and between the interstices of culture, outside the boundaries of society's normative structure" and as being "imbued with a tremendous magical potency" (Mascia-Lees et al., 1987, p. 104). Put simply, given our marginal stance as both Black and women in a white patriarchal society, Black women authors have found and continue to find ways to subvert the boundaries of hegemonic discourse.

Taken within this frame, there is no reaggregation at the end of the liminal phase, if liminality could be considered terminal at all for the Black woman author. In fact, it is argued that Black women authors' sense of communitas is at its height in the interstices. Given this, I use the concept of double liminality to analyze the rhetorical moves that author Angie Thomas uses in her novel, *THUG*. As discussed by Mascia-Lee et al. (1987),

> As women writers seek new ways of imagining women's experience, ways that do not imply accession to standard roles, critics are challenged to develop new strategies to read and understand these women's works. This is particularly true of Black women writers, who weave their experiences of racism and sexism as well as of their subculture and community throughout their stories.
>
> *(p. 102)*

Added to this charge is the consideration of an adolescent readership. It must be taken into account not only Black women authors' double liminality, but also the ethical responsibility that comes with writing from the vantage point of youth (Cadden, 2000). It is into the realm of young adult literature then, that I apply and extend this scholarship. From this study, I assert three main points: 1) Black women authors' liminality allows for the reconciliation of lived and imagined experiences as a Black girl. 2) Black women authors are afforded the space to subtly imbue their historical Black girls' literacies into their characters. 3) There is a racialized and gendered strain of defining, establishing, and participating in community as a Black girl.

## Methods

For this study, qualitative critical content analysis was used for its focus on analysis within literary texts (Johnson, Mathis, & Short, 2017). Critical content analysis is interested in "locating power in social practices by understanding, uncovering, and transforming conditions of inequity and locating sites of resistance and change" (Johnson et al., 2017, p. vii). Given this chapter's concern with context-appropriate tools and strategies to engage Black girls' literacies in YA literature and the importance of uptake in educational institutions, *THUG* was selected as the focal text based on the following criteria: 1) the presence of a teenaged African-American female protagonist, 2) authored by a Black woman, 3) contemporary realistic fiction, 4) written after 2010, 5) school-based settings within the story, and 6) awards of literary merit. These criteria were selected in efforts to capture an authentic snapshot of what a contemporary Black girlhood experience might be in the current sociopolitical landscape. Considering that this chapter focuses on *THUG* as a product of a social phenomenon (the doubly liminal experience), interviews, articles, and lectures with Thomas were analyzed as well.

I analyzed the data with the intent of identifying thematic recurrences across *THUG* and the experiences of Thomas in her own life and as she composed her novel. To begin, I read *THUG* with the intent of immersing and familiarizing myself with the story. As described in Johnson et al. (2017), it is important as researchers "to experience the whole before we start analyzing the parts" (p. 8). Upon completing the initial read, I selected a theoretical lens through which to read and analyze the book based on my research purpose. I then reread *THUG*, focusing on the critical issues that emerged by way of my theoretical stance. This was a close read, in which I began to take note of salient codes, which would subsequently be collapsed into thematic groupings. After completing the beginning stage of analysis with *THUG*, I explored content pertinent to Thomas. This data was then compared to the thematic data from the novel and coded appropriately. After collecting and coding this data, I returned to the theories undergirding the study, studying the relationship and emerging patterns between Thomas' novel and the life experiences and stories that she shared in relationship to her book. As argued by Mazzei and Jackson (2012), by intertwining data and theory, researchers are in an optimal position to push theory to its limit and subsequently extend scholarship into new terrain.

## Findings

From the analysis, there were a large number of issues addressed in the data, ranging from a sense of invisibility as a Black girl and the role of digital space in Black-centered activism, to the duality of being treated as both girl and woman. However, in the space of this chapter, I explore the three most salient thematic occurrences. Those are: Negotiation of Self in Schooling Context; Voice and Voicelessness; and Existing in Community and Collectivity. In the remainder of this chapter, I discuss each of my findings and offer a discussion of the study, followed by implications for literacy researchers and practitioners.

## Negotiation of Self in Schooling Context

Perhaps the most prevalent thematic occurrence of double liminality in *The Hate U Give* concerns Starr's understanding of herself as she moves between Garden Heights, an inner-city ghetto known for its notorious gang wars, and her predominantly white and affluent school community, Williamson Prep. This is unsurprising considering the large role that school plays in adolescents' social development as well as acculturation. The notion of carrying oneself differently in various parts of life is not limited to Black girls and women. However, within the context of *THUG*, Thomas' negotiation of identity weighs heavily on her schooling experiences, which consequently color heavily the nature and behaviors of Starr.

In an interview during the 2017 Chicago Humanities Festival, Thomas was asked why it was important for her to write *THUG*. Thomas makes mention of the book starting out as a short story she began writing to make sense of the world for herself while she mourned the death of Oscar Grant from her private

Christian and conservative high school in Jackson, MS (Chicago Humanities Festival, 2018). This juxtaposition in school and home communities reflects very closely that of protagonist Starr. The responsibility Thomas carried to make sense of the world for herself is reflective of what Wright (2016) refers to as the trope of the "self-reliant" Black girl. As a result of living through traumatic and often racialized experiences—in the case of Thomas having to sort through the pain of Oscar Grant's death in a space that felt contrary to grief—self-reliant Black girls are imbued with a *knowing* girlhood (p. 60) that blurs the lines of their experiences with those of mature, adult circumstances. However, liminal space away from the confines of societal expectation provides the room necessary for Thomas to renegotiate outcomes and circumstances. It is at this point we as readers must consider the junction between Thomas and Starr.

Considering Starr, it is important to recognize her character as prematurely knowing—"when Black girls gain independence or a deepened awareness of their precarious positions . . . through informal observations, such as witnessing the harmful actions" (Wright, 2016, p. 61). This position, particularly given her role as protagonist, suggests a sense of assuredness in the midst of grief and chaos. However, this outward presentation is complicated by the simultaneous voice of Starr's internal narration. Thomas, as author, makes an active decision to ricochet Starr between a desire for a youthful girlhood at school and the truth beyond its boundaries. Reflecting on going to school prior to her upcoming court appearance after the shooting of Khalil, Starr says:

> For at least seven hours I don't have to talk about One-Fifteen [the police officer]. I don't have to think about Khalil. I just have to be normal Starr and normal Williamson and have a normal day. That means flipping the switch in my brain so I'm Williamson Starr. Williamson Starr is approachable. . . . I can't stand myself for doing it, but I do it anyway.
>
> *(Thomas, 2017, p. 71)*

This notion of normality and the fact that Starr attributes it to Williamson Prep, of all places, reinforces the notion of traditional school literacies as being a direct reflection of the dominant white, middle-class culture. This moment, then, offers up an opportunity to use Black girls' literacies to discuss with students a critical evaluation of Starr's schooling experience, its relationship to her identities, and how exactly they fit into the scheme of "normality."

These instances of negotiation continue through the length of the book, although the complacency to which Starr resigns gradually shifts from resisting her marginal experience of trauma to a bold acceptance of magical potency and potential that accompany her life in the interstices. As Khalil's case comes to a disappointing close, Starr finally comes to terms with the power that lies in liminality. She proclaimed, "I was ashamed of Garden Heights and everything in it. It seems stupid now though. I can't change where I come from or what makes me, me. That's like being ashamed of myself. Nah. Fuck that" (Thomas, 2017, p. 441).

While there lies power in liminal space, it can serve doubly as a trap for erasure and invisibility in the absence of *communitas*—a cohort of *equals* with whom the transition (in this case from adolescence to adulthood) is made. For Starr, she has Black girlfriends, but they are limited to only one aspect of her being. This manifests in the sharp compartmentalizing of self in various spaces—code-switching. For Thomas, by engaging issues of police brutality as a Black girl in white spaces, the written word serves as her rejection of society's margins. In doing so, she emerges from the writing of *THUG* having done the work of considering her experiences without sacrificing herself.

## Voice and Voicelessness

Coming of age novels often describe a protagonist who is developing a sense of authority in what they say and how they are heard, and in the case of *THUG*, this holds true. However, in addition to budding autonomy, as readers we must also consider the culturally specific manner in which critical, political, and intellectual Black girls' literacies are invoked on behalf of Thomas and Starr alike (Brooks & Browne, 2012). Culture and positionality differentiate liminal space, because it is in that space that one prepares for who they must be in order to survive reaggregation into dominant societal structures. When asked in an interview with journalist Britt Julious just how much of herself she poured into Starr as a character, Thomas acknowledged a number of her own interests and quirks that were built into Starr: Harry Potter, Jordan sneakers, and even *The Fresh Prince of Bel Air* (Chicago Humanities Festival, 2018). However, Thomas also poignantly addresses how Starr's outspoken nature is very much unlike herself.

> I was not nearly as outspoken as Starr—or as she becomes in the book. I was not that at 16 at all. At 16, I did not think that anything I had to say mattered. I didn't think that my voice mattered or that my opinions mattered despite even having a mom who was very vocal about the fact that I should be vocal. But, I did not think that. I was different from Starr in that I did not have the confidence she has.
>
> *(Chicago Humanities Festival, 2018)*

Perhaps in her adolescence Thomas wasn't leading riots in the streets of her hometown, but as an adult, this need for voice and actively *giving* voice to the traumas and injustice facing Black people (and Black girls more specifically) shines through in her writing. *THUG* and Starr are both products of widespread trauma and a desperate call for change for Thomas. What began as a short story in response to the 2009 shooting of Oscar Grant quickly grew into a tool for Thomas "to show that these issues are happening to girls but to also show just how magical and real that Black girls are" (Chicago Humanities Festival, 2019). In this vein, it could be said that racialized and gendered trauma is in fact a catalyst for transition, shifting Black girls into the liminal state. That trauma served as a precursor for Thomas' writing is only amplified in her 2019 interview with Sam Sanders. Considering the reception of her novel in school spaces, she stated:

> You know why so many kids flocked to *The Hate U Give?* It was because it was getting banned left and right in schools. And when you're telling kids that this is something that we don't think you're ready for, that's the very thing that they feel they are ready for.
> *(It's Been a Minute, Sastry, 2019; Rissian, 2012)*

Books that reflect the current sociopolitical climate, particularly those written for young audiences, create opportunities for young people to grapple with the world's events through the lens of a same-aged peer. In the case of *THUG*, Starr is the peer in question, and her being a Black girl weighs heavily in the reception of the story. Starr struggles with voice as both narrator and participant, and this fluctuation between voice and voicelessness is indicative of her shifting world views.

Looking to the novel, Starr soon becomes a focal person in the eyes of not only the police conducting the case investigation, but also her community and the national media space after having been with Khalil on the night of his murder. As readers, we are intimately aware through narration of the burden that Starr carries as she decides whether to tell her story or not. From similar cases of police brutality, it now understood that the likelihood of Starr's testimony being sufficient for the indictment of the officer that killed Khalil is minimal, and that her Blackness, femaleness, and youth will all be used as a tool to further silence and invalidate her voice. However, to refer back to Mascia-Lees et al.'s (1987) explication of double liminality, "because liminality affords the opportunity for reordering reality, it provides a critique of [Black girls and] women's structural roles and holds open the possibility for change in these roles" (p. 106). Structurally speaking, we can predict that Starr's testimonies and interviews will not affect the outcome of the case itself, but the enactment of critical, political, and intellectual Black girls' literacies is powerful enough to incite change devoid of legal repercussions. We only have to consider Starr's realization that she is being called upon to speak to see the ways in which she straddles voice and silence. In contemplating her ability to tell the story of Khalil's death, Starr thinks:

> I've seen it happen over and over again: a black person gets killed just for being Black, and all hell breaks loose. I've tweeted RIP hashtags, reblogged pictures on Tumblr, and signed every petition out there. I always said that if I saw it happen to somebody I would have the loudest voice, making

sure the world knew what went down. Now I am that person, and I'm too afraid to speak.

*(Thomas, 2017, p. 35)*

This realization of the difference between speaking out through platforms of digital activism, or "slacktivism," and being called to the front lines in physical space cause a moment of pause. There is a certain level of invisibility and a perception of safety that comes with slacktivism (Mattson, 2017). While giving voice to one's concerns for social justice, there is also the affordance of logging off—of disconnection. For as much power is garnered through digital space, for as valid a Black girl digital literacy is in paying homage to Black lives by way of Tumblr, Starr recognizes that in this instance, there is no parallel for her spoken voice. Starr's ability to consider deeply and critically her digital involvement surrounding social issues of race, power, and the right to life, and how that differed from the ways that those very same issues were manifesting in her real life, indicates the emergence of opportunity to reorder reality and shift the role that she plays in just how Khalil's life will be remembered (Muhammad and Haddix, 2016; Mascia-Lees et al., 1987). Thomas' acknowledgement and treatment of voice through Starr's character as being in constant flux, and yet able to incite community-wide change for Garden Heights, is indicative of her attempts to "discover, direct, and re-create the self in the midst of hostile racial, sexual, and other forms of societal repression" (Rountree, 2008). Whereas Thomas was unable to reconcile her mourning of Oscar Grant's death with her white peers at school, she intentionally collapses Starr's separate lives into a single community bound by love, care, and demand for justice. Reemergence, then, for the Black woman writer, happens in collectivity by way of her story's resounding trauma and subsequent liberatory effects.

## Existing in Community and Collectivity

As discussed in the aforementioned section, Thomas shares a number of commonalities with *THUG* protagonist Starr, and yet, there are distinct boundaries drawn between them as concerns their engagement in activism against police brutality in Black communities. This dissonance between author and protagonist reflects the active establishment of communitas that is derived from liminal existence and culminates in one's identification of self. To illustrate this, for Thomas, there is no denial or silencing when it comes to the acknowledgment of her connection to the Black lives lost at the hands of white police officers (Chicago Humanities Festival, 2018). However, for *THUG* protagonist Starr, she uses denial of her involvement and connection to Khalil's death to maintain a sense of normalcy. The tension lies in the proximity to which Black girls align themselves to community and what comes of their membership or lack thereof.

Thomas, born and raised in Jackson, MI, speaks candidly regarding her relationship to her home state and how the stories of her family's lives there have influenced her development as a person. For instance, Thomas' mother heard the shots that killed Civil Rights activist Medgar Evers. These racialized experiences alongside Thomas' current life in Jackson call her to question the role of the Black community and how she navigates her current participation in it. In an interview with Sam Sanders, she speaks about the character development of Starr's father, Maverick, saying:

> I had to struggle like Maverick struggled in "The Hate U Give," you know. Like, if—does leaving change who I am? And I had to just realize that it doesn't, you know. The weird thing about specifically the metro Jackson area is that a lot of the nice neighborhoods and safe neighborhoods are gated.
>
> *(Sanders, 2019)*

There is a very clear case being made here, where Thomas is reconciling within herself, through the process of creating *THUG*, just what it means to be in community, in collectivity. She draws on political embodiments of Black girls' literacies as she reasons through both the importance of her proximity to Blackness in physical space while also desiring to live in a "better" area of the city, which requires her to move beyond those boundaries. This brings to the fore the problem of associating nice things and living spaces with whiteness. Thomas dwells in liminal space as a writer, but this also permeates how and *where* she is situated in the world. She explores this notion of community further by way of Garden Heights.

Black girls' literacies are political, and as a result, choosing to publicly engage social issues (particularly racialized ones) comes at a great price. While Starr feels strongly toward both the Garden Heights community and Khalil's death and the journey to securing justice for his life, she cannot immediately bring herself to publicly take claim of her neighborhood *and* fight for justice. Although we see Starr first come to this realization during her visit to Khalil's grandmother's home after the shooting, Thomas establishes this strained relationship as having roots much deeper. Explaining her status in the Garden Heights community, Starr shares: "I was born a 'queen' 'cause Daddy used to be a King Lord. But when he left the game, my street royalty status ended" (p. 17). Her father's leaving "the game," a Black cultural reference to gang life and affiliations that draw boundaries of access, status, and acceptance within Garden Heights, renders Starr a social peon. Coupled with her parents' decision to send Starr and her siblings to Williamson Prep in the outskirts of the city, Starr's connections to Garden Heights in her adolescence are limited. This is seen most poignantly after the shooting when Starr and her family visit Khalil's grandmother's house:

> Going up Ms. Rosalie's walkway floods me with memories. One time I was on my scooter, and Khalil pushed me off 'cause I hadn't given him

a turn. When I got up, skin was missing from most of my knee. I never screamed so loud in my life.

*(Thomas, 2017, p. 59)*

It takes Thomas' authorial choice of juxtaposing Starr's childhood and her own history for us to understand just why Starr is unable to make that initial connection between herself and her community. Ironically, Thomas centers the result of playground politics as the apex of pain in Starr's life in this passage, knowing that for Starr, child's play soon becomes a distant memory. This notion of community, it is important to add, is not bound by life. From this notion of community and collectivity, as readers we find ourselves challenged by the questions: What is community? How does the enactment of Black girls' literacies by both Angie Thomas and Starr reveal the potentiality of existing in liminal communities?

## Emergence of Critical Lenses for the Reading of Black Girlhood

This study set out to extend scholarship on the representations of Black girls in YA literature. Using the Black Girls' Literacies Framework alongside the theory of double liminality, I offered an analysis of Angie Thomas' novel *THUG*, exploring the relationship between her and her novel's protagonist Starr, and how that shapes her understanding of herself. To return to my initial research question, I asked: What can we as literacy researchers and practitioners learn from the relationship between Black women authors and their Black girl protagonists?

In focusing on Thomas' relationship to the text, there became room for the exploration of writing as a transitional ritual—a crossing into doubly liminal space. Whereas there are numerous studies and lessons regarding the teaching of authors' intent in literature, it is seldom that we consider how the writing perhaps was intended primarily for the discovery and liberation of the author themselves. Poet Audre Lorde captures this sentiment in her essay *Poetry Is Not a Luxury*, stating,

> As we learn to bear the intimacy of scrutiny and to flourish within it, as we learn to use the products of that scrutiny for power within our living, those fears which rule our lives and form our silences begin to lose their control over us.
>
> *(Lorde, 1977)*

Writing, particularly the writing of Black women, has never been apolitical. However, the politics behind their writing (particularly for young people) serve multitudes of purposes. As posited by Rountree (2008), these texts work to *teach* young Black girls how to navigate racialized and gendered encounters. Thomas (2019) and Toliver (2019) emphasize the way that speculative fiction helps us *reimagine* the realities of Black girls' power and potential. By reading and analyzing

Black women authors' experiences as liminal space, we learn to *empathize* with not only them, but also the Black girl characters that they create.

Black women authors' liminality allows for the reconciliation of lived and imagined experiences as a Black girl. Although the author may write from the contemporary time, there is undoubtedly negotiation of their own schooling experiences that shapes the outcomes and decisions of their written characters. Additionally, Black women authors are afforded the space to subtly imbue their historical Black girls' literacies into their characters. Earlier in the chapter, I briefly discussed the ethical responsibility of YA authors writing from the vantage point of adolescents. This is amplified for the Black woman author who is called to use the space of novel writing to both revisit and reimagine their own lived experiences and to offer direction to their Black girl readership without falling into the trap of didacticism. Finally, Black women authors make clear the racialized and gendered strain of defining, establishing, and participating in community as a Black girl.

So, in respect to the character development of Starr, while born in different times and having distinct identities, there is a clear alignment between the most prevalent thematic occurrences and Thomas' reconciliation of her own negotiation of these issues and how she is affected by them. This is not to say that Starr is an embodiment of Thomas' adolescent self; rather, she is a vehicle by which Thomas has explored alternative outcomes and potential selves. Elements of voice, community, and self-understanding are integral to the development of Black girls' literacies, and even more so to the writing of them for young people.

How, then, can double liminality be used for the benefit of literacy researchers and practitioners? The recent push for increased criticality and the strengthening of students' analytical skills in the Common Core State Standards is clear. But we must ask ourselves, what are we teaching students to be more critical of?

*THUG*, with its emphasis on police brutality against Black people in America, is a narrative with numerous entry points for readers from all walks of life, but ultimately this analysis was created to showcase meaningful consideration of Black girls and Black women authors.

From this analysis, there are benefits to applying theoretical lenses that are specific to Black girls and women. Unlike single identity approaches such as postcolonial and feminist lenses, the Black Girls' Literacy Framework and double liminality address the intersectional nature of Black girlhood and dive deep into aspects of our being that would otherwise be overlooked in a general reading experience. As literacy researchers and practitioners, I call for an increase in studies that further examine and theorize critical lenses for the reading, analyzing, and interpretation of Black girlhood. Given the multiplicity of Black girls' existence, there is room for various approaches to these texts, each with capabilities of revealing their complexities and depth.

# APPENDIX

The following material includes a transcription of interview questions directed at *THUG* author Angie Thomas. The first set of questions is derived from the Chicago Humanities Festival (2018) interview with journalist Britt Julious. The second comes from an interview with Sam Sanders on the NPR podcast *It's Been a Minute*. For the fuller context of the NPR interview, which was much more conversational in tone, the full transcript can be found from the citation information.

Chicago Humanities Festival. (2018). *Angie Thomas: The Hate U Give.* Retrieved from

www.youtube.com/watch?v=NICtpcJsP-o&t=750s&ab_channel=Chicago HumanitiesFestival

- Tell us a bit about growing up there [in Jackson, MS] and how being there really influenced the type of writing that you do.
- Knowing the impetus for why you wanted to write *The Hate U Give*, maybe can you go into why it was really important for you to tell this specific story, and not only that, but targeting it toward a young adult audience in particular.
- Tell me about the decision to explore those subjects through the protagonist of Starr. Was that a very conscious decision for you in terms of having a young girl as the protagonist for this story?
- Speaking of Starr, there are some elements to her that are kind of similar to your life, not to say that she's a complete composite of who you are but . . . she loves gym shoes, she loves hip-hop, loves Harry Potter so, tell me how much of yourself did you put into her as a character?
- Tell me about the decision to really focus on that [code-switching] a lot.

- Very recently Kendrick Lamar won a Pulitzer and I wanted to see what your thoughts were on that?
- Why was it really important for you to weave throughout the book the importance of hip-hop as a cultural touchstone, a philosophy of life. Why was that so critical for you in terms of creating your first novel?
- What do you think of people from places that are not the United States that maybe don't have the same sort of social and racial problems that are happening here? What do you think about them starting reading this very specific American story or/and taking certain things away from it?
- So maybe to move on a little bit from *The Hate U Give*, you have mentioned it a couple times, your upcoming book. It was scheduled to come out this year but is now coming out next year. Tell us what the writing process has been like, especially, you know, after your first book has been sort of exploded across the world.
- What advice would you have for any young writers who you know maybe feel like they have something to say but they don't know how to go about saying it?

NPR. (2019). Interview: Author Angie Thomas Talks "On the Come Up." Retrieved October 5, 2019, from www.npr.org/templates/transcript/transcript.php?storyId=690391879

- Speaking of rap, your new book, which I'm devouring, *On the Come Up*—how much of a description of this book can you tell all of your listeners, our listeners, without, like, spoilers?
- So, this book is set in the same neighborhood as your first book, *The Hate U Give*—Garden Heights. Describe that neighborhood for us, and then tell me why you chose the same neighborhood but a different character and a different plot for this new book.
- Do you feel that way about—I don't know—the news and things in the news tied to some of the stuff that you tackle, you know, in this book and the previous one?
- Because it's like I want to be encouraged, but I don't know. Do you think it's [police brutality against Black people] getting better?
- When do you know as a writer of young adult content when kids are ready for the serious issues you raise in your books?
- One of the things that I love about your career is that on top of just making good books, you are trying to make a good industry for books. And you have spoken out a lot about the lack of diversity in publishing, particularly the lack of diversity in publishing of children's books. You've even gone so far as to call out your own publisher, HarperCollins, and say, when you were a kid, they weren't making books for you. Years into this work now, do you think that's getting better?

- I also love, like, the entire backstory of *The Hate U Give*. Like—and I don't want to tell your story. I want you to tell it. But like, you started writing this book, like, in college at—what is it?—Belhaven University.
- Yeah. A thing I read about you was that since your career took off, you moved into a gated neighborhood. How does that feel? I mean, particularly writing about the communities that you write about in your books, did you feel like you were leaving some of that reality when you moved on up?
- Yeah. Yeah. I mean, you know, thinking about moving on up, like, I'm sure not just your location, but maybe everything about your life changed since the crazy, amazing success of *The Hate U Give*. Like, how different is your life, I guess, from, like, church secretary to now?

# References

Appleman, D. (2014). *Critical encounters in secondary English: Teaching literacy theory to adolescents.* New York, NY: Teachers College Press.

Bishop, R. S. (1990). Mirrors, windows, and sliding glass doors. *Perspectives, 6*(3), ix–xi.

Bishop, R. S. (1992). Multicultural literature for children: Making informed choices. *Teaching Multicultural Literature in Grades K-8*, 37–53.

Brooks, W., & Browne, S. (2012). Towards a culturally situated reader response theory. *Children's Literature in Education, 43*(1), 74–85. https://doi.org/10.1007/s10583-011-9154-z

Brooks, W., Sekayi, D., Savage, L., Waller, E., & Picot, I. (2010). Narrative significations of contemporary Black girlhood. *Research in the Teaching of English, 45*(1), 7–35.

Brooks, W. M., & McNair, J. C. (2015). "Combing" through representations of Black girls' hair in African American children's literature. *Children's Literature in Education: An International Quarterly, 46*(3), 296–307. doi:10.1007/s10583-014-9235-x

Brown, R. N. (2009). *Black girlhood celebration: Toward a hip-hop feminist pedagogy.* New York, NY: Peter Lang.

Brown, R. (2013). *Hear our truths: The creative potential of black girlhood.* Champaign, IL: University of Illinois Press.

Cadden, M. (2000). The irony of narration in the young adult novel. *Children's Literature Association Quarterly, 25*(3), 146–154.

Chicago Humanities Festival. (2019, May 10). *Angie Thomas: The Hate U Give.* [Video]. YouTube. https://www.youtube.com/watch?v=NICtpcJsP-o&ab_channel=Chicago HumanitiesFestival

Cueto, D. (2018). Contemplating and extending the scholarship on children's and young adult literature. *Journal of Literacy Research, 50*(1), 9–30. doi:10.1177/1086296X18754394

Daly, R. (1990). Liminality and fiction in Cooper, Hawthorne, Cather, and Fitzgerald. In K. M. Ashley (Ed.), *Victor turner and the construction of cultural criticism* (pp. 70–85). Bloomington: Indiana UP.

Gauthier, G. (2002). Whose community? Where is the "YA" in YA literature? *The English Journal, 91*(6), 70–76. https://doi.org/10.2307/821819

Gibson, S. (2010). Critical readings: African American girls and urban fiction. *Journal of Adolescent & Adult Literacy, 53*(7), 565–574.

Harris, V. J. (1990). African American children's literature: The first one hundred years. *The Journal of Negro Education*, (4), 540. doi:10.2307/2295311

Harris, V. J. (1992). African-American conceptions of literacy: A historical perspective. *Theory Into Practice*, (4), 276.

Johnson, H., Mathis, J., & Short, K. G. (Eds.). (2017). *Critical content analysis of children's and young adult literature: Reframing perspective.* New York, NY: Routledge, Taylor & Francis Group.

Lorde, A. (1977). Poetry is not a Luxury. *Chrysalis: A magazine of women's culture, 3*.

Mascia-Lees, F. E., Sharpe, P., & Cohen, C. B. (1987). Double liminality and the Black woman writer. *American Behavioral Scientist, 31*(1), 101.

Mattson, K. (2017). *Digital citizenship in action: Empowering students to engage in online communities.* Portland, OR: International Society for Technology in Education.

Mazzei, L. A., & Jackson, A. Y. (2012). Complicating voice in a refusal to "Let participants speak for themselves." *Qualitative Inquiry, 18*(9), 745–751.

Muhammad, G. E., & Haddix, M. (2016). Centering Black girls' literacies: A review of literature on the multiple ways of knowing of Black girls. *English Education, 48*(4), 299–336.

NPR. (2019). *Interview: Author Angie Thomas talks 'On the come up'*. Retrieved October 5, 2019, from www.npr.org/templates/transcript/transcript.php?storyId=690391879

Rissian, L. C. (Producer). (2012, May 4). *Twelve parsecs* [Audio podcast]. http://itunes.apple.com

Rountree, W. (2008). *Just us girls: The contemporary African American young adult novel*. New York, NY: Peter Lang.

Sanders, S. (Host). (2019, February 5). Author Angie Thomas writes to 'mirror' young, black readers [Audio podcast episode]. *It's been a minute with Sam Sanders*. WBEZ Chicago. https://www.npr.org/transcripts/690391879

Sastry, A. (Producer). (2019, February 5). *It's been a minute with Sam Sanders* [Audio podcast].

Sims, R. (1982). *Shadow and substance: Afro-American experience in contemporary children's fiction*. Urbana, IL: National Council of Teachers of English.

Thomas, A. (2017). *The hate u give* (1st ed.). New York: Balzer + Bray, HarperCollins Publishers.

Thomas, E. E. (2019). *The dark fantastic: Race and the imagination from Harry Potter to the Hunger Games* (1st ed.). New York: New York University Press.

Toliver, S. R. (2019). Breaking binaries: #BlackGirlMagic and the Black ratchet imagination. *Journal of Language & Literacy Education/Ankara Universitesi SBF Dergisi, 15*(1), 1.

Turner, E. (1990). The literary roots of Victor Turner's anthropology. In K. M. Ashley (Ed.), *Victor Turner and the construction of cultural criticism* (pp. 163–169). Bloomington: Indiana UP.

van Gennep, Arnold. (1960/1909). *The rites of passage*. Chicago, IL: University of Chicago Press.

Wright, N. S. (2016). *Black girlhood in the nineteenth century*. Champaign, IL: University of Illinois Press.

# 8

# BLACK GIRLHOOD ENTANGLED

## An Exploration of Nature, Magic and Community in Jewell Parker Rhodes' *Bayou Magic*

*Dahlia Hamza Constantine*

> I laugh as fireflies, streaking like lightning, surround me—head to toe, over, above, and about my body . . . I can do magic! I laugh out loud.
>
> (Rhodes, 2015, pp. 79–80)

In 2013, CaShawn Thompson first coined the expression "Black Girl Magic" as a way to capture the almost supernatural way in which Black girls and women persevere despite seemingly insurmountable obstacles. Within this concept is also the idea that Black girls not only survive, but thrive—creating art, music and literature that feels magical in its creativity. In her book *Bayou Magic* (2015), Jewell Parker Rhodes brings a different spin to the idea of Black Girl Magic by writing a story of magical realism where Maddy, a preadolescent Black girl, discovers her own magical abilities during a visit to her Grandmère's bayou community of Bon Temps, Louisiana. While Rhodes explores the coming of age of one unique and magical Black girl, she also weaves in the rich complexities of Black girlhood across time and space. Maddy's magic is not found in individual acts of survival or achievement; rather, we see that her girlhood is intimately entangled with nature, magic and the larger community around her.

In this chapter, I will explore the ways in which Jewell Parker Rhodes presents Maddy's agility with nature, magic and community as literacies that are multifaceted and entangled, woven together to create a rich tableau of Black girlhood. In an attempt not to separate out Maddy's literacies, but rather to highlight how each one is presented, I will use Muhammad and Haddix's Black Girls' Literacy Framework (Muhammad & Haddix, 2016). The Black Girls' Literacy Framework (BGLF) is rooted in the notion that Black girls' literacies are: a) multiple; b) tied to identities; c) historical; d) collaborative; e) intellectual; and f) political/critical.

Like Black girls themselves, each of these components is complex and multifaceted in its own right but also weaves together with other components as Black girls navigate their lives across time and space.

## "Read the bayou like Pa reads his newspaper . . ."

Muhammad and Haddix (2016) invite us to crack wide open the definition we have of literacy with their first component of their Black Girls' Literacies Framework (BGLF), in that literacies are multiple. Rather than limiting literacy to the lackluster version we currently hold so dear in school, relegating it to the humble words I use here to convey my meaning, we should think of literacy as multiple, as *literacies*. As various and intertwined talents and areas of expertise, working together as each Black girl navigates the world around her. Here, Jewell Parker Rhodes explicitly centers communion with nature—being able to *be* with it and understand it and also to harness its sheer power—as a powerful literacy that Maddy learns from her Grandmère. While I will also explore Maddy's literacies in magic and community leadership, these talents all stem from the deeper and interdependent relationship that she first builds with the natural world, and thus I will spend more time analyzing this area. As Maddy and Grandmère first sit out on the bayou, Maddy notes that they "read the bayou like Pa reads his newspaper" (Rhodes, 2015, p. 27). As a literacy, Maddy's connection to nature is a complicated combination of a skill and an art—something to practice and to be mastered. Something to learn from an elder but to explore on your own as well.

Throughout *Bayou Magic*, Rhodes interlaces Maddy's growth as a Black girl with her deepening relationship to the natural world. As she delves deeper and deeper into the natural world—from being greeted by a mysterious firefly on her drive to Bon Temps to sitting on the porch and studying the bayou to later swimming underwater with the Black mermaid Mami Wata—Maddy's confidence and sense of herself as a descendant of strong African girls grows. Early in the story, she leaves the city and family behind and notes that, "traveling deep into the country, the world seems huge. Miles and miles of open space" (Rhodes, 2015, p. 10). It is this wide-open space—and being away from the noise of the city— that Maddy needs to develop her magical abilities and her confidence in herself. Each time Maddy goes deeper into the unknown parts of the bayou, her ability to commune with the natural world and to read its signs and perform magic intensifies. "Your sisters saw the world too real. You need space in your mind. Space for imagination" (Rhodes, 2015, p. 49). Here, Grandmère directly connects Maddy's growth with the openness of nature and the chance to explore and *become*.

This is not a critique by Rhodes of cities or urban life. In fact, an exploration of Rhodes' many other books demonstrates that she chooses a variety of settings for her stories, exploring Black childhood across many spaces. Rather, Rhodes invites us to move past the national imagination that sees Black girls as *solely* synonymous with urban centers and instead to explore what Black girlhood might look like in the bayou. While the majority of Black girls in the United States *do* attend urban schools, over 20 percent live in small towns and rural parts of the country and engage with the natural world as part of their everyday life (NCES, 2014). Kids in urban settings are often bequeathed the title of "street smart" when they navigate complex urban networks of transportation, community norms, economics and surveillance by the state, amongst other factors. But we do not have a mainstreamed term for the type of literacy that is needed to engage with the natural world. Additionally, when we think of girls who are environmentalists and have strong literacies in relationship to nature, we rarely think of Black girls, despite the long international history of the incredible contributions they have made (Frazier, 2016).

Even more, as both Jewell Parker Rhodes and history show us, the story of Black peoples across the world has been intertwined with the landscapes in which we live. Both the wonders of Black agricultural practices and the horrors of the Black connection to southern plantations in the American South link the land deeply with the stories of the people who lived upon it. Even when the land was a source of terror, abuse and exploitation, Black Americans found a way not only to live miraculously *with* the land but also to turn to the land as a source of healing—creating herbal medicines and salves to treat both physical and emotional ailments (Harley, 2006). These elders bridged the ancient knowledges inscribed in their hearts and memories with the new plants and landscape of the Americas.

When we first meet Maddy, she is a shy and hesitant youngest daughter who is often afraid of speaking up for herself. But by the end of the story, Maddy feels at home in the bayou at night. What was previously scary feels natural, and she notes, "I run. It's dark but I know exactly where to go. My feet don't stumble. . . . I feel like I'm home" (Rhodes, 2015, p. 129). The natural world—and her freedom to explore it—is what allows Maddy to eventually become the quiet heroine who rallies the community to save the bayou from an environmental disaster. Mirroring the interdependence of the natural world, the bayou gives Maddy strength and confidence, and she reciprocates. First, she coordinates a massive cleanup effort to combat the effects of the destructive oil spill. When that is not enough, she initiates a chain of magic by calling on the fireflies and mermaids who build a levee to protect Bon Temps. She is a child of nature, and it is here that she fully comes into herself.

This idea that childhood is directly intertwined with the natural world is a recurring theme not only in children's literature, but also in childhood studies and childhood geographies. Many scholars have emphasized the importance of nature for the well-being of children (e.g. Kong, 2000; Kahn & Kellert, 2002; Faber Taylor & Kuo, 2006). Scholars of children's literature have long discussed the ways in which authors intertwine childhood and nature, with nature being the idyllic place for children (Jones, 2002). Nature is free and open and allows for independent mobility and discovery, while the city is positioned as dangerous and constricting for children. This duality, however, is not typically found in in

African American children's literature, as the rural landscape is not perceived as a tranquil place of freedom but a place where slavery, the Jim Crow South and the fight for racial equality are prevalent. Tamara Butler, in her work on Black girlhood and place, calls on scholars to open up "and mark the additional geopolitical spaces where Black Girls thrive, make meaning, care for one another, and negotiate (Butler, 2018, p. 39)." Rhodes does so here; while she does not shy away from the horrors of slavery, she does expand the possibilities of the rural bayou landscape by crafting it as a world where a young Black girl can be a magical heroine.

Turning to the second and third components of the BGLF, we see that communing with nature is also tied to identities and is historical as it brings together both an African and African American identity, integrating the oral traditions and the learning from elders and the land itself. Grandmère is a healer who has Maddy learn everything about the bayou, respecting it and observing it and understanding herself to be a part of it, while allowing the landscape to be a part of her as well. Literacies as presented in the BGLF and in *Bayou Magic* are not an "objective" and static set of skills that can be applied to everyone in the same way. Instead, we are invited to think of how our literacies interweave with the multiple identities and histories that Black girls hold within ourselves. In *Bayou Magic*, Maddy's literacy in nature is deeply interwoven with her identity as a Black girl, specifically a Black girl who is a descendent of both Grandmère and Membe. This adds the complex layer that is often stripped away from Black girls and other members of marginalized groups—the right to be an individual with your own personality and family history. For, while Rhodes shows us that Maddy's literacies are deeply tied to her identity as Black girl, they are related more specifically to her family's unique legacy and to her special place in the family. It is one thing for us to say that family is an important concept for Black girls and another to deeply and explicitly show how your lineage impacts but does not fully determine your literacies. Rhodes, after all, does not make every woman in Maddy's family magical; while she implies they all may access it, it is Maddy who chooses to pause and listen and feel the magic.

Maddy gets to be her own person with her own complex literacies and talents while still being a part of the Lavalier family and a Black girl. Nature is intertwined not only with Maddy's identity and sense of Black girlhood now, but also with her ancestry and heritage and all the Black girls who have come before her. As Grandmère tells Maddy of their family's history from slavery to the present, nature always plays a starring role. Membe, their ancestor captured on African soil and brought to the region as a slave when she was only 10 years old—the same age as Maddy—was from a great river tribe and used the water and earth to heal others. Grandmère asks Maddy:

> Did you know that when Africans were first captured, Nature cried. . . .
> Trees bowed down, their leaves falling, boughs scraping the ground. Mister
> Wind blew and blew, trying to whip women, men, and children free from

their chains. . . . clouds turned gray—sun slipped down into Mistress Earth. Lions roared, even though men had guns to bring them down. Gorillas, wailing, pummeled their chests. Elephants trumpeted horror. Earth trembled, but nothing, no one, could stop the slave trade.

*(Rhodes, 2015, p. 83)*

Here, nature is so intertwined with Black people and cherishes us so much that it feels our pain and tries to help us. Maddy realizes that as a Black girl, she should take comfort in the natural world, and that that the natural world is in tune with her, sending her signs of warning through spider webs, yellow moons and birds with broken wings. Of course, she has to be in the bayou and connected to nature to hear this. Her literacies here are intertwined not only with her family history, her identity as a Black girl and her own personal gifts but also with the landscape of the bayou itself.

## "In a Magical Cottage Deep in the Forest . . ."

Within the open and mysterious landscape of the bayou, Rhodes shows us that Maddy's Black girlhood and her literacies also live in relationship with magic and mythology. I want to pause here to explain that when I refer to mythology, I refer to the stories of a people. I do *not*, as it is studied in most American schools, consider mythology as something fictional, nor as a "primitive" way of understanding the world that modern adherents to atheism and Abrahamic religions have moved beyond. Our mythologies are our stories, our ways of understanding the world, no matter how many (if any) gods are involved. Our mythologies and stories are deeply rooted in the land, stemming from a time when nature, religion, magic and stories were all intertwined as a way of understanding that we are one *part* of a larger world, rather than superior creatures destined to conquer it.

It is no surprise then that Rhodes ties Maddy's magic to the landscape of the bayou itself. Early in the story, even as Maddy is a little unsure of her new surroundings, she tells us, "But I feel like I'm in a storybook, in a magical cottage deep in the forest" (Rhodes, 2015, p. 19), foreshadowing that magic resides in the forest, away from the noise of the city. In fact, the deeper Maddy delves into the bayou, the more she is able to communicate with Mami Wata and other magical creatures. As Grandmère reminds her, she needs to be out in nature for her magic to flourish because magic needs space for imagination. Maddy's first magical act springs from the natural world as Grandmère asks her to call Miss Firefly to her—this tiny part of nature, giving light, becomes Maddy's guide and helper. Similarly, Miss Firefly's ancestor firefly was a helper to Membe, Maddy's enslaved ancestor. Maddy's girlhood, magic and nature are constantly tied in with her history and heritage.

The BGLF reminds us that our literacies are historical—directly tied into the moment in history in which we find ourselves and layered with millions of other historical moments that led to this point. Black girls also employ their literacies in a political and critical manner, understanding the nuanced power structures in which they exist and exhibit agency as they attempt to make changes. Maddy's literacies in magic and communing with nature stem from her family's heritage in Africa, from Membe's horrific journey in a slave ship and through slavery in America to this moment. Her magic is reflective of the current moment and the need to save the bayou, but it also holds within it her family and people's history. She is able to bridge the past, present and future as well as structural racism, classism and environmental injustice as she navigates her role in protecting her beloved bayou.

Rhodes also celebrates the mythological mermaid Mami Wata, who followed Membe's slave ship to America and who is virtually unknown outside of the African continent, to show Black girls that some mermaids look just like us. W. E. B. Du Bois (1919), in creating *The Brownies' Book* magazine for Black children with Augustus Dill, cited the goal "to make them familiar with the history and achievements of the Negro Race" as one of the main reasons for creating literature for Black children. Rhodes embraces this idea by linking magic to Maddy's lineage and Black culture overall. But she also moves beyond the idea of "history and achievements" being locked into a traditional definition of scientific discoveries, literary merit or political gains (Bishop, 2007). She chooses to create a *magical* world that centers Black girlhood, Black histories and Black mythological beings. In the introduction to her groundbreaking work, *The Dark Fantastic: Race and the Imagination from Harry Potter to the Hunger Games*, Ebony Elizabeth Thomas deeply explores the dichotomy between magic and realism that many Black children are asked to choose between. Young Black girls are often made to feel like there is no room for magic because the *real* world "held trouble enough for young Black girls" without adding the complications and possible dangers of magic (Thomas, 2019, p. 7). Rhodes alludes to this in her story when she tells Maddy that her sisters "saw the world too real" (Rhodes, 2015, p. 49) and thus could not deepen their literacy in magic. Being able to see past (or alongside or underneath) reality appears to be essential to exploring your literacy in magic.

In addition to this dissuasion by concerned family members, the very White world of fairy tales and fantasy stories read in the United States adds another layer that shrouds the worlds of magic and magical realism even further. But in the racially diverse Bon Temps community, it is only Maddy and Grandmère who practice magic. Interestingly, it is only the *women* in Maddy's family, starting with Membe, who have magical gifts, and all are young when they start practicing their powerful and healing magic. There is something about girlhood, specifically *Black* girlhood, that drives this magic. Even the magical firefly and the African mermaid Mami Wata are girls. Maddy describes her as "a girl, beautiful, velvet black. Curls of blue-black hair fall to her waist . . . Mami Wata doesn't look any older than me" (Rhodes, 2015, p. 19). We see that magic and magical *literacies* are directly intertwined with Black girlhood and ancestry. Mami Wata, like Maddy, is born of a historical moment where she has to use her magic to protect those around her. While she is one of many mermaids, she emerges out of our cultural history as a source of comfort and love to accompany enslaved African peoples who were kidnapped, enslaved and brought across the Atlantic. Rhodes once again widens our vista as to what it means to be a Black girl and what Black girls' literacies can be, centering Black girls as magical heroines rooted in both the old ways and the current historical moment in which they live.

## "I'm Counting on You to Hold Together Bon Temps . . ."

While Maddy's girlhood is related directly to nature and magic, Rhodes shows us that Black girlhood also lives in the context of the larger community and in service of it. Black feminist scholars such as Patricia Hill Collins (2000) and others (Carby, 1987; Guy-Sheftall, 1995) have long written about the role of community and interdependence in the lives of Black women. That is, while Black women fight for their liberation as women, we also work in collective service of the entire community. Rhodes highlights the Bon Temps community as one of extreme interdependencies, with the people, landscape and wildlife living intertwined lives. In fact, when Maddy first discovers her magic by calling all the fireflies to her, she does so in the midst of the community, at a party in the bayou attended by all the residents. And it is these same fireflies who come back later to help save this same community.

The BGLF urges us to consider how literacy is collaborative, and Rhodes takes up this idea, by placing Maddy's literacies in both nature and magic not only in the context of a large community but also in collaboration with the landscape and other nonhuman actors. This collaboration moves beyond "modern"[1] ideas of human beings as the dominant creatures on earth and instead sees an ancient collaboration that is rooted in all the indigenous cultures of the world. It is not an accident that Maddy's magic flourishes outdoors in nature in harmony with the whole community rather than alone. Magic here is not self-serving or for playful exploration, but rather a great responsibility and a way to serve. While Maddy is curious about the mermaid Mami Wata and is thrilled to swim with her through the bayou, she only turns to Mami Wata for *support* when the community is threatened and needs help. As Maddy comes into her own, she learns that both Grandmère and Membe used magic as girls to support their communities. Even Miss Firefly and Mami Wata use their magic only in service of protecting others. Rhodes' message is that as a Black girl, you are part of a larger community and it is part of your heritage to protect this community. This is a coming of age story where Maddy finds her voice and strengths in a community of female characters—a community where nature and magic blend seamlessly.

Collins (2000) writes about the stereotypical media images of Black women, citing the Mammy role who takes care of everyone in a subservient way, and she challenges authors to compose literature as a way to debunk such images. However, Jewell Parker Rhodes makes caring for others not a burden that is imposed externally, but rather a powerful way of leading. Here we see that Maddy, Grand-mère, Mami Wata (and earlier Membe) all take care of their communities, but it is not in a subservient way. Grandmère is revered as Queenie in a racially diverse Bon Temps; she reigns over her kingdom because she has magical ways of knowing the world and uses them to care for and heal everyone. Membe, as a young slave, was still a leader of her people, and Mami Wata is a celebrated mythical figure who provided care and comfort. For these characters, caretaking comes in the form of community leadership and happens on their own terms; it is what gives them strength and status.

This caretaking and community leadership is yet another literacy that Black girls throughout time have practiced but that rarely receives attention as its own form of literacy. The BGLF asks us to consider that Black girls' literacies are also intellectual, and Maddy's community leadership rooted in nature and magic exemplifies many aspects of this, such as pattern recognition and the ability to evaluate, connect and synthesize different ideas. While intellect is often positioned as distinct from the natural world and magic, as Rhodes demonstrates, there is a deep level of study and intellectual prowess that Maddy exhibits as she launches her effort to protect the bayou. Patricia Parker's in-depth and interdisciplinary research on Black women executives highlights the way in which Black women, more than White men, White women and Black men, are able to combine traditionally "masculine" strategies of leadership such as autonomy, strength and confidence with what is thought of as "feminine" strategies of support, care and consideration (Parker, 2004; Parker & ogilvie, 1996). Black women also add in creativity, risk taking and boundary spanning as a way not only to combine different leadership styles but also to constantly innovate. As the BGLF incorporates the idea that Black girls' literacies are also political and critical, it becomes crucial for us to explore the idea that providing care and leading a community are literacies that Black girls have always excelled in. It is not leading merely out of a sense of power or domination, but rather a leadership that emerges from a deep sense of love for your community and the ability to collaborate with others. Both American and world history have shown us countless examples of Black girls and young women who have led political and social movements rooted in a sense of community and care. From the countless young girls who desegregated American schools; to the Martinican sisters Paulette and Jane Nardal, who as young students at the Sorbonne in the 1920s created literary salons that brought together African American, Caribbean and African scholars, helping to launch the Negritude movement; to Tarana Burke, founder of the #MeToo movement; and Alicia Garza, Patrisse Cullors and Opal Tometi, who founded the Black Lives Matter movement, Black girls and young women have led the charge on issues both local and global.

And while *Bayou Magic* is a coming-of-age story of one young Black girl who explores her own voice and gifts and magic, it is also the story of a Black girl who leads a massive environmental justice movement to protect the bayou. Rhodes does not shy away from discussing the evils of slavery nor the impact of global greed on the environment, but weaves this in as Maddy's literacies in communing with nature, her magic and her community leadership aid her in taking a stand and having an impact on both historic and current political issues. Maddy's literacies are both intrinsic and also guided and supported by her elders and the community. Her deep knowledge of the literacies of nature and magic and community leadership emerge from her own unique place in her family, as well as her unique family and her as a Black girl. Rhodes beautifully crafts in Maddy these layers of individuality and family and the larger community. Maddy gets to be her unique self, even in the midst of leading a larger community effort, and works from within the community to address the fears faced in an interconnected world. While the oil spill is the result of global economic interdependence and the damages it can wreck on the local landscape and the people and other beings who live within it, Maddy's relief effort also brings in the local community as well as the larger global mermaid and firefly community. There is a constant and intricate interweaving of individuality and community that allows Maddy to be literate in multiple components of the BGLF while still retaining her own unique personality and story.

Part of the magic that Rhodes weaves into her story is the creation of space for us to consider a different kind of Black girlhood. A Black girlhood that may be quieter, more rural and involve magic. A Black girlhood that is not meant to replace the representations of Black girlhood more popular in today's media but one that expands our collective imagination of who we were, who we are and who we might become. Black girls are not a monolithic collective of interchangeable people, but rather unique and complex individuals with traits and stories and literacies that weave together and apart. As Marilyn Nelson reminds us in her poem, "Thirteen Year Old Negro Girl," each of us is layered with a unique interwoven tapestry of stories and experiences and desires, and the mask we wear is "just the top-of-the-iceberg me" (2014).

Maddy, in the last few lines of the story, is indeed a newsworthy girl, though she never takes credit for the incredible work she has done in leading a community relief effort. Instead, she smiles to herself and knows she has changed as she drives back into the city with her mother. Not only did she conquer her own individual challenges, but she was also a critical part of a monumental community relief effort. The openness of nature—and the magic and community she finds within it—allows her to grow not just as a girl, but as a Black girl. Riding back, she calls on her magical fireflies with confidence and without hesitation, ready to take on the city as she awaits her next summer with Grandmère.

This moment of Maddy recognizing her power and her magic is mirrored daily in the lives of Black girls across the country and the world. Girls who are using their multiple and interconnected literacies to challenge established systems. Girls who are simultaneously being unique individuals with a set of collaged identities while cracking open for all of us what it means to be a Black girl. Girls who remind us that our literacies are part of our heritage, but that we can also seamlessly weave together our ancient and embodied cultures alongside the new ones that we inhabit. It is time for all of us to listen to their stories.

## Note

1. I use the word "modern" here instead of Western because this line of thinking is dominant in those who follow Abrahamic religions (which all emerged outside the "West"), regardless of their geographic location. Additionally, *pre*-Christian European religions more closely align with every other indigenous culture across the world in seeing people as *one* part of a large and interconnected world.

## References

Bishop, R. S. (2007). *Free within ourselves: The development of African American children's literature.* Portsmouth, NH: Heinemann.

Butler, T. T. (2018). Black girl cartography: Black girlhood and place-making in education research. *Review of Research in Education, 42*(1), 28–45.

Carby, H. (1987). *Reconstructing womanhood: The emergence of the Afro-American woman novelist.* New York: Oxford University Press.

Collins, P. H. (2000). *Black feminist thought: Knowledge, consciousness, and the politics of empowerment* (2nd ed.). New York: Routledge.

Du Bois, W. E. B. (1919). The true brownies. *The Crisis, 18*, 285–286.

Faber Taylor, A., and Kuo, F. E. (2006). Is contact with nature important for healthy child development? State of evidence. In C. Spencer, & M. Blades (Eds.), *Children and their environments: Learning, using and designing spaces.* Cambridge: Cambridge University Press.

Frazier, C. M. (2016). Troubling ecology: Wangechi Mutu, Octavia Butler, and Black feminist interventions in environmentalism. *Critical Ethnic Studies, 2*(1), 40–72.

Guy-Sheftall, B. (Ed.) (1995). *Words of fire: An anthology of African-American feminist thought.* New York: The New Press.

Harley, D. A. (2006). Indigenous healing practices among rural elderly African Americans. *International Journal of Disability, Development and Education, 53*(4), 433–452.

Jones, O. (2002). Naturally not! childhood, the urban and romanticism. *Human Ecology Review, 9*(2), 17–30.

Kahn, P. H. Jr., & Kellert, S. R. (Eds.) (2002). *Children and nature: Psychological, sociocultural and evolutionary investigations.* London: The MIT Press.

Kong, L. (2000). Nature's dangers, nature's pleasures. urban children and the natural world. In S. L. Holloway, & and G. Valentine (Eds.), *Children's geographies. playing, living, learning.* Critical geographies 8. London: Routledge.

Muhammad, G. E., & Haddix, M. (2016). Centering Black girls' literacies: A review of literature on the multiple ways of knowing of Black girls. *English Education, 38*.

National Center for Education Statistics, U.S. Department of Education (NCES). (2014). *Rural education in America.* Washington, DC: National Center for Education Statistics.

Nelson, M. (2014). *How I discovered poetry.* New York: Speak.

Parker, P. S. (2004). *Race, gender, and leadership: Re-envisioning organizational leadership from the perspectives of African American women executives.* Mahwah: Erlbaum.

Parker, P. S., & ogilvie, dt. (1996). Gender, culture, and leadership: Toward a culturally distinct model of African-American women executives' leadership strategies. *The Leadership Quarterly*, 7(2), 189–214.

Rhodes, J. P. (2015). *Bayou Magic*. New York: Little, Brown Books for Young Readers.

Thomas, E. E. (2019). *The dark fantastic: Race and the imagination from Harry Potter to the Hunger Games*. New York: New York University Press.

# 9

# BEYOND THE PROBLEM

## Afrofuturism as an Alternative to Realistic Fiction About Black Girls

*S. R. Toliver*

Dr. Mae Jemison was the first Black woman to journey into space, and her inherent curiosity for science was a major influence on her journey to become an astronaut. But what most inspired her to reach for the stars was seeing Nichelle Nichols play the character of Nyota Uhura, a communications officer on the USS Enterprise who translated numerous written and spoken languages; was adept in mechanical, computer, and software engineering; and reported directly to the captain of the ship. Moreover, Nyota Uhura was the sole Black female character on Star Trek in the 1960s and the first Black person to be centered as a major character in an American television series. In an interview with CNN ("Then & Now," 2005), Jemison reminisced about the diverse composition of the Star Trek crew and how this vision helped her to understand that she, too, could be involved in space exploration and other scientific endeavors. More importantly, she was able to look at Uhura and see a promising future in a time when it was uncommon to see Black women in roles that showed them reaching the outer limits of the Earth and pushing past stereotypical characterizations. Thus, in many ways, Uhura represents a visual and embodied manifestation of an expanded future, a representation of unfettered Black womanhood.

Jemison's accomplishment as the first African American female astronaut forged a new pathway for Black women and girls, and the impact of speculative fiction on her trajectory should not be ignored. Yet, in the last 20 years, research centering Black girls in fiction texts has overlooked speculative fiction as a genre worth investigating, as scholars conducting content analyses of fiction and analyzing Black girls' responses to fiction consistently focus on realistic narratives (Toliver, 2018). Of course, the realistic text choices used most often in literacy research address common topics associated with Black girlhood, such as colorism, body image, and resistance, but in centering these works, the possibilities inherent in speculative fiction are overlooked. However, because Black girls' identities are not restricted or monolithic, it makes sense to broaden the current boundaries to include complex, multidimensional, and multilayered genres of literature.

Speculative fiction covers a vast range of imaginative texts, including fantasy, science fiction, cyberpunk, sword and soul, and various others; therefore, examining each subgenre would be impossible within one chapter. However, Afrofuturism is specifically suited for a discussion of Black girls, as it is written for and by Black people. Afrofuturist authors place Black characters in lead roles, attend to African Diasporic cultural dispositions that affect the characters, and examine social and political events that currently affect Black people (Nelson, 2002; Womack, 2013). Additionally, authors who write Afrofuturist narratives critique the environmental, social, racial, economic, and political orders of society (English & Kim, 2013). Therefore, Afrofuturism is an aesthetic in which Black authors can reimagine how Black people have traditionally been presented.

The purpose of this chapter, then, is to center the following research question: How can Afrofuturist literature expand representations of Black girlhood? To address this question, I first discuss the connections between Afrofuturist literature and the Black Girls' Literacies Framework (BGLF) (Muhammad & Haddix, 2016). I then provide a critical content analysis that highlights prominent themes within six Afrofuturist young adult novels as examples of texts that represent nuanced depictions of Black girlhood. Lastly, I discuss how the books highlight the many facets of Black girlhood.

## Afrofuturism and Black Girls' Literacies

Afrofuturism combines science fiction, fantasy, magical realism, horror, history, and imagination to critique oppressions and imagine unbound Black subjectivities in future or alternate worlds (English & Kim, 2013; Womack, 2013). It is a way for Black writers to combat socially constructed realities that converge Black identities with calamity and to contest stories where imaginative spaces align the persistence of Black lives with a disastrous future (Yaszek, 2006). Essentially, Afrofuturism forms a foundation to disrupt modern, racist ideology that exists to restrict Black imaginations, and it also provides a space for Black people to envision the tools (Eshun, 2003; Hopkinson & Nelson, 2002) necessary to subvert oppressive paradigms and create the futures and worlds they wish to see.

Although Afrofuturism is a space for all Black authors to rewrite and revise stories told about Black people, Black women writers use the aesthetic as a place to critique and create as they construct Black women and girls' identities (Barr, 2008; Pough & Hood, 2005). Specifically, they often centralize Black women and girls, using Afrofuturism to redefine how Black girls' racialized and gendered identities are depicted in text. Through Afrofuturism, Black female writers have a physical and symbolic space where they can explore their identities, dig behind societal ideas about what it means to be Black and female, and create room for

Black women and girls to define their own existence in numerous and nuanced ways (Morris, 2016; Womack, 2013). Thus, Afrofuturism is a radical movement that defies dominant ideologies by not only centering Black people, but also highlighting the voices of Black women, disrupting intersected forms of oppression simultaneously.

The creation of more Black female characters by Black female authors and the teaching of these texts is necessary for Black girls because speculative fiction has historically created a dismal view of the future for this group. Specifically, speculative fiction has a history of being primarily created by, for, and about white men (Hopkinson, 2005; Obeso, 2014), and when Black girls are included, they are often used as fodder for the progression of the plot (Morris, 2016). Alternatively, Afrofuturism is dedicated to the creation of an egalitarian environment that is accepting of Black female bodies and all the diversity they can encompass (Womack, 2013). This freedom expands the ways in which Black girls can understand their position in identity creation, showing them alternatives to the roles that are stereotypically handed down to them.

By focusing on Black girls, Afrofuturism intricately aligns with the BGLF. Particularly, Afrofuturism layers multiple genres and focal points, so the texts are never solely determined by one specific genre. This means that Afrofuturism cannot be classified as science fiction, fantasy, or horror because it uses a combination of speculative subgenres. Additionally, with its explicit focus on Black people and their ability to imagine alternate worlds and futures, Afrofuturism is tied to identities. Particularly, as the writers create Afrofuturist worlds within their stories, Black characters, Black cultures, Black communities, and Black journeys toward selfhood are never abandoned. Instead, the authors use the stories to better understand their positionalities as Black people in the modern world.

Moreover, Afrofuturism is historical, as each author "actively draw[s] on Afrodiasporic history and culture to tell complex and sometimes contradictory stories about how and why race relations might continue to matter in the future" (Yaszek, 2006, p. 55). That is, Afrofuturist texts purposefully highlight the histories of Black people and make those histories a prominent focus in the plot of the story. Also, by focusing on the ancestral roots of various Black cultures, Afrofuturism is collaborative, as creators use numerous Black cultural histories in the invention of futuristic and alternative worlds. In this way, Afrofuturism is socially produced and co-constructed by various groups of Black people as they examine the past and present to create imaginative possibilities.

Furthermore, as Afrofuturism attempts to combat oppressive representations and critique past and present social history, it is inherently intellectual, political, and critical. It critiques modern conceptions of Black identities and the subjugation of Black people by highlighting the numerous systemic, institutional, and individual biases that create the foundation for many social justice issues in society (Everett-Haynes, 2017). Through a metaphoric rendering of modern social ills, the texts often act as experiential portals that guide readers to reflect on the current state of the world, to hypothesize about the trajectory of society, and to challenge any possible future that continues the subjugation of Black people. In this way, Afrofuturism highlights society and social problems and uses the supernatural, magical, and/or futuristic to discuss power, misrepresentation, falsehood, and the need for social transformation.

Because Afrofuturism is multiple, tied to Black identities, historical, collaborative, intellectual, political, and critical, it can be examined through the BGLF. Therefore, in the following sections, I provide explicit examples of the connections between Afrofuturism and the BGLF by conducting a critical content analysis of six young adult Afrofuturist texts—*Binti* by Nnedi Okorafor (2015), *Parable of the Sower* by Octavia Butler (1993), *The Summer Prince* by Alaya Dawn Johnson (2013), *Breaking Free* by Alicia McCalla (2012), *Orleans* by Sherri Smith (2015), and *The Chaos* by Nalo Hopkinson (2012). I chose texts written by Black female authors to highlight the contributions of Black women to the genre and to show how the genre is being co-constructed by established, fledgling, and indie authors.

## Analyzing the Texts

Qualitative content analysis is a highly flexible method that requires researchers to systematically analyze a body of texts to make valid inferences (Krippendorf, 2004). This form of analysis is inherently intuitive and interpretive, requiring the researcher to read through and scrutinize the data, identify concepts and patterns, draw conclusions about the text, and situate those conclusions in some larger context (White & Marsh, 2006). Thus, researchers conducting qualitative content analysis work to connect their interpretations to the larger societal context, situating meaning as existent outside of the text.

By adding the word "critical" to content analysis, researchers are assuming a questioning stance that will guide all aspects of the interpretation process in hopes of transforming spaces of inequity (Short & World of Words Community, 2017). However, instead of only focusing their analysis on issues of literary misrepresentation and stereotypes, they also look for reconstruction, "for the ways in which texts position characters as resistant to existing stereotypes and representations in order to develop counter-narratives, and to offer new possibilities for how to position ourselves in the world" (p. 6). For this analysis, I focus on the reconstruction element of critical content analysis by analyzing the positioning of Black female characters in Afrofuturist texts.

To ensure that the content analysis focused on representations of adolescent Black girls, I chose to only include texts with adolescent female protagonists. Additionally, because I aligned my research with Afrofuturism, I ensured that each text depicted well-rounded Black female characters in futuristic and/or fantastic settings and contained metaphors for and about Black life, history, and social justice. I understand that many scholars state that Afrofuturism centers futuristic settings (Eshun, 2003; Morris, 2016; Nelson, 2002); however, other scholars include fantasy (Newkirk, 2018), magical realism (Sorensen, 2014), and horror (Northington, 2018) as part of the aesthetic. For this analysis, then, I chose to include various speculative fiction subgenres to ensure that both definitions are acknowledged, as the nomenclature is still evolving.

I used critical content analysis (Short & World of Words, 2017) to analyze these texts. First, I immersed myself as a reader rather than a researcher to create an interpretation of the text. Then, I immersed myself in the BGLF, and I listed major tenets of the framework to guide my second reading and focus my research questions. From this point, I conducted a final close reading in which I wrote theoretical memos about each major category and placed these in a chart to better identify connecting themes among the novels.

Using this method of critical content analysis, I found similar themes across each text. These themes include creating and maintaining community to ensure survival, representing cultural diversity within Black girlhood, and critiquing and challenging pervasive oppression. In the following sections, I provide examples of each of the themes, highlighting two Afrofuturistic young adult texts for each section. I then discuss how each of these components enables a larger discussion of Afrofuturism as layered, historically framed, tied to identities, socially involved, grounded in the critical thought, and focused on subverting domination, discrimination, and misrepresentation.

## Findings: On Community and Survival

Throughout history, Black women have constructed communities based on shared characteristics and geographical location (Hine, 2007). These communal entities were essential as Black women developed "innovative strategies of political engagement and community mobilization and remained demonstrably committed to improving the welfare and enlarging opportunity structures for the people with whom they identified, represented, and served" (p. 17). That is, the communities in which Black women participated were collaborative and co-constructed based on shared experiences and goals, and the women used the communities to create opportunities for everyone who identified with or participated in the communal space. Just like Black women, Black girls also have a need for co-constructed and collaborative spaces through which to form their communities, and the Afrofuturist texts selected for this analysis build on the historical relevance of community by showcasing how various groups help the protagonists progress and thrive.

In *Binti*, a mathematical genius, named Binti, leaves her home in Naimib, Africa to pursue her education, and she must use the lessons learned from her homeland to survive in an alien world. However, even though Binti makes the decision to leave her homeland, she remains connected to it through her use of otjize, a mixture used by the Himba people to protect themselves from the desert climate. Before leaving her home to attend Oomza University, Binti mentions the longevity of her bloodline in the village, noting that six generations of her family have lived in the same house in the same location. She knows that leaving the community may result in her dismissal from the tribe, especially since she mentions that the Himba "don't travel. We stay put. Our ancestral land is life; move away from it and you diminish. We even cover our bodies with it" (pp. 12–13). The earthly blend that covers their bodies is used for a practical purpose, but Binti connects the use of otjize with her ancestral lifeline, a connection symbolized through the physical covering of her body with the land.

Later in the story, Binti's life is threatened by the Meduse, a militant alien group who realizes the healing potential of her otjize. The Meduse want the mixture for their own medicinal purposes, but Binti argues that she could not give all of her otjize to the aliens because of its connection to her culture. In fact, she says, "if your chief knows my people, then he will have told you that taking it from me is like taking my soul" (p. 49). Essentially, when presented with the decision of dying or keeping the otjize, Binti chooses the latter. She does not hesitate to note her cultural history even in the face of danger, suggesting her acknowledgement of the necessity of maintaining the connection to her Himba community as essential for her individual and spiritual survival.

Ultimately, African Himba land covers Binti's body even when she decides to leave home. It is important enough to her that she brings it with her on her journey into space. It is significant enough that she is willing to deny alien beings the medicinal benefits of her homeland in order to keep her community with her as long as possible. The otjize is representative of the cultural link she has with her Himba community even though she has left the village to pursue an academic life. It is a metaphorical mobilization of her community as she tries to create more opportunities for herself. In essence, her communal history is embedded in her skin and woven into the braids in her hair, and she would rather face death than to lose this connection.

Whereas Binti refused to sever communal ties to her Himba village, Lauren, the protagonist in *Parable of the Sower*, addresses the community in a vastly different manner, with Lauren choosing to alter her communal ties as necessary. At the beginning of the novel, Lauren lives with her father, stepmother, and two brothers in a walled community in the ravaged state of California. The community is made up of a patchwork of individuals that cross racial, gender, and religious lines, but they work together to ensure the survival of their community, especially in an area where arson, robbery, and murder are rampant. In one internal musing, Lauren analyzes the community in which she lives, noting the need to come together and evolve under changing circumstances.

> Civilization is to groups what intelligence is to individuals. It is a means of combining the intelligence of many to achieve ongoing group adaptation. Civilization, like intelligence, may serve well, serve adequately, or fail to

serve its adaptive function. When civilization fails to serve, it must disintegrate unless it is acted upon by unifying internal or external forces.

*(p. 10)*

In this statement, Lauren recognizes that adaptation is a requirement in the survival of civilization, and she compares this notion of adjustment to her current community. She mentions the need to combine the intellectual capabilities of all people, children and adults, because she knows that all have a purpose in the stabilization and future existence of the community. Sadly, she also feels as though her community may not come together or adapt to the increased violence, so it may cease to serve its function as a safe place for the residents. If this occurs, she is willing to let the community disintegrate to allow a better community to form and function.

Lauren is right in her presumption, for after her community is destroyed by an arsonist terror group that infiltrates her community, she must learn to survive in the wasteland that America has become. Instead of trying to make it on her own, she realizes the need to maintain a community, not only with the remaining members of her former living space, but also with trustworthy new people that have useful skills. For example, when she meets her initial group of travelers, Lauren understands the need to work together for the collective good of the new community. She reminds her group members of this need by saying, "We're a pack, the three of us, and all those other people aren't in it. If we're a good pack, and we work together, we have a chance" (p. 183). Later, she says, "If we work together, we can defend ourselves, and we can protect the kids. The community's first responsibility is to protect its children—the ones we have now and the ones we will have" (p. 321). In these two statements, Lauren shows her dedication to the community in the present and the future, focusing on collective effort as a means for future sustenance.

In the beginning of the text, Lauren's community is based on location, and when the community is burned, Lauren's community is changed as she joins with two survivors and picks up six other travelers. Her goal is not to find an already established community with which she can identify. Instead, her goal is to create a community in which she feels safe, a collective group that is dedicated to their survival and the survival of future communal members. This takes a collaborative effort from every person in the group, as the community is co-constructed to become a protective space for all people involved.

Both Binti and Lauren think differently about the ways in which community is created and maintained. For Binti, community connections are rooted in ancestral cultural practice, and they are an integral part of the community members no matter where they travel. Contrastingly, Lauren believes that community is relative. It can be adjusted, depending on the needs of the communal members. While Binti believes that community should be maintained at all costs, Lauren believes that communities can be created, destroyed, and recreated to suit the individual's purposes. Yet, even though there are differences, the two protagonists share one, important similarity. They each rely on community for their own progression and survival.

## Findings: On Diversity in Black Girlhood

Culture is unsteady and evolving; yet, when specific racial groups are discussed, they are often depicted as monolithic, static, and unidirectional (Paris & Alim, 2014; Johnson-Bailey, 1999). However, even though racial group members have some commonalities, their experiences should never be homogenized. Factors such as the political landscape, economic context, time period, and individual experience all create a foundation for people within the same racial group to have vastly different experiences (Palmer, 2018). Thus, even though Black girls are a part of a specific racialized and gendered group, they often have distinct ideas, beliefs, and characteristics.

June Costa is a budding young artist and the Afro-Brazilian protagonist of *The Summer Prince*, and she is a resident of the matriarchal pyramid city of Palmares Três, where there is constant surveillance by the government as well the paparazzi. The matriarchs, known as Aunties, control every aspect of the society, maintaining control through rigged elections, fear tactics, and historical precedence that ensures they keep their power. The citizens are divided in numerous ways to ensure the Aunties' complete control of the city. First, the city is spatially divided in tiers, with politically and financially affluent citizens living on the highest levels of the pyramid and the disadvantaged members of society forced into the depths of the city, surrounded by sewage.

The citizens are also divided into two age groups: the under-30 Wakas and the over-30 Grandes. Wakas are granted less privileges than those who have passed the threshold of true adulthood because the Aunties believe that people younger than 30 have not lived long enough to reach maturity. Wakas cannot have a place in government, and they are considered societal leeches, rather than contributing members of society. Beyond these age groups, the citizens are segregated by skin color because the Aunties have forbidden anyone from having skin that is too light or too dark. In fact, to ensure that people are within the required "color scheme," genetic modifications are often required. Anyone who is deemed too light or dark is considered an outcast, a lowly person in the color hierarchy.

In one scene, June describes the culture present in the city by acknowledging the chain of events that resulted in their current state. She recognizes the perfectly even gender demographics of the city created by the Aunties of the past and present, and she also states that she can "feel the strength of all our ancestors bearing us up. They are the heavy trunk and thick boughs of a tree on which I am only the tiniest budding leaf" (p. 23). In this excerpt, June seems rooted in her culture by the direct comparison of her ancestry to the roots of a tree, suggesting that she believes roots and ancestral guidance are important to the balance of her community. She knows the importance of her ancestors to Palmares Três, noting that they support and strengthen the city even though they have left the mortal world. In comparison to her resilient ancestors, however, she feels underdeveloped, a tiny sprout in a community of full-grown trees.

June's feelings of insignificance are upended, however, when she meets Enki, the Summer Prince, who forces her to think differently about her world. She says, "I love Palmares Três, but how I have begun to hate the Aunties who run her" (p. 206). It is here that June acknowledges her dislike of the current culture upheld within the city she loves, especially since the Aunties show everyone just how much they devalue the lives of others. She knows that the segregation of citizens by skin color, class, and age must be changed because the city, as a whole, should prosper, which means that every single person, regardless of their status, should also thrive. As the stepdaughter of a high-ranking official, June knows that she will have to subvert the current cultural milieu to ensure that her city flourishes, rather than falters. Even though she feels small, she is willing to subvert authority to ensure a prosperous future for all residents. That is, she honors and respects her history and the values of her city, but she also knows that cultural elements can be changed.

Although June embraces activism in order to make necessary changes in her world, XJ Patterson, the protagonist in *Breaking Free*, rejects her family's history of activism. The novel takes place in a futuristic Atlanta, Georgia, where genetically enhanced people (GEP) are killed or forced to assimilate. The Coalition to Assimilate Genetically Enhanced persons (CAGE) is responsible for enforcing government rule, but there are pockets of activists who want all GEPs to maintain their freedom. As a GEP, XJ rejects the government's history of violence against people like her. Yet, even though her mother, Dorothy, is a leader of the revolution, as was her grandfather, XJ would rather live the life of a "normal" teenager instead of fighting for the revolution.

At the beginning of the story, Dorothy is pursued by CAGE, but before she is imprisoned by the task force, she pleads with XJ to continue the fight she is no longer able to pursue. She knows that XJ does not want to be in the spotlight or fight for the GEPs, but Dorothy also knows that XJ may be the only person capable of assuming a leadership role in the revolution. Dorothy pleads with XJ as she's being captured, saying:

> Our family made sacrifices for the freedom of all GEPs. This time, to protect us all, I'm sacrificing myself. It's the only way. . . . You must fulfill your grandfather's mission. You must become a revolutionary. You're our last hope. Your generation must carry on where ours ends.
>
> *(loc. 152)*

Dorothy knows that being captured by CAGE implies she will be murdered or forced to alter her way of thinking. She knows that the revolution could cease to continue without leadership. So, she calls on XJ to continue the legacy of the family, carrying on the mission to ensure the freedom of all GEPs, XJ included.

However, instead of embracing this task, XJ replies, "All my life you talked about my destiny and our family's legacy! I'm only 17 years old! I need you. . . . It's crap trying to live up to the legacy of dead people!" (loc. 159). XJ's response suggests that although her people (GEPs) are being persecuted for merely existing, she is not willing to follow her family's activist endeavors. She thinks it is unfair for her to have so much weight placed upon her because she is young and in need of support and guidance. In fact, as she talks to a friend about her thoughts, she says she is sick of the revolution because of the strain it placed upon her family. Thus, even though the group to which XJ belongs is faced with oppression, and even though her family has a history of helping to combat that oppression, XJ would rather remove herself from the fight. She wants change, but she does not want to be the person responsible for making that change happen.

Both June and XJ are young, Black girls who live in futuristic, oppressive societies, and they both witness the persecution of people based on their perceived status in the world. Additionally, they both feel inconsequential in the larger narrative of their worlds, wanting things to change, but not knowing if they have the power to actually make that change happen. However, although there are similarities, June and XJ's geographical locations and individual experiences create different depictions of Black girlhood.

Specifically, June lives in a post-apocalyptic Brazil, and because she is considered privileged in her society, she is afforded certain rights and freedoms. She speaks against the Aunties and their discrimination against minoritized populations without fear of repercussion. She is defiant and wants to see change, and she is willing to fight for what she wants. XJ, on the other hand, lives in a futuristic version of the state of Georgia and has no power, for she is considered to be a lower-class citizen, and she has no access to influential government officials. Additionally, her identity as a GEP puts her at risk for forced assimilation or death, and her mother's status as a revolutionary makes her a government target. XJ would rather remain peaceful and avoid the revolution in order to ensure her safety.

Fundamentally, although both characters are Black girls, they have different cultural experiences that could never be homogenized just because they share a race and gender identity. Black girls are numerous. They can be African, Afro-Caribbean, Afro-Brazilian, African American, multiracial, etc. They can come from Haiti, Cuba, Australia, China, France, and beyond. They have myriad political, economic, societal, and individual experiences. Their identities cannot be restricted to one perspective because there are nuances in Black girlhood that must always be acknowledged. June and XJ exemplify the nuances of Black girlhood. They are both Black girls, but their differences create a uniqueness that cannot be standardized.

## Findings: On Critiquing Oppression and Envisioning Change

Afrofuturist authors do more than portray nuanced representations of Black girl-hood; they also critique and challenge the ways in which Black girls are oppressed in society. Eshun (2003) notes that Afrofuturism "is concerned with the possibilities for intervention within the dimension of the predictive, the projected, the proleptic, the envisioned, the virtual, the anticipatory and the future conditional" (p. 293). That is, Afrofuturist authors reconstruct the current speculative visions that align Blackness with calamity. They critique the present and provide counterstories that depict potential spaces of hope, rather than despair.

In Sherri Smith's *Orleans*, numerous hurricanes have devastated the Gulf Coast, and the combination of stagnant water, chemical runoff, and dead bodies cause the creation of an intense strain of disease known as Delta Fever. When the first few hurricanes hit the area, the government agrees to help the people of Orleans, but they later decide it would be easier to quarantine the whole region and remove the people's citizenship. The government builds a barrier around the entire territory to prevent residents from escaping and suspends aid and resources to prevent the residents from helping themselves. Further, armed guards are stationed atop the walls with direct orders to kill any person who tries to gain entry into the other states.

While the residents are restrained, medical researchers travel to and from Orleans to conduct experiments that may rid Orleans of the fever, but although outsiders believe the scientists are looking for a cure, the trapped residents know the evil of their intentions. This is shown in a conversation between the two central characters, Fen de la Guerre, a 15-year-old Black female resident of Orleans, and Daniel, a White male researcher who hopes to find his own cure for Delta Fever. Like Daniel, Fen's parents traveled to the Delta region to join a research facility in hopes of finding a cure for the residents. However, Daniel discovers that they left the facility after falling out with the management. When Daniel finds out about this, he is confused and asks Fen about why her parents left the research organization.

FEN: Why you think my parents left? They ain't working on a cure here, Daniel. Orleans just a lab to them. We ain't people, we rats.

DANIEL: If they weren't looking for a cure, what is all this for? . . .

FEN: You from the other side of the Wall. Don't you know? . . . Dr. Warren's pet project,

He ain't interested in the Fever. He studying tribes.

DANIEL: Ending racism. For the most part, the rules of blood make race irrelevant. Blood types cross all ethnicities.

FEN: If folks stop hating each other 'cause of skin color, the only difference be blood type.

DANIEL: A new form of racism. It's like Tuskegee all over again.

*(p. 210)*

Basically, the organization wanted to see what would happen to the concept of race if the disease continued and separated people based on their blood type. They wanted to experiment on the people without actually trying to find a cure for them. Thus, Orleans citizens were used as an experimental research group, just like rural Black men in Alabama were used by the U.S. Public Health Service and the Tuskegee Institute.

Fen is unaware of the Tuskegee experiment, but she notes that people in power are always going to abuse their control over others. She also notes that even through societal abuse and horrendous living conditions, the people of Orleans continue to fight for their survival and dignity. This is shown through makeshift Mardi Gras celebrations some residents participate in every year after the storm season is over. Fen explains this tradition to Daniel by saying:

> Somebody found an old Mardi Gras warehouse or something, and he pull out some costumes and go riding through the streets. Just one man holding up a lantern, saying "We still here, we still here, thank Lord almighty, we still here." . . . And other people started, too, 'til they all been wading along, with they flashlights and torches and all kinds of things, and they start singing and dancing, 'cause this be New Orleans and that be what we do.
>
> *(p. 173)*

In this excerpt, Fen explains that one person decided to celebrate the life and resistance of the citizens instead of lamenting over their situation, and others joined in the celebration. Regardless of what was happening and how they were ignored, they still lived. They were still there, whether the government was trying to eliminate them or not. Although the author could have centered the people's hopelessness and desolation, she chose to challenge the portrayal by highlighting a community act that brought the people together, despite their struggles.

Another example is shown in Nalo Hopkinson's novel, *The Chaos*. The story centers Sojourner "Scotch" Smith, a young Black girl who is trying to better understand herself in a world that seeks to define her. At the beginning of the story, the reader learns that she has recently moved to a new city and is attending a new high school. Her family chose to move because of the constant harassment Scotch faced at her former school, LeBrun High. LeBrun is a predominately White school in Guelph, Canada, and Scotch was one of only five Black people who attended. At the school, she was bullied because of the shape of her body. She was called a slut and a skank. She was cornered in a parking lot after school, held down, and spit on. She had rocks thrown at her as she tried to return home from school. As she recounts her experiences, she states the following:

> once people decide you're the school slut, it sticks. It gets tangled up in you like the chewed-up gum in your hair. It's like you're wearing a big S

on your forehead, and no matter how much foundation you put on over it, eventually it shows through. Eventually somebody'll look at you a certain way, or a bunch of girls will laugh as they walk past you, and even if that look doesn't mean anything and those girls aren't laughing at you, in your mind you'll be the school slut all over again.

*(loc. 1775)*

Scotch's former classmates assigned a scarlet letter to her body, positioning her as the school harlot because her body did not mirror the bodily form of the school's majority White population. Sadly, she also comments on the lasting effects of her exclusion and ridicule, stating that once the bullying begins, it is difficult to move beyond those feelings.

To protect her from the bullies, Scotch's parents decide to move to Toronto in hopes that their daughter could attend a more diverse school. Scotch enjoys her new school and is no longer ashamed of her body or her sexuality, and she represents her body comfortability with more revealing clothing. However, she is afraid to tell her strict parents about her newfound freedom. Although they knew the bullying was not her fault, Scotch's parents consistently tell her to act modest and remain hidden, not presenting herself as a target. They want her to cover up any part of her that could be sexualized by the dominant gaze, because they want her to be safe. However, Scotch says, "They didn't really understand what I'd learned at LeBrun High; being good didn't make me safe" (loc. 219). In other words, hiding from others was not going to stop her from being derided. The only way to combat the ridicule was to be comfortable with herself, despite the words of others.

To avoid the gaze of her mother, Scotch dresses conservatively while she is at home. Each day, however, she brings a change of clothes to school, deciding to wear clothes that are more revealing, but also more comfortable for her. She embraces her physical structure and no longer hides it for fear of bullying because she knows that covering her body will not stop others from eschewing negativity. So, even though dominant forces have resulted in a system that could make any young, Black girl hate her outward features, Scotch reclaims her body and her sexual identity, refusing to live within the constraints provided by larger society. Thus, Hopkinson refuses to focus the story on the bullying and oversexualization of the main character. Instead, she reimagines what the reclaiming of Black girl sexuality could look like.

Both *Orleans* and *The Chaos* provide commentary about the ways in which Black people and Black girls have faced oppression. However, instead of only highlighting subjugation, the authors depict Black characters who maintain hope, agency, and self-love even in the face of hardship. Both authors present narratives that do not equate Black existence with hardship. Instead, they offer counterstories, where Black people celebrate and smile in the midst of societal and governmental oppression.

## Afrofuturism and BGLF

As mentioned previously, Afrofuturist texts are intricately aligned with the BGLF, and the content analysis further bolsters this alignment. For instance, each text covers an array of speculative subgenres, including science fiction (*Binti, Breaking Free*), magical realism (*The Chaos*), and dystopian (*Orleans, Parable of the Sower, The Summer Prince*). Moreover, the stories within each category are layered. *Binti* and *Breaking Free* are both science fiction, but one takes place in Africa and outer space, while the other is set in a futuristic Georgia with GEPs. There are three dystopian books, but they have different settings, the characters speak different languages, and the imperfections within the societies differ. Thus, there are multiple theoretical and practical access points into the texts, and they cannot be analyzed simply.

Additionally, each story is focused on various representations of Black female adolescence because the protagonists within the texts represent many geographical locations, family compositions, class statuses, and capabilities. Particularly, the stories take place in Africa (*Binti*), the United States (*Breaking Free, Orleans, Parable of the Sower*), Canada (*The Chaos*), and South America (*The Summer Prince*). Binti, Lauren, Scotch, and June all come from two-parent households, while XJ comes from a single-parent home, and Fen lives with community members. Also, while June is financially and socially advantaged, the other protagonists do not have the same advantages. Binti is mathematically intelligent and earns a scholarship to an interplanetary university for her ability. XJ has genetically enhanced capabilities that grant her telekinesis and telepathy. June is an artist who uses her creativity to construct socially informed art. Scotch is a hip-hop dancer who uses dance as artistic freedom. Fen is multi-lingual and perceptive, so she is able to survive in multiple environments. Lauren is intuitive and calculating, enabling her to prepare for numerous possibilities in advance. Collectively, these stories depict myriad Black girl identities, suggesting the many selfhoods of Black girls.

Moreover, as each story represents the multiplicity of Black girlhood, the authors are also portraying the history of diversity within Black cultures. Namely, Nalo Hopkinson includes Caribbean folklore, Alaya Dawn Johnson incorporates Brazilian history, and Nnedi Okorafor depicts Himba tradition as prominent aspects of their novels, highlighting the diversity of Black girlhood outside of the United States. Alternatively, Sherri Smith, Octavia Butler, and Alicia McCalla show varied portrayals of Black girlhood within the United States, with Fen living in New Orleans, XJ residing in Northeast Georgia, and Lauren inhabiting various sections of California. By representing Black girls in various parts of the world, the authors attend to the myriad and collective histories of Black people and denote the expansiveness of Blackness.

Of course, representing Black people in various parts of the world requires a discussion about why people were forced to move in the first place and how the movement has impacted the descendants of African people, and the authors attend to this fact. Specifically, Smith writes about governmental oppression; Hopkinson discusses the prevalence of respectability politics and colorism; Johnson confronts classism and heterosexism; Butler challenges ageism and religious oppression; Okorafor critiques colonialism; and McCalla focalizes racism and self-care. Each author reflects on the social problems that plague Black people in general and Black girls specifically. Yet, the authors also counter oppressions they notice with varied representations of joy, celebration, agency, and drive. Thus, the authors critique and challenge social issues and provide counterstories of Black girlhood, suggesting that oppression does not have to be the only concept that represents Black children (Hood, 2009).

Together, the authors of Afrofuturist young adult texts are collaboratively (re) constructing representations of Black girls by providing multiple combinations of Black girlhood that are unbound by location, characteristic, ethnicity, family, etc. They show that Black girls are not restricted to homogenized ideas that limit how Black girls can exist in the world. That is, the Afrofuturist authors presented in this chapter provide another frame upon which Black girlhood can be depicted. They present a way for readers to critically think about how Black girls can, have, do, and will exist in the world.

As English educators prepare to teach literature that features Black girls, it is imperative that they include speculative stories that present a broadened view of Black girlhood. This is essential because representations of Black children are often "limited to the townships of occasional historical books that concern themselves with the legacies of civil rights and slavery but are never given a pass card to traverse the lands of adventure, curiosity, imagination or personal growth" (Myers, 2014, para. 7). This means that most Black girls are erased from imaginative literature, eliminating them from stories in which their dreams, hopes, and aspirations for the future matter. Ultimately, this erasure narrows the depictions of Black girlhood to specific narratives, bounding them to the present or the past.

I am not insinuating that Afrofuturism is superior to realistic genres, but I am advocating for researchers and educators to begin expanding what texts we consider when we teach Black girls or teach about Black girls. I am advocating for the use of texts in which the conflict that guides the narrative is not based on the cultural, gendered, and linguistic differences the protagonist has in opposition to dominant society. I am advocating for stories that portray Black girls as warriors, princesses, ambassadors, and revolutionaries in the future, sustaining their culture in ways currently unfathomable in realistic portrayals. Black girls need more. Black girls deserve more. Black girls need access to stories depicting the past, the present, the future, and the fantastic.

## Conclusion

When Mae Jemison was an adult, she was granted the opportunity to be featured in a Star Trek episode that was all about "the fact that our fantasies lead our realities and our realities lead our fantasies and it comes full circle again" ("Then and Now," 2005). Jemison's dreams were initiated by Nyota Uhura, a fictional character, and that vision became a reality. She looked at her surroundings and realized that she needed the fantastic to help her see another way of being in the future. She took that fantasy and made it a part of her future existence, helping other young Black girls to see that being an astronaut was no longer a fantastic possibility.

Muhammad and Haddix (2016) recommend that teachers create "opportunities for Black girls to read and respond to literature in ways that help them to critique, negotiate, or mediate selfhood" (p. 323). Afrofuturism can assist Black girls in completing all of these tasks, as Afrofuturist authors create texts that provide nuanced depictions of Black girlhood. Additionally, the ways in which the authors highlight alternate or imaginative futures can counter the identity-constraining box into which society tries to force Black girls. If Uhura helped Jemison reach the stars, imagine what Fen, XJ, June, Binti, Scotch, and Lauren could do for our Black girls.

## References

Barr, M. S. (2008). "All at one point" conveys the point, period: Or, Black science fiction is bursting out all over. In M. S. Barr (Ed.), *Afro-future females: Black writers chart science fiction's newest new-wave trajectory.* (pp. ix–xxvi). Columbus, OH: The Ohio State University Press.

Butler, O. (1993). *Parable of the Sower.* New York, NY: Grand Central Publishing.

English, D., & Kim, A. (2013). Now we want our funk cut: Janelle Monáe's neo-afrofuturism. *American Studies, 52*(4), 217–230.

Eshun, K. (2003). Further considerations of afrofuturism. *The New Centennial Review, 3*(2), 287–302.

Everett-Haynes, L. M. (2017, February 21). Afrofuturism: Where science fiction meets social justice. *UANews.* https://uanews.arizona.edu/story/afrofuturism-where-science-fiction-meets-social-justice

Hine, D. C. (2007). African American women and their communities in the twentieth century: The foundation and future of Black women's studies. *Black Women, Gender Families, 1*(1), 1–23.

Hood, Y. (2009). Rac(e)ing into the future: Looking at race in recent science fiction and fantasy novels for young adults by Black authors. *The ALAN Review, 36*(3), 81–86.

Hopkinson, N. (2005). Afrofuturism: Womanist paradigms for the new millennium. *Femspec, 6*(1), 103–110.

Hopkinson, N., & Nelson, A. (2002). "Making the impossible possible": An interview with Nalo Hopkinson. *Social Text, 20*(2), 97–113.

Hopkinson, N. (2012). *The chaos.* New York City, NY: Simon & Schuster.

Johnson, A. D. (2013). *The summer prince.* New York City, NY: Scholastic, Inc.

Johnson-Bailey, J. (1999). The ties that bind and the shackles that separate: Race, gender, class, and colour in the research process. *International Journal of Qualitative Studies in Education, 12*(6), 659–670.

Krippendorf, K. (2004). *Content analysis: An introduction to its methodology* (2nd ed.). Thousand Oaks, CA: Sage.

McCalla, A. (2012). *Breaking free*. Stanwood, WA: Heart Ally Books.

Morris, S. (2016). More than human: Black feminisms of the future in Jewelle Gomez's The Gilda Stories. *The Black Scholar, 46*(2), 33–45.

Muhammad, G. E., & Haddix, M. (2016). Centering Black girls' literacies: A review of literature on the multiple ways of knowing of Black girls. *English Journal, 48*(4), 299–336.

Myers, C. (2014, March 15). The apartheid of children's literature. *The New York Times*. www.nytimes.com/2014/03/16/opinion/sunday/the-apartheid-ofchildrens-literature.html?smid=fb-share&_r=0

Nelson, A. (2002). Introduction: Future texts. *Social Text, 20*(2), 1–15.

Newkirk, V. (2018, April). Where fantasy meets Black lives matter. *The Atlantic*. www.theatlantic.com/magazine/archive/2018/04/children-of-blood-and-bone-tomi-adeyemi/554060/

Northington, J. (2018, May 10). 8 Great reads to get into afrofuturism. *Book Riot*. https://bookriot.com/2018/05/10/best-afrofuturism-books/

Obeso, D. (2014, October). How multicultural is your multiverse. *Publisher's Weekly*, 25–31.

Okorafor, N. (2015). *Binti*. New York, NY: Tom Doherty Associates.

Palmer, C. A. (2018). Defining and studying the modern African diaspora. *Journal of Pan African Studies, 11*(2), 214–220.

Paris, D., & Alim, H. S. (2014). What are we seeking to sustain through culturally sustaining pedagogy? A loving critique forward. *Harvard Educational Review, 84*(1), 85–100.

Pough, G. D., & Hood, Y. (2005). Speculative Black women: Magic, fantasy, and the supernatural. *Femspec, 6*(1), ix–xvi.

Short, K. G., & Worlds of Words Community. (2017). Critical content analysis as a research methodology. In H. Johnson, J. Mathis, & K. Short (Eds.), *Critical content analysis of children's and young adult literature: Reframing perspective* (pp. 1–15). New York, NY: Routledge.

Smith, S. (2015). *Orleans*. New York, NY: Penguin Young Readers Group.

Sorensen, L. (2014). Dubwise into the future: Versioning modernity in Nalo Hopkinson. *African American Review, 47*(2/3), 267–283.

Then and Now: Dr. Mae Jemison. (2005, June 19). *CNN*. www.cnn.com/2005/US/01/07/cnn25.tan.jemison/

Toliver, S. R. (2018). Imagining new hopescapes: Expanding Black girls' windows and mirrors. *Research on Diversity in Youth Literature, 1*(1), Article 3.

White, M. D., & Marsh, E. E. (2006). Content analysis: A flexible methodology. *Library Trends, 55*(1), 22–45.

Womack, Y. L. (2013). *Afrofuturism: The world of Black sci-fi and fantasy culture*. Chicago, IL: Chicago Review Press, Incorporated.

Yaszek, L. (2006). Afrofuturism, science fiction, and the history of the future. *Socialism and Democracy, 20*(3), 41–60.

# KITCHEN TABLE TALKS

## Reading Texts and Black Girlhood

*Dahlia Hamza Constantine, Melanie A. Kirkwood-Marshall, Detra Price-Dennis, Ebony Elizabeth Thomas, and Stephanie Toliver*

The authors in this section gathered around a virtual kitchen table, using the online platform Zoom, to engage in conversation around shared ideas and guiding questions about Black girls' digital literacies practices. They participated in a conversation where they talked across their respective work as children's literature scholars and literacy educators who foreground Black feminist/womanist epistemologies in their personal, social, and professional lives. Genius poet Gwendolyn Brooks, considering the great actor Paul Robeson, wrote, "We are each other's business; we are each other's harvest; we are each other's magnitude and bond." Black women have taken that quote to heart, and use it to express our responsibility to each other. We are each other's business, harvest, magnitude, and bond. That "magnitude and bond" extends to reading texts, including the representation of Black girls in literature for children and young adults, as well as in school curriculum, media, and the Web. While most research and scholarship on Black girls rightly focuses on the experiences, needs, and outcomes of living Black girls, past and present, in this kitchen table talk, we focus on Black girl readers, as well as the mirrors, windows, and sliding glass doors into their storied experiences. For how Black girls show up on the page and on the screen matters for the ways that Black girls are treated in real life.

In honor of this themed issue, this kitchen table talk is organized around these sub-questions:

- Why is it critical that all educators acknowledge Black girls' literacies in their work?
- Why does representation in literature matter for Black girls?
- How are Black girls' digital literacies honored in your work?

- When you think about how Black girls are represented in literature, what are important considerations for the field of literacy education and classroom practice?

In the sections that follow, we highlight our dialogic exchanges in response to these questions and conclude with final words of wisdom. We invited an esteemed sista scholar, Ebony Elizabeth Thomas, to provide an introduction to this KTT as well as to offer responses to the transcribed discussion about Black girls' representation in literature.

To re-create our kitchen table talk, we video-recorded our Zoom chat and transcribed the video. Each section that follows captures key points transcribed that were made to address the guiding questions.

## Acknowledging Black Girls' Literacies

### Why Is It Critical That Educators Acknowledge Black Girls' Literacies in Their Work?

EM: It's critical that we acknowledge Black girls' literacies because it makes literacy researchers and practitioners more effective, empathetic, and introspective in their work. I have also been thinking about the ways proximity to Black girls and their literacies matter and how educators need to ask themselves, "Where do you position yourself in society and what are the ways that you connect to Black girls?" Because that's going to look different for each person and you can't just have one seminar on, say, Black girl literacies, and each person receive it in the same way.

DAHLIA: If we think about this question from a US perspective, it's a part of the US story and so you can't have the study of literacy without the study of Black girl literacy because that's from the beginning of our history. But, it is also in the history of the world because when you think about early literacy in the world and places where storytelling has been kept for a long time, Black girls were part of that tradition. And storytelling, whether it comes through dance, or through the oral tradition, or through connection with nature and herbalism, it's been there. So it would be incomplete not to have Black girl literacies. Our understanding of literacy would not be rigorous if it doesn't include Black girl literacies. And so, it's for Black girls, but it's also for the world to engage in more rigorous and rich literacy practices.

STEPHANIE: I agree with Em that Black girl literacies enable educational stakeholders to be more effective, empathetic, and introspective. Black girls often exist as corporeal sites of struggle, where our physical presence and intellectual complexity stands in opposition to stereotypical and narrowed descriptions that have historically confined our personhood in educational spaces. Because of this, I believe that honoring Black girl literacies is a critical facet in activist work that can combat these stock narratives of Black girl-hood. Knowing that Black girls' literacies are historical, multiple, political, critical, and tied to identities sets the stage for educators to begin dismantling some of the oppressionist views that have burdened our girls for far too long. When educators acknowledge Black girls' literacies in their work, they begin to lift that burden, and that's what educators should be doing.

EBONY:  In my work on science fiction and fantasy stories for children and teens that make it to film or TV, also known as transmedia, most of the Black characters are young girls. Even in comics, perhaps the most famous Black character of the past 50 years is mutant heroine Ororo Munroe, best known as Storm from Marvel's lucrative *X-Men*. Clearly, there is something about endarkened girlhoods that especially anchors storytelling (and restorying) in the West. It's my opinion that #BlackGirlMagic stories and views ought to be studied from the perspectives of Black girls themselves.

## Making the Case for Representation

### Why Does Representation in Literature Matter for Black Girls?

EM:  Why literature matters for Black girls, I think it's because it allows us to be seen in our entirety. I honestly feel that we're allowed more of an opportunity to be humanized on the page and [entered in words?] than in person. And so as a society, even though we're in the midst of technological revolution and all these things, of course, we covet these traditional modes of learning and knowledge acquisition. And so Black girls, simply put, we're more reputable in books and in stories than we are in our presence. And that feels weird to say out loud but that's how I feel I've experienced the world.

DETRA:  So, literature from Black girls matters because it writes our stories and realities into the fabric of the American life. That is beautiful. I also love what you said, Em, about who's more reputable on the page, who gets more multiple iterations of ourselves on the page, and I kept thinking of people who read these books in a book club, versus how they treat Black women in real life. Or teachers who can read Black characters and oh, tell you, "I saw *The Color Purple* on stage", and then turn around the next day and can't treat a Black girl with respect in the classroom.

DAHLIA:  I think there are a few issues to unpack. One is seeing ourselves in books. Second issue is understanding and seeing what has been there (how we have been represented across time). And then third, what's possible and what we can imagine. I also think in any society, whoever is on the margins gets relegated to a few perspectives, and not full personhood, and every story has to represent a whole race. But if you're white, every story gets to be about that character, not about the whole group. So, I think the more we have representation, the more we can just crack open what it means to be a Black girl.

DETRA: I think both of you are just nailing it on the head about representation. I agree with you that the more stories we can tell, the more we can keep pushing those boundaries, especially around intersectionality. I also think the more people can keep dreaming about what's possible opens up space for when they meet a Black girl who doesn't fit "the mold," they don't automatically make her a unicorn. She can just be another really awesome Black woman.

STEPHANIE: I think of Dr. Rudine Sims Bishop's windows and mirrors metaphor. Every child should have the ability to see themselves in literature, and every child should be able to use literature as a way to see into the lives of others. Black girls' mirrors have often been minimized, cracked, or distorted. They may see themselves in texts, but these representations often show only one window into Black girlhood when there are many ways to be Black and girl. Like Dahlia mentioned, whoever is on the margins gets relegated to few perspectives and not full personhood, and that correlates to how Black girls are often treated in school spaces. Black girls occupy the full spectrum of intersecting identities, but that is not shown in the literature that has historically been available in schools. That's why it's essential to not only have representation, but to have nuanced depictions of Black girlhood so that we can push the boundaries of what being Black and girl means in and out of schools.

EBONY: Black girls' underrepresentation in stories of all kinds—books, comics, television, films, and around the Web—has implications for the ways that we're treated in the real world. All too often, in stories, Black girls are both the resolution to the narrative problem—from helper characters like "magical Negroes" who only exist to further the story of white protagonists—and *the* problem to be solved. (DuBois, "How does it feel to be a problem?") When Black girls and women engage in reading, all too often, we see our real-world social status mirrored in the purported escapist realm of the fantastic, all while other readers complain that Black girl characters are neither likable nor relatable. Accurate and authentic representation of Black girls in literature will not only positively influence the self-esteem of Black girls themselves but has the potential to shift how others view us in the real world.

## Honoring Black Girls' Literacies

### How Are Black girls' Literacies or Literary Interests Honored in Your Work?

DAHLIA: For me, the international perspective is really important as well as thinking across different regions and looking at what's been here historically. I love archives, so I love digging deep into the stories. This idea started in my Harlem stories class digging in archives. I was looking at yearbooks and trying to understand where Black girls have always been present, documenting their untold stories and histories. So I was looking at one Black girl who was the student council president. This is in the late 1800s in New York in an integrated school. And she was the student body president at this all-girls' school. But these stories, it's not that they're exceptions, it's that there's so many of them and they're just untold. And those are the stories I just love focusing on, kind of everyday things Black girls do. Not necessarily someone who led this whole movement, but she was a student body president. So what does that mean to be doing that in the late 1800s?

I am also interested in nature-based ways of knowing. That's something that's really important, the connection back with land because I do think a big stereotype of Black girls and girls of color, is they tied to an urban space. That's a big part of this story, but it's not the only story. And especially when we look at the literacies of Black girls and Black women in conversation with nature and healing. That is also a huge part of the American story that rarely gets told. So nature, naturalism, environmentalism becomes a very white space, and it doesn't include the voices of Black girls. That's something that I've just been really into the last few months, of looking at Black women naturalists, Black women environmentalists, and girls who are leading movements.

EM: I want to emphasize the necessity of praxis. Even with studying literature, I know a lot of times that research that is literature-based can be just—you think it's rooted in the book and the reader, but, I think, for me, it's important to share space with Black girls actively. And that informs my research, and so I honor Black girls by listening to Black girls both in the text but also in real life. And so I think that's also going to be important for our practitioners, for researchers, for everyone. It's not enough to just read the books and read the representations. Oh, I know Black girl literacies. We need to know Black girls. Praxis is also here.

STEPHANIE: I believe that Black girl literacies are imaginative and communal. What I mean by this is that Black girls dream, and we often dream in community with other Black girls. In my work, I center these two facets of Black girl literacies by examining speculative fiction texts, including science fiction, fantasy, and horror. I look for the ways that these texts position Black girls, and I look for the ways that it intertwines the past and the present to create the future or the fantastic. I didn't have many book options like this when I was younger, and now that these books exist, I want to explore them and find ways to bring them to other Black girls who need to see themselves fighting dragons, flying through the air, or journeying into Wonderland. Additionally, I want to help Black girls to find community through dreaming, so I create spaces for Black girls to come together, engage with speculative fiction texts, talk to each other, and write with each other. They may talk or write about what's in the text. They may talk or write about what's going on in their lives. They may connect what's happening in the text to what's happening in their own personal stories. Whatever they choose to talk or write about, I want to ensure that they have safe spaces to dream. I want to help create hush harbors for collective dreaming where they know their dreams are valued.

EBONY: As stated before, I didn't initially set out to focus on Black girls in youth media and young adult literature. I wanted to look at how Black children and teens were being positioned in these texts. This is because during my era, so much focus was on the so-called Black male crisis. There was a broad assumption that Black girls were going to be alright. There wasn't as much conversation about Black girls being at risk, or underrepresented, until the 21st century.

During the process of researching and writing *The Dark Fantastic*, I experienced a Black feminist awakening, and began to learn more about the excellent and necessary work of the Black Girl Literacies Collective. Going forward, I will be looking forward to highlighting the stories that Black girls and women tell, both for children and teens, as well as through our scholarly contributions. We have given so much to the world, but all too often, our contributions are overlooked during our lifetimes, then forgotten or "hidden" after we're gone. I want to help write us back into the narrative.

## Considerations for the Field of Literacy Education

### When You Think About How Black Girls Are Represented in Literature, What Are Some Important Considerations for the Field of Literacy Education and Classroom Practice?

EM: Selection. How are we choosing these books? Every book is not for every person just because it has a Black girl. We don't exist in the monolith. So I think it's important, one, for teachers to know how to choose or select books, but also it's important for literacy educators or teacher educators to be well-read in Black girls' literacies and this literature so that we can actually impart that knowledge to the teachers.

I'm even thinking in terms of pedagogy, how we're teaching pedagogy. How do we break out of that single narrative when we're talking about the implementation of Black books, Black girls, or Black girls' literature? So I'm thinking about that, but also genre. What does that look like in terms of Black girls' representation, authorship, cultural insiders and outsiders. Don't just pick a book because it has a Black girl. Teachers have to consider how we approach the book. It makes me wonder, what is the stance that we're bringing to the book in the same way we think about maybe a feminist lens?

We also have to think about reader response. Are we giving agency to Black girls in these spaces? We can't even assume that they're always there, but when we're thinking about response and activities, who's leading conversations and shaping them? Are we prioritizing Black girls' voices, their experiences and expertise? Also how do we encourage students who aren't Black girls to engage these texts, right? How do we negotiate those silences, grapple with their identities and how those identities influence what they're reading and how they understand Black girlhood? So those are some things to consider.

DAHLIA: I love that because it could be, and we've talked about this today, that these books aren't just for Black girls or these literacies aren't just for Black girls. They're important. They create an opening for everybody to learn and to grow, but what's our responsibility when we have Black girls in the class and we read these books to the girls and to everyone else so that it doesn't become an exhibitionist kind of thing. What is the ethics of care around reading certain books with girls?

EM: I feel like Black girls in literature, particularly in contemporary realistic fiction, become these cultural artifacts. Right now, I am really interested in this literature as a form of solidifying our history of Black girlhood, how it manifests, what the literacies are, and how even across time. I'm sure they will maintain. I'm sure the Black Girls' Literacies Framework will still apply, although by what means it might look different. So, I'm just saying Black girlhood seems to be timeless.

STEPHANIE: I'll separate my response into three categories even though I know that they are all intertwined, and their roles often overlap. As Em noted, I think teachers need to think through their selection of texts, not only the ones that are chosen as class reads, but also those that are placed on bookshelves. When students go to select books to read independently, what windows and mirrors are present in the classroom? How recent are the books available? What genre options are included? How many books are there for Black girls to choose from? Thinking through these questions is essential because Black girls are not monolithic. We have such varied interests in our reading choices, so having a Black girl as the protagonist of the story does not automatically correlate to a Black girl liking the story. I think it's also important to think about the novels selected for whole class reads. Too often, books with Black female characters are read in small groups, while canonical texts are taught to the whole class. What does that say about whose representation is most important?

Of course, teachers may not know how to teach non-canonical texts or where to find them, so I think this is where teacher educators come in. We have to think about how we are helping teachers to think about text and the reading of text in our classrooms. We have to think about whether we are helping teachers to locate new books. I know that there are courses on young adult literature and courses on how to teach reading, but are we really assisting preservice teachers to develop the skills needed to approach the teaching of diverse texts that center Black girls? If we aren't, how can we make sure that our future teachers have the knowledge needed to teach these texts? How can we make sure that our future teachers understand the need to learn the history of others as well as their own history before teaching these texts in their classrooms? For us to do this, both teachers and teacher educators must read fiction and nonfiction work written by Black women and girls. We must read about the history of Black women and girls in the United States. We must connect these readings so that we can present this information to our students.

I think this is where literacy researchers come into the picture. We often read the literature and connect it to history and other theoretical and conceptual ideas. We then send our work out to academic journals in hopes that it will be read and implemented somewhere. Still, I think we should make more attempts at creating scholarship that engages different audiences. I love writing academic articles, but I know that the number of readers for the articles will be low because that is the nature of academic writing, especially when so much of it exists behind paywalls. But, what if we summarized our work in a few tweets on Twitter? What if we wrote an op-ed every few articles or so, summarizing our ideas for a different audience? What if we guest blogged on a teacher website as a way to transfer our theoretical implications to a practitioner audience? This is not to say practitioners and other stakeholders cannot read our academic articles, but it is saying that it would be much more efficient to read a short editorial instead of a 25+ page academic treatise. If they want to learn more, then our articles are there. I think this would help various stakeholders in working with Black girl literacies because we could ensure that people in various positions can access the work.

EBONY:  Centering Black girlhood literacies—as well as the literacies of all Black children of marginalized genders—will require broad recognition that there can be no salvation for cisgender Black men or boys unless or until all of us are free. This is not to erase the important foundations laid by Dr. Alfred Tatum, Dr. Jawanza Kunjufu, and other elders whose names we speak, but to build upon their good work by presenting a fuller picture of what our communities have been contending with for centuries here in the United States and throughout the Atlantic world. This will be essential for moving Black education forward from 20th century "endangered Black male" rhetoric. By no means will we abandon our precious boys, just that our future considerations must contain a focus on Black childhood. Black girl literacies research is a vital part of this new paradigm.

It has been said recently that representation in literature, media, and culture isn't enough—that it is not liberatory. However, the fight for representation is vital when the lack of it has implications for the real-world treatment of Black girls. Stories matter. They are how humans share their hopes and fears, their realities, and their dreams. They teach us how to treat each other. If we can provide our young people with a balance of stories showing the full constellation of Black girlhoods, it would do much to shift the perception of our Black girls in the popular imagination.

# SECTION 4

# Centering Black Girls' Digital Literacies

# 10

# URBAN YOUNG ADOLESCENT BLACK GIRLS' DIGITAL MEDIA PRACTICES

## Humanizing the Digital Experience

*Tonya B. Perry, Kristie Williams, and Jameka Thomas*

The 21st-century lifestyle includes the use of technology in almost every aspect. From the timed coffee alarm to the tracking of our steps, our lives and careers are intertwined with science, technology, engineering, and mathematics (STEM) in ways that we have come to take for granted. Although STEM innovations impact our lives in a multitude of ways, women of color are still underrepresented in STEM careers as producers of new ideas and possibilities for the use of technology in society (Espinosa, 2011; Malcom & Malcom, 2011). According to the National Science Foundation Report (NSF) (National Science Foundation, National Center for Science and Engineering Statistics 2013), there were 4,874,000 employed scientists and engineers (both male and female) across all occupational levels in business or industry. However, only 75,000 were Black females, which is less than 2%. The absence of women of color in STEM fields may be attributed to several interrelated problems of support (McPherson & Fuselier-Thompson, 2013): first, girls of color may underestimate their ability to be successful with required academic work (Clewell & Ginorio, 1996); second, girls of color may lack mentorship, role models, and preparation that would sustain their involvement in STEM fields (Hill et al., 2010); and, third, the overall *science culture* (isolationist) is not inviting for girls of color (Guynn, 2019; Espinosa, 2011; Leskin, 2019; Ong, 2005). To create a more open and inclusive STEM community for girls, including girls of color, out-of-school organizations have formed groups such as Black Girls Code, Girl Scouts of America, GEMS (Girls Excelling in Mathematics and Science) and others. Although these groups are intended to support girls' engagement in STEM experiences, we must also examine how such experiences might become more prevalent and valued in school settings (Li, Snow, & White, 2015). We can miss opportunities to cultivate Black girls' agency if we do not understand how to engage them fully to teach them wholly.

The first step in transforming educational contexts around STEM exposure is to understand Black girls' experiences with technology, from their perspectives, based on their ongoing practices (Williams et al., 2019). In the context of in-school and out-of-school settings, we also need to understand any underlying strengths in the ways female students use technology for personal and academic purposes to "read the world" (Freire & Macedo, 1987). Such evidence may support new directions for creating greater equity and more robust interventions in the use of STEM resources in school for Black girls. Price-Dennis (2016) states, "in a world that is rapidly changing and engaging in more multimodal interactions, exploring the digital literacies practices of Black girls is a necessary next step" (p. 338). Through an examination of Black girls' digital media practices, we may be able to establish a "pipeline" across content areas to the STEM field that will build on the skills they enjoy, extend those skills to other new practices, and transform those practices into more relatable academic and creative practices. Digital media are ubiquitous resources for creating, producing, and consuming information and ideas (Hull & Schultz, 2001). For example, during an event to celebrate young writers, one young, soft-spoken Black girl who seemed reluctant to share read her original poetry, "I Am One of a Kind," a powerful rendition of Black girl strength, empowerment, and spiritual quest for self. As we applauded her for her rich writing and delivery, her church member, who also attended the celebration, revealed that her teachers did not know that she was a writer, that her Google Drive was filled with original pieces, and that she wrote but never published her words. It was a missed opportunity, not only in the school environment but also in the community, to tap into her strength and give her an outlet to share her words and to build her digital literacies and, at the same time, to find ways to spread her voice using technology. In a study of critical digital literacy practices with Garcia et al. (2020), black girls used technology to leverage their identity in the world. They sourced technology to create activist identities and utilized technology to express agency. More examples are needed for Black girls to connect STEM to relevance and purpose.

As a beginning point for understanding the ways technology is used among Black girls, we examined their use of digital media in school and out of school. This research is informed by affirming and assets-oriented theories of pedagogy (Jackson, 2005), multimodal learning (Voss, 1996), and Black feminist thought (Collins, 2002), combined to create the Framework for Supporting Black Girls' Digital Media Practices. This framework is closely tied to Muhammad and Haddix's Black Girls' Literacies Framework (2016), which includes six components that are important for engaging Black girls in literacy pedagogies: multiple (multilayered), intellectual, tied to identity, historical, collaborative, and political/critical. This framework ties Black girls to the digital literacies, explicating the ties between being fully human and the use of the technologies as a tool to achieve some level of wholeness and humanity. This chapter merges three theoretical frameworks: Pedagogy of Confidence (Jackson, 2005), Multiple Literacies (Voss, 1996), and Black Feminist Thought (Collins, 2002) to discover how Black urban middle school girls engage in digital media practices via their body, mind, and heart. In this chapter, we will 1) define the Framework for Supporting Black Girls' Digital Media Literacies; 2) review a study of Black girls' digital use; and 3) explore through a case study how effective digital use in the urban middle school classroom can speak to the humanity and wholeness of Black girls.

## BTS: (Behind the Scenes)

Three theoretical frameworks inform this study to construct one larger framework that addresses the potential for teaching Black girls. The first theory, Pedagogy of Confidence (Jackson, 2011), speaks to students taking learning risks outside of their comfort zones, which represents the engagement of the body. The second, the work in Multiple Literacies (Voss, 1996; Kist, 2005; Gee, 2000; Moje, Dillion, & O'Brien, 2000), explains how students see the world from their own perspective and then connect it to academic and transformative practices, which engages the mind. The third theory, Black Feminist Thought (Collins, 2002), discusses the importance of self-empowerment as a Black female, critically thinking about significance of self beyond institutions and other structured systems, which engages the heart. The Framework for Supporting Black Girls' Digital Media Practices encompasses the three major theoretical underpinnings for understanding and promoting Black girls' digital media practices.

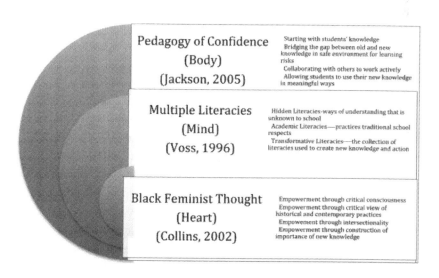

**FIGURE 10.1**   Framework for Supporting Black Girls' Digital Media Practices

Pedagogy of Confidence is the expectation that all students will learn. This is an important theory in the education field because it directly addresses having high expectations for Black students and respecting differences (Jackson, 2011; Ladson-Billings, 2009). This theory uses culture, language, and cognitions to construct an instructional model for students. According to Jackson (2011), Pedagogy of Confidence includes characteristics that strengthen student learning by: 1) finding instructional techniques that address students' learning needs; 2) bridging the gaps between the content students need to know and the students' understanding of concepts using prior knowledge—using cultural experiences and content to enhance the learning; 3) teaching for critical understanding in different disciplines; 4) allowing and facilitating student discovery and inquiry in the learning process; and 5) designing tasks that are performance-based to demonstrate and evaluate student learning. To build this confidence and extend student knowledge, a teacher should affirm students and use their understanding of their culture in the classroom, challenge students beyond their basic skills or comfort levels, connect learning to real life, and create a caring environment for students—an environment that promotes positive interactions (body) to increase various types of activities within the learning process. When students have developed the confidence to learn information, they are more likely to take risks, initiate their own practices, and respect those of others (Jackson, 2011). In the Muhammad and Haddix (2016) model for teaching Black girls, there are six components; two components, collaborative learning and intellectual development, sync well with the model, connecting the Pedagogy of Confidence and the construction of the body—the act of readying, doing, participating, developing, creating, and engaging the body actively in the work of learning.

A second theory, a framework for understanding Multiple Literacies, is premised on the assumption that words and worlds are interrelated; and that meaning-making systems (print and non-print) are deeply enmeshed in the culture and everyday life of people (Voss, 1996; Kendrick, Early, & Chemjor, 2013; Kist, 2005; Gee, 2000; Moje, Dillion, & O'Brien, 2000; Muhammad & Womack 2016). Garcia (2002) explained this concept as how students understand their world is influenced by who they are, what they believe, what they value, how they see themselves in the world, their cultural background, and their interests. The way in which students "see" the world is based on their experiences, ensuring students know that the knowledge (mind) they bring to the classroom is valued and respected (Price-Dennis & Carrion, 2017). Digital media practices and exposures can impact how children view the world. Access to technologies and interaction with digital media allow students to experience their worlds in multiple ways. For example, if a student is a chef, she may use technologies in various ways. A student chef may use digital practices to research information, read the review of other recipes, watch cooking techniques on YouTube, or build her own blog to share cooking tips with other young people. Students can use their multiple "hidden literacies" (the ones rarely recognized in traditional schooling spaces) in school to build "academic literacies" (school application of their ways of understanding by connecting their everyday knowledge with inquiry and problem-solving), as they also rework their new conceptual understanding into "transformative literacies" (learning to use their hidden and academic literacies to create new learning for the world) that impact the larger world (Perry, 2006). For instance, "hidden literacies" (cooking) can build "academic literacies" (problem-solving caloric intake for food recipes) that will grow "transformative literacies" (creating diabetic recipes) (Perry, 2006). Muhammad and Haddix (2016) call this learning "multiple, layered learning," the ability to learn in different modalities and "intellectual stimulation," constantly building new knowledge for yourself and others. The development of the mind, learning in different ways, is important to engage Black girls in the learning process and in transformative practices to create meaningful, impactful learning.

A third lens, Black Feminist Thought, supports an understanding of Black girls' digital media practices in relation with their efforts to withstand oppression. To see oneself as unworthy or incapable is a type of societal oppression that keeps one from learning or attempting new opportunities (Collins, 2002). One form of empowerment is through knowledge development; a second form is active engagement, experiences that counter systemic forms of oppression (Collins, 2002). Through both of these forms of empowerment, Black girls can develop an awareness of and confidence about who they are in order to deconstruct ideologies. "Coming to recognize that one need not believe everything one is told and taught is freeing for many Black women" (Collins, 2002, p. 286), and this happens through increased knowledge, experiences, and interactions that allow one to question and think critically. This permission to learn the way you understand and love who you are in the process is just as important to the learning journey as the engagement of the mind and body. When a Black girl has high expectations of herself and engages this belief (her heart) in this process, she then feels empowered, which leads to the construction of additional new knowledge. Creating a new way to look at learning and life and to challenge the status quo can allow Black girls opportunities to tear down paradigms that do not fit them as learners and develop new ways of thinking and being. Muhammad and Haddix (2016) refer to this as the development of healthy identities, linking the past to the present and creating a critical and political stance. This is the development of the heart of Black girls, building resilience, purpose, self-love, and empowerment in their lives.

Black female urban middle school students, in particular, need to know that they have valuable and unique ways to understand academic and nonacademic worlds. This also suggests that middle school students should be encouraged to see the world through different digital practices, such as building websites, creating blogs, and designing music. However, Black girls are sometimes limited by their own confidence levels, perceived and real, limited access to opportunities, identities related to who they are as learners, and thus, their choices as contributors to fields such as STEM (McPherson & Fuselier-Thompson, 2013). Engaging in respectful and appropriate active learning processes that scaffold their level of involvement, engaging the mind in meaningful and connected learning that builds to transformational learning practices, and engaging in the work that affirms who they are, not only changes them personally, but can also be a helpful framework for building our teaching and learning with and for Black girls (Collins, 2002; Li, Snow, & White, 2015).

## JSYK (Just So You Know): This Is How We Collected the Info

Administering survey data in one urban emergent middle school with a predominantly Black and Latino population, 150 urban middle boys (75) and girls (75) in seventh grade were the participants. (For this study, however, the data collected from the girls will be examined.) The school is located in an urban community in a mid- to large school district in the South. The school housed approximately 400 students and 36 teachers, administrators, and support staff members. About 80% of the students qualified for free or reduced lunch.

The mixed-methods sequential explanatory study included data collection that occurred in two distinct phases: student surveys and teacher interviews. Students in one urban middle school in seventh grade completed a survey that was distributed in English classes. The survey included questions about students' in-school and out-of-school digital media practices. Seventh-grade students responded based on the frequency of each digital practice. For example, students were asked if they updated their status on Facebook and how often (never, once a week, every other day, every day, and more than once a day). The survey included questions for response to frequency scale questions. In addition, two seventh-grade teachers were interviewed about the types of assignments and other digital literacies in which students participate. Also, teachers shared their perceptions of adolescent girls' and boys' digital literacies practices from their perspectives.

The 150 self-reported surveys were coded and input into an Excel database and uploaded to SPSS software. The data were also identified as "female" or "male" when entered. An average score (1–5) for each of the 43 items was calculated. For quality control, this survey was first piloted with a small group of students (10) in a middle school program with different demographics. As the researcher, I wanted to pilot the study in a school that was similar to the targeted group, but I was unable to access another similar school. From the pilot, I learned that the questions were not worded in child-friendly language. As a result, we reworded the questions and added more recent digital practices to the questionnaire (changed BeBo to Facebook, for example). Two seventh-grade teachers were interviewed in 45-minute increments. I then analyzed the quantitative data in three different forms. First, the difference between the male and female score for each response was determined. This information indicated the differences in performance between males and females. Using a T-Test, nine areas show significant differences. Using a nonparametric test, Chi-Test, five areas emerged as showing significant differences. The five significant areas are listed in the next section.

In the second phase, the interview questions for the teachers were semistructured, allowing for follow-up conversations and discussions between the interviewer and participants. Interviews were captured on a digital recorder so that the researcher could refer to the conversation and check for understanding. Transcribing the data was the next step in this process. The researcher transcribed the audiotaped interviews, then converted them into text data. After re-reading the document several times, the researcher conducted the member checking strategy, sending transcripts to participants to verify that the message intended by the participants was accurate in the transcription of the data. After receiving verification feedback from participants, the researcher added or deleted changes to the transcript. Questions and response/clarification statements were highlighted, so as not to confuse the interviewer's words with the participants' words (Creswell, 2002). The researcher coded one document in "text segments," working with participants for member checking (Creswell, 2002), but the primary purpose for the collected information for this study was to examine how, if at all, Black girls in the urban middle school used digital practices in different ways. The primary research questions were as follows:

1.  What types of digital media practices do Black girls engage in during school?
2.  What out-of-school digital literacies practices do Black female students engage in?
3.  How are both the in-school and out-of-school digital practices used?

## ICYMI (In Case You Missed It): This Is What We Found Out

The findings from the study were divided into in-school and out-of-school digital media practices. The two types of in-school digital media practice for girls were *social/communication* and *academic*. Based on the survey, of the 43 indicators, girls participated mostly in the social/communicative digital practices: writing on Facebook by updating their status pages and sending messages to others through the Chat feature, even in school on cell phones and computers. Text messages and emailing were other ways that girls were writing with digital tools. Boys, on the other hand, participated in these types of digital activities less than girls. The survey responses from the boys were more frequent than the girls in academic use of digital in-school practices (even if at inappropriate times such as instructional times during school); boys reported creating animated videos, creating online graphics, posting comments to blogs, and updating and creating their own websites.

Teacher interviews revealed that girls preferred to write essays in class in their paper journals when given a choice of other digital project choices, such as website or blog designs. Also, according to the teachers, Facebook and other social networking tools emerged in discussions among the girls in class, sometimes used as distracting and diverting tools to the academic conversations.

The survey indicated five types of out-of-school digital practices for girls: social/communicative, musical/visual/performative, interactive with technology (non-social), designing, and informative. The girls in the surveys scored most frequently in out-of-school literacies in the performative arts: listening to music, watching YouTube videos, and taking pictures/videos using phones and digital cameras. Also, girls reported watching online television, reading websites, using Facebook, and sending text messages. Many of the adolescent boys also reportedly participated in these same activities as the girls, but the boys had a higher frequency than the girls in the designing and interacting with technology subgroups: recording videos, creating animated videos, drawing animated figures, performing skits/videos, reading and posting to blogs, playing games online, instant messaging, and creating websites.

Based on the study, five areas of performance between males and females were measurably significant:

1. Girls listened to music more than boys (.024).
2. Girls read Facebook more than boys (.003).
3. Girls took pictures with digital cameras more than boys (.002).
4. Girls used cell phones for pictures more than boys (.011).
5. Girls watched online television, especially movies, more than boys (.002).

Although not statistically significant according to the Chi Square-Test, it is worth noting here that boys played online games more than girls (.064), according to this sample. The act of creating a persona, designing strategy, and implementing tactics would be considered a producer skill for this study. Teachers reported that girls liked to write essays in class but opted not to design animation tools or even write their essays outside of a "comfortable" digital genre (preferred Word document to wikis).

## FOMO (Fear of Missing Out): Here's a Recap of What We Learned

Overall, it appears that Black girls in this study were digital consumers, whereas boys were more creators (Table 10.1). For this study, "consumer" is defined as the act of using an existing platform or practice of one skill. In the "consumer" stance, the learner mainly performs one basic act, such as read a blog, take a picture, open a website, or watch a video. The "creator" is defined as the act of using an existing platform or practice and adding to it or changing it. In the "creator"

**TABLE 10.1** Survey Findings

| | Question | Average female score (1–5) | Average Male score (1–5) | T-Test | Chi-Square Test |
|---|---|---|---|---|---|
| 1 | Listening to music | 4 | 3.61 | .018 | .024 |
| 4 | Reading Facebook status | 3.07 | 2.44 | .004 | .003 |
| 23★ | Playing games online | 2.75 | 3.05 | .193 | .064 |
| 25 | Taking pictures with a digital camera | 3.02 | 2.27 | .0002 | .000 |
| 27 | Taking pictures with a cell phone | 3.34 | 2.64 | .003 | .011 |
| 42 | Watching movies on television | 3.76 | 3.05 | .001 | .0002 |

★ No significant difference in this category.

stance, the learner mainly interacts with the digital practice and adds to it, such as reading a blog and posting, taking a picture and posting it on the blog, opening a website and creating a response or creating a website, or watching a video and then posting another one. Young adolescent girls participated in digital literacy practices that were more social as a consumer. Young adolescent boys, however, participated in digital literacy practices that allowed them to create.

## SWYD (Stop What You're Doing): Black Girls' Media Practices Matter

Digital literacies practices can be divided into two different categories: consuming and creating/producing practices. Based on this study, Black girls tended to participate in digital practices that positioned them as consumers. These types of activities required participants to "take-in" and "respond" to the existing digital practices. Boys, however, tended to participate in literacies as creators. In this position, boys actually designed and implemented practices that led to the creation of new practices or products. More of their out-of-school literacies also seemed to involve higher-level interaction and design (responding to blogs, creating an animation video, website design, playing games online, etc.).

It is unclear from this study exactly the type of girls' responses to Facebook friends or the types of text messages they were writing. It could be that they were very much "creator" responses, such three-part mini-videos. This, however, did not emerge in this survey as an activity in which the girls were engaging. What is clear, though, is that overall, Black girls' consuming approach to the literacies may impact the race/gender gap we see in the research, especially tied to STEM-related fields. It is possible that Black girls may not see themselves as scientists, mathematicians, or computer specialists in middle school at such an early age for a variety of reasons (McPherson & Fuselier-Thompson, 2013), thus they tend to choose consuming digital media practices. However, it is possible for Black girls to see themselves in these roles in future careers and in middle school when given roles as digital producers, not options, to develop these skills.

This information can be helpful to teachers and parents of young adolescents as we design academic and out-of-school learning opportunities for students, especially Black girls. Based on this research, I purport that Black girls should be given opportunities, not options, to participate in the types of learning activities that will mold the creator in them and allow active participation and problem-solving, thinking about the larger possibilities of the work, and development of a stronger sense of self-worth. Instead of giving options for the types of projects in class, some consuming and some creating, we should consider designing assignments as "creator" projects, which will encourage girls to hone the digital skills that may or may not be the most comfortable, such as creating an animation video in English class, developing a website for the group in social science, or coding for an app in business class. This is especially important for Black girls, as engaging the body actively in the digital learning process, engaging the mind in how to create transformative work that uses the skills, and engaging the heart in work that affirms their "inner and outer self" are all important.

## IRL (In Real Life): Application of Research With Black Girls in an Urban Middle School Environment

In this section, we will share a case study of a Black girl who was in a seventh-grade English classroom. When conducting this research, we then began to ask the questions, "So what does the Framework for Supporting Black Girls' Digital Media Practices look like in practice? How do we create opportunities for Black girls in a regular classroom setting that provides opportunities for them to develop as digital learners?" The research was conducted by Tonya, and her experience will be reflected in this section.

In response to the research, Mr. Lee, a seventh-grade English teacher, and Tonya created a social justice unit with digital components in which all students participated. The purpose of the critical thinking social justice unit was to create an opportunity for students to engage actively in their world. Students first examined topics around social issues that were important to them. Students then participated in online research and café conversations (with orange juice and doughnuts) in class to dialogue about social issues in the community. After watching online videos about different topics, students each selected one issue for inquiry. After discussing and finalizing a topic, each student was given a camera to take pictures of objects to persuade their audience about their issue. Students researched their topics, wrote argumentative letters, and created an action plan. Some students were able to create digital animations and work with equipment, such as videoing and recording devices. Although Tonya participated with all students, she focused on the development of the Black girls, particularly Leah, during this social justice unit and their growth as users of digital devices. Below is her story.

Leah, a personable 14-year-old, arrived to class late two days in a row. When she arrived, she immediately began to talk to classmates near her seat, even if the teacher was instructing. When the teacher asked her why she was late, she referred to her locker as the culprit for her tardiness: "You know my lock has problems, Mr. Lee." After explaining this to the teacher both days, she proceeded to talk to her classmates and find her mirror and brush in her purse. "Girl, how does my hair look? Is it too much out?" She groomed daily in class after her arrival.

She was also absent for three days at the beginning of the social justice media project. After observing Leah for the first two days and working with classmates, Tonya worked directly with Leah as she decided on her social justice project. She was highly intelligent and engaged in the work. Even though she was late and absent, she was able to catch on very quickly to the assignments, although she was frequently distracted by talk with other young ladies that she often initiated.

Her dialogue consisted of local school gossip that she missed because of tardiness or absences. For example:

"He is seeing her? No way. What?"
"Yes, Girl," a friend whispered. "I know."

She also had a phone that she hid in her pocket because they were not allowed in school, but Leah discreetly removed it from her uniform jacket when no one was looking. The teacher would remind her, though, that his eyes were everywhere in the classroom. She laughed, not shyly, but complied. The teacher shared with the researcher that Leah was very bright but had become more concerned with school social life recently.

Leah and Tonya began working together on her project during the first week. She selected a topic for her social justice unit based on her personal experience. She chose to discuss homelessness that was experienced by children because of family drug use, abuse, and/or abandonment.

I chose this because I see people come into my mom's store who ask for pens. I asked my mom why they need pens. She says that if you are on drugs, you can clean out the inside ink and use the pen to snort cocaine.

Leah continued, "I think that we should do something to help people who seem so helpless. I want the children at least to have something."

During the café conversations, she had an opportunity to talk with partners, including Tonya, about her plan to make a difference. During the activity, she was focused and engaged. At first, she would create a large project in the community to impact homelessness of children who experience trouble because of parents' addiction to drugs. Tonya found Leah very caring and focused on the problem and solution. They worked together to narrow her scope to something that she could better control. Through conversations, she decided on a school-wide coat and sock drive for children.

Leah discussed her plans with Tonya to make a difference. The school-wide coat and sock drive would be supported by the school administration. Leah's argumentative essay would be written to the principal of the school to request support and airtime on the intercom and student morning show to advertise the drive. To champion her cause, she took pictures of "crack cocaine" but really sugar in a spoon, boxes homeless children and families live in, empty pens, and trash cans.

Leah and Tonya also created an animation video about homelessness on Xtranormal/Go Animate to use as advertisement for her coat and sock drive. She selected the characters, their voices, and the dialogue to demonstrate the difference students can make in the lives of others by participating in the drive. Her characters were brown teenagers with jeans and T-shirts, talking as they were walking down the street. The female character was the one talking about the drive, convincing the male character to participate in the worthy project. The animation ended with the male character agreeing to help collect the items for the homeless children who have experienced such difficult circumstances. The language she chose was contemporary and informal.

At the end of the project, Leah wrote that she learned that children could make a difference in the lives of others. She felt good about her choice and her project. She stated, "This project taught me never to look down on anyone in that type of manner." Another young lady commented on homelessness: "the number of foreclosed homes I see in my neighborhood is just plain pitiful. I mean sometimes it's not their fault." Leah ended her work with, "We might be kids, but we can still make a difference." Leah did implement her clothes drive during the school year, as reported by her teacher.

After the social justice project, Leah connected her hidden knowledge (work in the store) with her academic task (writing and research). This interest in knowing more about homeless children was developing into an inquiry-based process. A sense of empowerment was developed as she established a critical understanding of the social issue. We observed the development of her "heart" in this project at this point. She started to feel empowered as a learner as she thought about transformative literacies related to her topic.

Leah's collaboration with others to work actively allowed her to create new knowledge. This building of confidence allowed her to take risks, ask questions, and reformulate her understanding of her project. At this point she was also creating transformative literacies, a project or understanding that reaches beyond the desk at school to the school community. Leah used digital practices to write her essay on the computer, research her topic and learn facts about her project, advertise her drive, and create a commercial for her collection efforts. The focus of the project itself was not digital literacies, but digital tools were used to empower her as a learner and activist.

Leah used technology to construct her message to classmates about her social justice topic. Her increased confidence led her to take "learning chances" and delve into digital platforms that were new to her. Because she felt connected to her topic (relevance) and had experienced some success in class sharing her topic (collaboration and academic knowledge), Leah's level of empowerment increased. This made it easier for her to develop her cartoon piece.

The highest level of learning is transformative practices. Leah was able to identify something she liked and cared about that was "hidden" from the usual school environment, applied "academic" practices to her topic through research and collaboration, and created a "transformative" project that reached beyond paper and desk. Digital practices played a role in every step of her work. As a result, the work was enhanced and Leah's interaction with technology had perhaps increased her willingness to learn more digital practices, developing an increased sense of empowerment.

After Tonya analyzed her interactions with Leah in Mr. Lee's class, she found Leah was social (not an isolationist) and preferred to interact with others. A career working alone, which is how girls may perceive the STEM field, might not capture Leah's attention. Learning segments in class that are perceived as individual or less collaborative did not appeal to Leah. In response to this knowledge, in class, whenever possible, the teacher and Tonya provided opportunities for the girls to interact and develop socially. Tonya and Mr. Lee realized this choice created opportunities for students to chat about other topics and move away from academic discussion (as seen earlier with a discussion about hair). Peer-mediated talk, though, is an important part of the learning process and requires students to learn how to navigate their own language and the timing of tasks. This is also an important part of learning to implement digital practices, which are collaborative and discursive practices that require peer and self-regulation. If we want them to be successful with building this skill set, we need to entrust learning to the girls using gradual release practices as they move more to independence.

We also noticed the use of digital tools in school varies from school to school. In this environment, digital devices are seen as a distraction. However, the girls had to participate in digital practices; there were no options to use only paper and pencil for this assignment. In this social justice unit, digital tools were just that: tools for learning. The focus was on the research and writing; digital platforms helped the girls do the work and there were choices for them to select.

Creating policies that allow digital tools in school takes a shift in mindset. Viewing the tool as an asset-based, out-of-school, "hidden" literacy practice of value that can easily translate into academic school practices can be difficult, especially when the teacher and student view the use of the device differently. What would happen if devices were seen as friendly and helpful as opposed to distractions? As 21st-century teachers, our practices should reflect students' needs to incorporate technology. Our data has helped us to understand the importance of supporting students in developing healthy strategies to incorporate digital media practices.

From the three-week project and working with Leah closely, three themes emerged: increased student engagement, relevancy to life, and purposeful, empowered learning of new skills. Leah engaged in class, and her attendance increased during the project. Also, the number of tardies decreased and the number of classroom interruptions were minimal as the project continued. The student overall was very focused on her individual project and the implementation plan. She sometimes asked, "When are you coming back so we don't have to do work?" From this statement, it was implied that the social justice project did not seem like "work" because there were no worksheets. The student did not perceive this as learning because it was engaging. School had taught her that learning was not engaging. Engaging work was fun, which was not school. Therefore, the social justice project was not really schoolwork, according to the information she relayed to her teacher, which was eye-opening: school is not synonymous with engaging and insightful learning.

What does impactful learning look like? Leah found a larger purpose for learning through the social justice project. She developed a project that could impact the larger community, which required research of the topic, argumentative letter writing, and plan development. She used her learning for a cause that she considered worthwhile. Leah used animation to take her project one step further. She used non-traditional school practices to impact and persuade. The data suggests she learned without *realizing* she was learning.

## BTW (By the Way): Let's Talk About It

Overall, Leah did not see herself as a change agent prior to the project. When asked how students use out-of-school literacies or "things they like to do at home," most responded to uses for entertainment and informal communication. After the project, however, the girls did begin to use media, writing, and visual literacies to impact change, whereas before the project, most girls used the literacies for mainly entertainment/recreational/communicative purposes. There was little connection between what students like to do at home and their in-school practices.

All of the girls in the class, but particularly the ones engaged most intently, felt as if their voices were heard by their classmates and someone in the community. The teacher reported that the students wanted to continue to do this type of learning, but the reality of test preparation and other mandates kept him from structuring his class in an inquiry-based manner to build their critical literacy skills for the rest of the term.

As we think about educating our Black girls and cultivating their bodies, minds, and hearts for what is ahead of them as young women, we must also think about redesigning curriculum and teaching pedagogies that challenge yet support learning. Teaching Black girls deliberately and purposefully to engage in digital practices can expand their knowledge base and their voices beyond the consumer stance. Teaching Black girls digital media practices expands their horizons as they too can participate in producing their own knowledge and creating their own futures with opportunities (McArthur, 2016).

The development of successful digital practices can be aligned with the engagement of the mind, body, and heart. When teachers and community leaders build around these three components, the humanization of digital learning can create an engaging space for Black girls. Technology then becomes doable, understandable, relatable, purposeful, and interesting instead of isolationist (Espinosa, 2011) and difficult to achieve (Clewell & Ginorio, 1996). Black girls can see themselves as producers of knowledge and not just consumers, developing new opportunities to share their voices and design new knowledge through digital media practices. Opportunities for them to develop as critical, self-assured, multi-layered digital learners comes from a humanizing experience to build their minds, body, and hearts, creating a wholeness in the process.

## Middle School Assessment Media Practices Survey

**What you do:** Read each statement and fill in the circle that best describes your answer. Please mark how often you do the following activities

| Question | Never | Once a week | At least every other day | Every day | More than once a day |
|---|---|---|---|---|---|
| **When you are not at school, how often do you . . .** | | | | | |
| 1.   Listen to music on the radio/internet? | | | | | |
| 2.   Write your own songs? | | | | | |
| 3.   Listen to music on an iPod/phone? | | | | | |
| 4.   Read someone else's Facebook status? | | | | | |
| 5.   Update your status on Facebook? | | | | | |
| 6.   Look at someone else's pictures on Facebook? | | | | | |
| 7.   Create photo albums on Facebook? | | | | | |

| Question | Never | Once a week | At least every other day | Every day | More than once a day |
|---|---|---|---|---|---|
| 8.  Message on Facebook Messenger? | | | | | |
| 9.  Watch YouTube videos? | | | | | |
| 10. Record your own videos using camera? | | | | | |
| 11. Watch Xtranormal/ animated videos? | | | | | |
| 12. Create Xtranormal/ animated videos? | | | | | |
| 13. Watch cartoons? | | | | | |
| 14. Draw cartoons? | | | | | |
| 15. Watch graphic novels/ comic as a series on TV or on the internet? | | | | | |
| 16. Create graphic novels? | | | | | |
| 17. Watch TV? | | | | | |
| 18. Perform skits? | | | | | |
| 19. Read text messages? | | | | | |

**When you are not at school, how often do you. . .**

| | | | | | |
|---|---|---|---|---|---|
| 20. Send text messages? | | | | | |
| 21. Read other people's blogs? | | | | | |
| 22. Post comments on a blog? | | | | | |
| 23. Play games online? | | | | | |
| 24. Make phone calls on Skype/Google? | | | | | |
| 25. Take pictures with camera? | | | | | |
| 26. Share digital pictures online? | | | | | |
| 27. Take pictures on a cell phone? | | | | | |
| 28. Send pictures on a cell phone? | | | | | |
| 29. Receive pictures on a cell phone? | | | | | |
| 30. Read emails? | | | | | |
| 31. Send emails? | | | | | |
| 32. Instant message? | | | | | |
| 33. Look at websites? | | | | | |
| 34. Create or update your own website? | | | | | |
| 35. Use the internet to help do homework? | | | | | |
| 36. Watch the news? | | | | | |
| 37. Watch TV while doing homework? | | | | | |

| Question | Never | Once a week | At least every other day | Every day | More than once a day |
|---|---|---|---|---|---|
| 38.  Listen to the radio while doing homework? | | | | | |
| 39.  Listen to an iPod while doing homework? | | | | | |
| 40.  Go see a movie at the movie theater? | | | | | |
| 41.  Rent movies? | | | | | |
| 42.  Watch movies on TV? | | | | | |
| 43.  Watch TV or movies online? | | | | | |

**More about you.** Please choose the response that describes you.
I am
- Male
- Female

_____

I am _____ years old.
My race is
- White
- White, non-Hispanic
- **African American**
- Hispanic
- Asian
- Pacific Islander
- Native American
- Other _____

My grade in Language Arts is closest to
- A
- B
- C
- D
- F

Language
- I speak English only
- I can speak more than one language

Which language or languages? _____

I can get on the internet at home
- Yes
- No
- Sometimes

## References

Clewell, B. C., & Ginorio, A. B. (1996). Examining women's progress in the sciences from the perspective of diversity. In C. Davis, A. B. Ginorio, C. S. Hollenshead, B. B. Lazarus, P. M. Rayman, & Associates (Eds.), *The equity equation: Fostering the advancement of women in the sciences, mathematics, and engineering* (pp. 163–231). San Francisco: Jossey-Bass Publishers.

Collins, P. H. (2002). *Black feminist thought: Knowledge, consciousness, and the politics of empowerment* (2nd ed.). New York, NY: Routledge.

Creswell, J. (2002). *Educational research: Planning, conducting, and evaluating qualitative research.* Columbus: Merrill Prentice Hall.

Espinosa, L. L. (2011). Pipelines and Pathways: Women of color in undergraduate STEM majors and the college experiences that contribute to persistence. *Harvard Education Review, 81*(2), 209–240.

Freire, P., & Macedo, D. (1987). *Literacy: Reading the word and the world.* South Hadley, MA: Bergin & Garvey.

Garcia, D. (2002). Making multiple literacies visible in the writing classroom: From Cupareo, Guanajuato, to Cal State, Monterey Bay. *Social Justice, 29*(4), 122–136.

Garcia, P., Fernández, C., & Okonkwo, H. (2020). Leveraging technology: How Black girls enact critical digital literacies for social change. *Learning, Media and Technology,* 1–18.

Gee, J. P. (2000). *Knowing in and through discourses.* Presentation, National Council of Teachers of English 90th Annual Convention, Denver, CO.

Guynn, J. (2019, January 24). Good ol' boys network, meet Black girl magic: Black, female entrepreneurs are changing Silicon Valley. *USA Today.* www.usatoday.com

Hill, C., Corbett, C., & St. Rose, A. (2010). *Why so few?: Women in science, technology, engineering, and mathematics.* Washington, DC: American Association of University Women.

Hull, G., & Schultz, K. (2001). Literacy and learning out of school: A review of theory and research. *Review of Educational Research, 7*(4), 575–611.

Jackson, Y. (2005). Unlocking the potential of African American students: Keys to reversing underachievement. *Theory Into Practice, 44*(3), 203–210.

Jackson, Y. (2011). *The pedagogy of confidence: Inspiring high intellectual performance in urban schools.* New York, NY: Teachers College Press.

Kendrick, M., Early, M., & Chemjor, W. (2013). Integrated literacies in rural Kenyan girls' secondary school journalism club. *Research in Teaching of English, 47*(4), 391–419.

Kist, W. (2005). *New literacies in action: Teaching and learning in multiple media.* New York: Teachers College.

Ladson-Billings. (2009). *The dream keepers: Successful teachers of African American children.* San Francisco: Josey-Bass.

Leskin, P. (2019, September 20). Google sued by engineering executive alleging she was paid "hundreds of thousands" less than her male peers and demoted for complaining. *Business Insider.* www.businessinsider.com

Li, Jia, Snow, C., & White, C. (2015). Urban adolescent students and technology: Access, use and interest in learning language and literacy. *Innovation in Language Learning and Teaching*, *9*(2), 143–162. http://dx.doi.org/10.1080/17501229.2014.882929

Malcom, L., & Malcom, S. (2011). The double bind: The next generation. *Harvard Educational Review*, *81*(2), 162–172.

McArthur, S. A. (2016). Black girls and critical media literacy for social activism. *English Education*, *48*(4), 362–379.

McPherson, E., & Fuselier-Thompson, D. R. (2013). Minority women in STEM: A valuable resource in the global economy. *Journal of the International Association for the Study of the Global Achievement Gap*, *5*(1), 45–58.

Moje, E. B., Dillion, D. R., & O'Brien, D. (2000). Reexamining roles of learner, text, and context in secondary literacy. *Journal of Educational Research*, *93*, 165–180.

Muhammad, G., & Haddix, M. (2016). Centering Black girls' literacies: A review of literature on the multiple ways of known of Black girls. *English Education*, *48*(4), 299–336.

Muhammad, G. E., & Womack, E. (2016). From pen to pin: The multimodality of Black girls (Re)writing their lives. *Ubiquity: The Journal of Literature, Literacy and the Arts*, *2*(2), 6–45.

National Science Foundation, National Center for Science and Engineering Statistics. (2013). *Women, minorities, and persons with disabilities in science and engineering: 2013*. Special Report NSF 13-304. Arlington, VA. http://www.nsf.gov/staistics/wmpd/

Ong, M. (2005). Body projects of young women of color in physics: Intersections of gender, race, and science. *Social Problems*, *52*, 593–617.

Perry, T. B. (2006). Multiple literacies and middle school students. *Theory into Practice*, *45*(6), 328–336.

Price-Dennis, D. (2016). Developing curriculum to support Black girls' literacies in digital spaces. *English Education*, *48*(4), 337–361.

Price-Dennis, D., & Carrion, S. (2017). Leveraging digital literacies for equity and social justice. *Language Arts*, *93*(3), 190–195.

Voss, M. M. (1996). *Hidden literacies: Students learning at home and at school*. Portsmouth, NH: Heinemann.

Williams, W. S., & Moody, A. L. (2019). Analyzed selfie: Stereotype enactment, projection, and identification among digitally native Black girls. *Women & Therapy*, *42*(3–4), 366–384.

# 11

# BLACK ADOLESCENT GIRLS' MULTIMODALITIES IN OUT-OF-SCHOOL LITERACY SPACES

*Delicia Tiera Greene*

The emergence of digital technologies has greatly impacted the literacy teaching and learning landscape. Despite the potential and possibilities digital literacies afford Black girls in the urban secondary literacy classroom, school spaces deem their literacy practices, historical traditions, and cultural nuances invisible. As double minorities, both Black and female, Black girls are confronted with various forms of oppression that work in conjunction with other forms of oppression to produce social injustice and marginalization. In a society designed to oppress them, Black girls often draw upon their out-of-school digital literacy practices, steeped in activism, to serve as tools of survival and resistance to disrupt and counter dominant narratives of who they are (Collins, 2000; Price-Dennis et al., 2017). There continues to be a tremendous gap between Black girls' in-school and out-of-school digital literacies.

## Disrupting Traditional Models of Digital Literacies in Schools

Traditional models of literacy instruction often privilege canonical texts, teacher-centered instruction, and print-based activities and assessments (Haddix & Sealey-Ruiz, 2012; Price-Dennis & Matthews, 2017; Vasudevan, 2006). In instances in which technology is incorporated into the curricula, literacy teachers often do not use the platform for students of color to focus on agency, identity construction, or meaning making, but instead use it solely to complete tasks (Dooley, Ellison, & Welch, 2016; Ellison, 2017; Vasudevan, 2006). Literacy teachers often incorporate digital technologies in school spaces in ways that it is decontextualized and not grounded in the lived experiences and literate lives of students of color.

> Digital technologies are used in formal institutions in urban communities as a curricular tool to educate students about new literacy, instead of being used in a transformative and emancipatory way to engage the critical capabilities that students already bring to new literacy.
>
> *(Vasudevan & Hill, 2008, p. 2)*

Historically, Black adolescent girls' literacy practices in digital spaces are often lumped together with mainstream populations, resulting in the invisibility of Black girls' literacy practices in digital spaces.

In addition, Black adolescents often do not see themselves represented in traditional forms of literature, which further silences their voices. However, Black girls are represented and engaged in more culturally conscious forms of texts, such as street literature texts (Gibson, 2010; Greene, 2015). Black girls tend to be drawn to the textual features, recurring themes, and cultural practices embedded in street literature texts (Morris, 2012), including storylines situated in urban communities in major cities (Morris, 2012); linguistic styles rooted in African American Vernacular English; female protagonists faced with life experiences often considered taboo, such as sexual abuse, teen pregnancy, and physical abuse (Morris et al., 2006); and popular culture elements, specifically hip-hop aesthetics (Jocson, 2005; Mahiri, 2005; Morrell, 2004), as well as the social issues present in urban communities (Jocson, 2005). This allows Black adolescent girls to engage in lived experiences and language practices rooted in their own cultural backgrounds (Sims-Bishop, 1983; Brooks, 2006).

Digital spaces provide opportunities for Black adolescent girls to experiment with their multiple identities, allowing opportunities for them to shape and reshape their representations of self and the world around them (Greene, 2015). Despite Black girls' appeal to street literature texts and digital technologies, there continues to be contention between their out-of-school and in-school literacies. The purpose of this study is to explore the ways in which Black adolescents enact their literacy and language practices in an online out-of-school street literature book club. This chapter is significant because it examines a growing yet underdeveloped body of scholarly work focusing on Black girls' digital literacies in an out-of-school street literature book club.

## Black Girls' Literacies Framework

The Black Girls' Literacies Framework is a theoretical framework that centers Black girls' racialized and gendered identities in an effort to engage them in literacy pedagogies in the urban secondary literacy classroom (Muhammad & Haddix, 2016). Muhammad and Haddix (2016) identified six components that center

Black girls' ways of knowing and engagement of literacy practices. They identify that Black girls' literacies are (1) multiple; (2) tied to identities; (3) historical; (4) collaborative; (5) intellectual; and (6) political/critical. The Black Girls' Literacies Framework encompasses the racialized and gendered experiences of Black girls within a digital literacy context. This framework also accounts for Black girls' ways of being and knowing in an effort to develop pedagogical strategies that honor Black girls' literacy practices, cultural nuances, and historical traditions in the digital age. According to Richardson (2003), Black girls' literacies entail "enacting special knowledge and ways of being to navigate the world" (p. 329). Richardson (2003) further argues that Black girls' ways of being and knowing entail their "cultural identities, social location, and practices that influence how they make meaning and assert themselves socio-politically in out-of-school and in-school contexts" (p. 329). This framing also provides insight into embedding cultural and equity-based pedagogies into literacy instruction to support Black girls. In this qualitative inquiry, I draw upon this framing because it informs my understanding of the many ways Black girls engage in literacy practices across spheres.

## Black Girls' Literacies

Black girls' literacy experiences are important to explore because they have historically been left out of engagements with literature (Brooks, Browne, & Hampton, 2008; Henry, 1998; Richardson, 2002; Sutherland, 2005; Wissman, 2011). Gibson (2016) explored the ways in which African American girls engage with street literature texts. Gibson explored Black girls' appeal to street literature, as well as their perceptions about the street literature text, *Supreme Clientele*. Drawing on a conceptual framework at the intersection of Reader Response Theory, Critical Literacy, and New Literacy Theory and employing a literature circle instructional model, Gibson (2016) found female participants drew upon gendered roles within their own lives to make meaning of female and male relationships in street literature texts. Gibson (2016) also found female participants held contradictory views about the representations of women in the texts, often viewing them as both "powerful and foolish." Gibson (2016) also found participants were critical of the female protagonists' choices and learned from the protagonists' experiences, which allowed them to view the texts as cautionary tales.

Henry (1998) examined Black girls' use of voice in a reading and writing program in a middle school classroom and found that participants displayed difficulty using their own voices in their writing. Drawing upon a Black Feminist framework, Henry (1998) found that Black girls often conformed to patriarchal norms in society and drew upon issues critical to their own lives. Similarly, in a qualitative study, Sutherland (2005) examined societal norms and documented the literacy practices, identity, and social positioning of Black girls as they discussed Toni Morrison's *The Bluest Eye* in their high school English classroom.

Sutherland (2005) found that Eurocentric views of beauty served as boundaries in their lives. Sutherland (2005) also found that other people's assumptions about Black girls served as boundaries as well. The participants in the Sutherland study viewed the text as a tool for understanding, questioning, and positioning themselves in the world. Sutherland (2005) also argued that texts with characters that are from the same racial and gender group are self-affirming for Black girls. Sutherland (2005) further asserts that Black girls should see themselves reflected in the literature through the implementation of more inclusive, culturally relevant, and girl-centered curricula.

Gibson (2016), Henry (1998), and Sutherland's (2005) studies highlight the importance of Black girls seeing images of themselves, in order to draw upon their racialized and gendered positionalities to make meaning of texts and shape and reshape their female identity formation. Sims-Bishop (1990) argues that

> literature transforms human experience and reflects it back to us, and in that reflection we can see our own lives and experiences as part of the larger human experience. Reading, then, becomes a means of self-affirmation, and readers often seek their mirrors in books.
>
> *(p. x)*

Hence, Black adolescent girls should find characters and thematic elements that reflect their personal interest and lived experiences.

## Black Girls' Digital Literacies

Employing Muhammad and Haddix's (2016) conceptual framework, Price-Dennis (2016) examined the ways in which nine Black girls took up critical literacies across various modalities to address social issues in a 5th grade language arts classroom. Price-Dennis (2016) and her team implemented multimodalities into the curriculum units, including poetry, children's literature, song lyrics, Ted Talks, music videos, Web 2.0 apps and platforms, tablets, and desktop computers. Price-Dennis (2016) found that "developing curricula that focused on social issues stemming from current events created spaces for Black girls to draw on critical literacy practices with digital tools to reshape how they demonstrated their thinking about social justice, power, and activism" (p. 348). Price-Dennis (2016) highlights three approaches to developing curricula with digital tools for Black girls' literacies: (1) promoting exploration of social issues that affect the lives of Black Girls; (2) providing opportunities for Black girls to exercise agency and confidence with digital literacies; and (3) creating space across modalities for Black girls to (re)imagine what it means to be a learner (Price-Dennis, 2016, pp. 348–353).

Similarly, Hall (2011) examined the literacy practices of three African American girls and their multiple identities as digital storytellers in a preparatory summer program. Employing a Critical Literacy and Black Feminist Thought framework, Hall (2011) also examined how their digital literacies practices informed their historical legacies. The girls used digital tools, including the Internet, and culturally relevant narratives that were steeped in cultural and linguistic histories (Hall, 2011) and composed a digital video response. Hall (2011) found that Black girls used digital technologies as counternarratives as they negotiated their identities around instances of pain, suffering, and healing. Hall (2011) also found that the interplay of linguistic styles was indicative of multiple subject positions.

Kendrick, Early, and Chemjor (2013) examined the writing practices of Kenyan girls in an afterschool secondary journalism club situated in a rural Kenyan secondary school. Kendrick, Early, and Chemjor (2013) implemented multiple modalities into the club, including digital cameras, voice recorders, and laptops. The scholars co-constructed their new literacy practices, new identities, and linguistic histories. Kendrick, Early, and Chemjor (2013) found that Black girls' competence as writers occurred gradually when they were given opportunities to experiment and construct identities as journalists (journalistic ways). They also found that writing served as counternarratives and provided affordances to speak back to dominant narratives.

Muhammad and Womack (2015) examined how Black adolescent girls make sense of representations of Black girlhood through the use of multimodal literacy. Muhammad and Womack (2015) examined their print texts ("penning"), as well as multimodalities ("pinning"), including Prezi, Pinterest, images, and video. Muhammad and Womack (2015) found that representations in both studies revealed that girls penned or pinned against three types of representations: (1) physical beauty and health: portrayals of being viewed as unpretty or unhealthy; (2) sexualizing and objectification: portrayals of being overly sexual; and (3) education: portrayals of being uneducated (p. 20).

Muhammad and Womack (2015), Hall (2011), Kendrick, Early, and Chemjor (2013), Hall (2011), and Price-Dennis, 2016 highlight how Black girls use digital technologies to construct their identities and counter dominant narratives. Their work also (re)imagines literacy teaching and learning where Black girls assume agency and autonomy as they engage in digital technologies and teachers accommodate Black girls academically by shifting their roles to a support capacity.

## Critical Discourse Analysis Framework

The Critical Discourse Analysis (CDA) framework was the method employed to frame the study and interpret data (Fairclough, 1989; Gee, 2005; Rogers, 2003). Chouliaraki and Fairclough (1999) argue that discourse is inherently political and rooted in social relationships and social identities, with a focus on patterns of power and privilege. Hence, language cannot be considered neutral because it is situated within political spheres with focuses on social, racial, gender, economic, and religious influences. I drew upon CDA because it accounted for the socio-political influences embedded in Black adolescent girls' literacy and language practices, which are often vastly different from dominant literacy, linguistic, and discourse patterns (Rogers et al., 2005). CDA also accounted for the ways in which Black girls negotiate their identities within and across literacy contexts. CDA also accounted for the gendered and racialized identities of Black girls and the socio-political influences embedded in their literacy and language practices.

## Methodology and Research Design

A qualitative research design was selected for this study. A qualitative research design was most appropriate since the study was context-specific, specifically focusing on how digital literature discussions influence Black adolescent girls' meaning making processes. A qualitative research design was also selected to examine how Black adolescent girls make meaning of literacy and make sense of their lives and the world around them, as well as how the meaning making process shapes their representation of self (Bogdan & Biklen, 2007). A qualitative research design was also selected to focus on how Black girls address social injustice.

The primary focal site was the online social networking site Facebook, and the secondary focal site was an urban public library. Dunbar Public Library, nestled in a small urban community in the northeastern region of the United States, was the community space used to conduct focus group interviews. Facebook was selected as the most appropriate online social networking tool because it did not have character limitations, which allowed for richer data. The selection of Dunbar Public Library fulfilled a community need, providing an opportunity to increase literacy programming that was teen-focused, girl-centered, and culturally relevant.

## Data Collection

Data were collected for a month and a half (six weeks). The pool of data derived from a range of data collection sources: (a) online Facebook discussion; (b) semi-structured focus group interviews; (c) field observations; and (d) researcher journal.

### Facebook Online Street Literature Book Club

The online discussions served as the primary source of data in this study. The online discussions occurred over an eight-week period. The online discussions were asynchronous and occurred over the course of two weeks during a book cycle. The facilitator's level of engagement entailed posing discussion prompts during each online discussion, as well as engaging in online discussions. Each discussion prompt focused on a particular social issue based on a prevalent theme in a particular text. The participants contributed approximately 3–4 posts during a two-week book discussion cycle.

## Selection of Street Literature Texts

Drawing upon a Black Feminist epistemology, participants were provided a level of self-expression, autonomy, and choice in selecting street literature titles. Participants selected four texts from a list of ten street literature texts. This chapter focuses on one of the four street literature texts selected, which includes *PUSH* by Sapphire.

## Semi-Structured Focus Groups

Focus group interviews supplemented the online discussions and served as "targeted data" (Morgan, 1997; Rubin & Rubin, 2005), providing opportunities to clarify responses, for follow-up questions, and for the probing of responses (Stewart & Shamdasani, 1990). The interviews also provided an opportunity to further engage in intimate conversations with participants about their online experiences. Drawing upon a Black Feminist perspective, focus groups provided a space of group resistance narratives, which validated Black girls' everyday experiences. Participants met face-to-face once in a book cycle at the end of a week of online discussions. Focus group discussions occurred over a four-week period and lasted about an hour. In their spare time, participants regularly frequented the library; however, they did not usually frequent this particular library prior to the study because it had limited teen programs. Participants built rapport prior to the beginning of the study through a book club meet and greet that the facilitator organized.

## Field Observations

Field observations entailed immersing myself in the day-to-day lives of adolescent participants and examining their literacy and language practices across contexts, specifically digital and face-to-face spaces (Creswell, 1998; Dewalt & Dewalt, 2002). Field observations provided a rich source of data in the virtual environment, including linguistic styles and literate subjectivities, as well as in the face-to-face environment, including multimodal data such as facial expressions, voice intonations, nonverbal cues, and other forms of body language.

## Researcher Journal

In a study focused on race and gender, the researcher journal was auto-ethnographic in nature and used as a self-reflexive tool designed to balance and account for my multiple identities as an African American woman, community-engaged researcher, facilitator, and book club participant (Fetterman, 2010).

Turning the lens on myself and examining my social location through auto-eth-nographic accounts served as a means of balancing my biases and accounting for how my positionality functioned in my role as book club facilitator, participant, and researcher and impacted my interaction with Black girl participants within and across contexts.

## Participants

Six female adolescent participants between the ages of 12 and 17 participated in the research study. The study employed two types of sampling: purposive sampling and convenience sampling. Employing a purposive sampling (Patton, 1990), the selection criteria included the following: (1) Black adolescent girls between the ages of 12 and 17; (2) Black adolescent girls that were avid readers of street literature texts; (3) Black adolescent girls that were users of digital tools, specifically the social networking site Facebook; and (4) Black adolescent girls that had immediate access to technology. Employing a convenience sampling entailed selecting participants that I had worked with on previous community literacy projects. Each participant brought rich perspectives and experiences to the research project.

## Critical Discourse Analysis: Orders Across the Institution

Fairclough's (1989) three-tiered analytical framework examines the interplay of the text and the social world by focusing on the linkages between talk at the situational, institutional, and societal level across three levels of interacting or orders of discourse: genre, discourse, and style. This study focuses specifically on the institutional level, which consisted of the out-of-school digital and the face-to-face spaces, focusing on the way in which context influences how Black girls construct their identities and represent self through their discussions of street literature texts. Orders of discourse each represented a particular aspect of representation of self.

Genres are "ways of interacting" and represent Black girls' use of linguistic devices in discussions, such as agreement, disagreement, interruptions, or use of pronouns (Chouliaraki & Fairclough, 1999). Discourses are "ways of representing" and describe how knowledge is represented and from what perspective. Luke (2000) argues that discourses are "systematic clusters of themes, statements, ideas, and ideologies" (p. 456) that detailed Black girls' positioning around social issues depicted in street literature texts. Styles are "ways of being" and represented Black girls' position taking (Rogers, 2003) through the use of local and dominant linguistic strategies (Richardson, 2007; Smitherman, 2006). The first level of analysis was initial coding and entailed multiple readings of the data sets. The second level of analysis entailed coding data for each order of discourse (genre, discourse, style) across the institutional context. Data were transcribed manually.

## Findings

Online book club discussions, as well as face-to-face focus group interviews, around street literature texts served as safe spaces for Black girls to represent self and construct their identities. It is important to highlight that digital technologies served as a critical tool that allowed Black girls to engage in activist and social justice work by addressing the Black female protagonist's experiences, as well as reflecting on their own lived experiences. *PUSH* by Sapphire was the street literature text that participants read. The story details the experiences of an illiterate 16-year-old African American girl named Claireece Precious Jones, who endures hardship at the hands of society, her parents, and the school system. Precious endures being physically abused by her mother and sexually abused by her father, which resulted in birthing two children by her father. In this section, I illustrate how Black girls self-represent through their discussions of two prominent themes in the text *PUSH*: the Black female condition and Black motherhood.

## Finding 1: Representations of Self Re-Imagined by the Use of Multiple Literacy Practices (Multiple, Tied to Identity, Collaborative)

I posed the following question to the online Facebook group: *What was your initial reaction after reading PUSH?* The discussion below details a conversation exchange between Vanessa and Denise.

1  **Vanessa:** *When reading the first few chapters in my head I was just watching*
2  *Precious the movie but then it got more in depth than the movie about her*
3  *life and I learned things I didn't know. Although I haven't gone through the*
4  *same things as precious I felt a connection just being a girl. We are all*
5  *teenagers and go through obstacles at school and we still face rejection at*
6  *some points. I really liked the book.*

Vanessa represents self through literacy practices that are multiple and tied to her own identity, as well as collaborative. Although the initial discussion was based on the book *PUSH*, Vanessa's discourses around literacy are multiple, relating the text *PUSH* to cinematic elements in the movie *Precious*. Vanessa draws upon both the narrative elements in the text and cinematic elements in the movie to make sense of Precious and the world around her. As Vanessa engaged in multiple literacy practices, she also centered her own gendered identity in relation to Precious. Vanessa employs both distancing language ("I haven't gone through the same things as Precious") as well as gendered associating language ("I felt a connection just being a girl") to represent self. Vanessa also represents self by highlighting a personal connection with Precious and participants in the online book discussions ("We are all teenagers") and employs genre devices to co-construct the similarities in their experiences ("We . . . go through obstacles at school and we still face rejection at some points"). By employing the pronoun "we," Vanessa co-constructs knowledge with the female protagonist Precious as well as with other Black girls in the book club. Their experiences affirm Vanessa's representation of self.

## Finding 2: Representations of Self Grounded in the Collective Black Girl Experience (Collaborative, Tied to Identity, and Intellectual)

7 **Denise:** *I agree with Vanessa; Our experiences as young Black women in*
8 *society is somewhat similar. Although our situations are not as deep as*
9 *Precious' we still have similar experiences. It also shows me that being*
10 *Black is somewhat looked at as a downfall or a disadvantage. That*
11 *we cannot really even count on society & be so dependent on*
12 *them but on ourselves*

Denise represents self through literacy practices that are collaborative, tied to identity, and intellectual. By agreeing with Vanessa, Denise responds to her attempt at solidarity and illustrates her own gendered positioning in relation to Precious' and Vanessa's gendered positioning. Denise takes solidarity a step further and co-constructs knowledge through her position of Black female solidarity with Black girls via the use of gendered and racialized associating language, as well as the pronoun "our" ("our experiences as a young Black woman in society is somewhat similar"). Denise employs genre devices through her use of the pronoun "our." Denise demonstrates that she self-represents individually as well as collectively. It is both the individual representation of self and the shared narratives of the Black female condition that confirms for Denise Black girls' position in society. Denise represents self and society by highlighting personal connections with Precious' lived experiences and society's perceptions of Black girls (Brooks, 2006; Richardson, 2008). Denise's discourse further highlights the hegemonic ideologies at play and their impact on Black girls (Richardson, 2008). She highlights how being a Black girl is viewed negatively and that self-reliance is the only means of survival and security.

Denise uses Precious' experiences as a lens to make meaning of the texts, but also to assess how Black females in the 21st century are treated in society (Muhammad & McArthur 2015; Richardson, 2007). She uses her experiences and Precious' experiences to draw closer to selfhood and to highlight the way society views her own Blackness. ("It also shows me that being Black is somewhat looked at as a downfall or a disadvantage"). Denise engages in critical discourse at the societal level as she dismantles hegemonic ideologies and its impact on Blackness and femaleness (fieldnotes, September 10, 2013). She assumes Black female solidarity through the use of the pronoun "we." Denise further establishes how her representation of self, one of being Black and female, is intertwined with societal perceptions of Black girls (fieldnotes, September 10, 2013). Through the genre device "we," she highlights the consequences that come with being both Black and female and declares self-reliance as her act of resistance ("We cannot count really even on society & be so dependent on them but on ourselves"). According to Black Feminist scholar Patricia Collins (2000), Denise's emerging power is described as an agent of knowledge. In exhibiting self-defined and self-reliant qualities confronting race, gender, and class oppression, that knowledge empowers Denise, as well as the other participants on the online thread. Through social and cultural awareness, Denise offers a counternarrative about what it means to be both Black and female in society. Denise's intellectual thought is a reflection of the societal and social ills that impact the lives of Black girls.

## Finding 3: Representation of Self Influenced by Society's Neglect of Black Girls (Multiple, Intellectual and Political/Critical)

On the same discussion thread, Keisha and Nicki's initial reactions focused predominantly on Black motherhood. Keisha and Nicki represent self through literacy practices that are multiple, intellectual, and political/critical. Keisha and Nicki's responses entailed a character analysis of Mary, Precious' mother. The following exchange details their unique perspectives on Black motherhood.

1    **Keisha:** *the first couple chapters had me riddled with emotion. Like for*
2    *example I was angry for the fact that Precious's mom is so cruel to her and*
3    *tries to break her down with everything she has. Like when she calls Precious*
4    *inappropriate names, that can break down a person's self-esteem*
5    **Nicki:** *it was sad because from what I've seen precious is being abused and when*
6    *precious was being abused I didn't like it at all when she was getting hit by the skillet*

Keisha's literacy practices are political/critical, analyzing the power dynamics present in the mother–daughter relationship. Keisha highlights how the verbal and physical abuse that Precious endures at the hands of her mother negatively impacts her self-image (fieldnotes, September 15, 2013). By comparing and contrasting the text *PUSH* with the movie *Precious* and detailing visual images of abuse, Keisha displays literacies that are multiple and that contribute to her own heightened emotional state of sadness. Nicki and Keisha's dominant discourse of motherhood is loving, protective, and understanding.

In the following text, Tammy's literacy practices highlight how society contributes to Precious' life experiences. She offers a perspective on Black motherhood focusing on the conditions that society creates that oppress teen mothers. She alludes to the cycle of dysfunction that plagued Precious' mother as a teen mother and now Precious as a teen mother. Tammy's literacy practices are tied to identity, intellectual, and political/critical.

8   **Tammy:** *The story of Precious makes me sad. I wanted to jump in the book,*
9   *scream, and try and save her. How can so many people in her life, in*
10  *society watch this girl slip through the cracks. The question again I asked*
11  *why does society put on blinders and say its not my child. But it's our*
12  *problem and it becomes our issue when tax payers say that they have to*
13  *help our teen moms who have to get on public assistance. So I say to*
14  *society it takes a village to raise a child.*

Tammy represents society by reversing roles with society and interrogating the very system that perpetuates Black girl's oppression and vilifies teen mothers. Tammy's discourse on mothering is deeply rooted in her own lived experiences as a teen mother. She then personalizes the oppression that Precious experiences and details how systematic oppression functions on critical social issues like teen pregnancy. Tammy's concept of motherhood is expansive and highlights the systemic factors that perpetuate Black teen mothers "slipping through the cracks." Throughout the online discussion, Tammy interrogates society and holds them accountable for the oppressive conditions that teen mothers are confronted with.

## Finding 4: Self-Representation Based on Perspectives Around a Traumatic Experience (Collaborative, Intellectual)

In the face-to-face discussion group, I posed follow-up questions focusing on Black motherhood. I posed the following question: *What was Precious' relationship like with her parents?* Denise, Lisa, and Tammy each discussed their perspectives on Black motherhood:

1   **Denise:** *(sits up and repositions herself in the chair) She was born into*
2   *dysfunction. Her motha was sexually abusing her. Her motha allowed her*
3   *husband to abuse Precious. Her motha was sick in the head!!*
4   **Lisa:** *(holds head down, slouches in the chair, folds arms, and lowers voice) It*
5   *was nasty. Her father abused Precious. Her [Pause] well at the end her father*
6   *died. It was like the relationship was [Pause] it was not like people's*
7   *relationship with dere father is. Precious said it felt good!? (frowns her face)*
8   **Denise:** *(looks at Lisa and repositions herself in the chair) I always try to*
9   *figure out what options they had in that particular situation. I can't judge*
10  *a character negatively if circumstances led them down the wrong path and*
11  *they didn't really have no options to turn their life around.*
12  **Tammy:** *(looks at everyone in the group) Her mom wasn't really a mother*

13 *figure to her. She was by herself. Even with the adults that were in her life.*
14 *Becuz her mom didn't play the mother role. Her mom play [Pause] of. I*
15 *don't know her mom just broke her down. She wasn't a mother that help you*
16 *and build you up and support you. It was all caused by Precious' upbringing*

Similar to their previous discussion comments, Tammy and Denise's discourse highlights the circumstances that led to Precious and Mary's strained relationship. Tammy attributes the strained relationship to Precious' "upbringing," while Denise attributes it to being "born in dysfunction." Tammy and Denise's discourse focuses on the cause of Precious' circumstance and highlights a familial history of dysfunction and a cycle of abuse (fieldnotes, September 15, 2013). Denise positions Precious' mother Mary as both a willing participant and an accessory, associating her actions to mental illness (fieldnotes, September 15, 2013).

Despite Lisa's knowledge of the years of sexual and mental abuse Precious endured, she is unable to account for the lasting effects such a traumatic experience has (fieldnotes, September 25, 2013). This is evident in Lisa being perplexed when Precious states that sex with her father became normal to her. In response to Lisa, Denise acknowledges that a character's circumstances may be a result of external factors that make it difficult for them to turn their life around. Denise's "ways of interacting" reveal that she disagrees with Lisa's perspective. This indicates Denise's understanding of how external factors may be outside of a person's control and may determine their fate. Over the course of this research study, Lisa and Denise shared their personal stories of sexual trauma. Their discourse reveals that their "ways of representing" regarding Precious' sexual trauma is vastly different.

## Finding 5: Self-Representation Influenced by Social Norms Around Literacy and Language (Political/Critical, Tied to Identity, Historical)

Over the course of this research study, Black girls' "ways of being" often entailed engaging in literacy practices via vastly different linguistic strategies in the online discussion group, as well as in the face-to-face discussions. For example, Denise and Lisa represented self through linguistic strategies rooted in African American Vernacular English (AAVE). Grounded in literacy and linguistic strategies of African American people of the past, Black girls' practices were historical. They often code-meshed ("dere," "be" copula, and the use of double negatives), blending both AAVE and Standard English. However, Denise and Lisa often employed linguistic strategies rooted in Standard English in the online discussions. Separate and apart from this study, I was Facebook friends with all of the participants and observed their digital practices outside of the online book club. Despite the participants employing Standard English in our Facebook book club, they employed

AAVE in their Facebook conversations with their friends outside of the study. Although this study was situated in an out-of-school digital space, this revealed that Black girls' literacy practices were tied to their identity, as well as to social norms around literacy, learning, and language. This further reveals that literacy is a political tool that holds an enormous amount of power. The political nature of literacy also contributed to in-school social norms being present in an out-of-school digital space.

## Implications for Literacy Teacher Educators in Centering Black Girls' Literacy and Language Practices in School Spaces

The focus of this study was to examine the literacy and language practices of Black adolescent girls in an out-of-school street literature book club. In doing so, this study highlighted the ways Black girls represented self through discussions of culturally relevant texts mediated via digital technologies. The implications for literacy teacher educators highlight pedagogical strategies designed to create culturally relevant, literacy-focused digital learning experiences for Black girls.

## Literacy as a Digital Practice

In school spaces, technology is not often incorporated into the curricula in ways that allow Black girls to focus on agency, identity construction, or meaning making. Hence, technology tends to not be grounded in the lived experiences and literate lives of Black adolescent girls. Literacy educators should try to mirror the level of freedom of expression and autonomy often present in Black girls' digital practices in out-of-school spaces. It is these experiences that help Black girls to shape and reshape their identities.

Literacy educators should create opportunities for Black girls to engage in digital literacy practices with a socio-political agenda at the forefront. This can be achieved by creating opportunities for Black girls to address socio-political issues via digital technologies. Black girls engage in socio-political issues via digital technologies in out-of-school spaces; however, this is not often as prevalent in school spaces. Literacy educators can embed digital technology platforms, such as zines, digital storytelling, blogs, podcasts, digital memoirs, and digital storyboards. Although the digital platforms offer different features, each platform allows Black girls to engage in critical literacy and to create and co-create digital imagery that offers Black girls the opportunity to develop counternarratives that challenges dominant narratives of who they are. In these opportunities to be creators lie opportunities for Black girls to engage in agency, identity, and meaning making. This also allows literacy educators opportunities to support Black girls as they engage in socio-emotional development.

## Literacy as a Socio-Political Act

In the age of school mandates and scripted programs, school spaces often do not reflect the academic needs of Black girls. School spaces often do not account for the multiple home and cultural traditions and literacy experiences that shape who Black girls are and how they see the world. Hence, Blackness and femaleness are socio-political acts in themselves. Literacy educators can support Black girls' experiences by developing opportunities for them to discuss social issues that affect their personal lives, as well as their communities. This entails employing a critical literacy approach to texts, allowing Black girls to engage with the ways power, privilege, and positionality shape the experiences of the character and his/her conditions throughout the texts. Such an approach constantly serves to support Black girls in the shaping and reshaping of self. It also allows Black girls to engage with texts that draw on textual features, such as thematic content, cultural ties, and linguistic strategies. Teaching literature from a racialized, gendered, and cultural perspective affirms Black girls' experiences in both in- and out-of-school spaces. Literacy as a socio-political act also entails literacy educators aligning texts with present-day conditions, specifically current issues of injustice that impact the lives of Black girls, and allowing them to speak back to these injustices. Literacy as a socio-political act also entails literacy educators creating spaces for Black girls' roles in curriculum development to be participatory in nature, so that their experiences, voices, and perspectives are embedded in instruction.

## Conclusion

Traditional conceptions of literacy, specifically canonical texts, individualized instruction, and decontextualized technology practices, have been prevalent in school spaces. These narrow conceptions of literacy continue to widen the gap between Black girls' out-of-school and in-school literacy and language practices. Literacy educators are positioned to embedded critical digital literacy practices into their curricula. Literacy educators infusing such an approach in the classroom promotes digital literacy practices that honor and cultivate cultural nuances, historical traditions, and the legitimacy of Black girls' representations of self and lived experiences.

With the emergence of digital technologies that greatly impact the teaching and learning landscape, teachers must reassess their role in the literacy classroom to deliver 21st-century literacy instruction (Greene, 2021; Haddix & Sealey-Ruiz, 2012; Price-Dennis & Matthews, 2017). Literacy mediated via digital technologies create opportunities for youth to engage in forms of experimentation and social exploration in support of their digital literacy practices (Dooley et al., 2016; Ellison, 2017; Ellison & Wang, 2018; Price-Dennis et al., 2017). This allows literacy teachers to assume a co-participative role that decenters teacher authority and fosters youths' creativity, critical thinking and collaborative engagement (Dooley et al., 2016; Ellison & Wang, 2018; Greene, 2021; Price-Dennis et al., 2017).

According to Price-Dennis (2016), the decentering of teacher authority and fostering of youth interests entail drawing on the daily experiences of Black girls to inform curriculum development.

## References

Bogdan, R., & Biklen, S. K. (2007). *Qualitative research for education: An introduction to theories and methods* (5th ed.). Boston, MA: Pearson.

Brooks, W. (2006). Reading representations of themselves: Urban youth use culture and African-American textual features to develop literary understandings. *Reading Research Quarterly, 41*(3), 372.

Brooks, W., Browne, S., & Hampton, G. (2008). "There ain't no accounting for what folks see in their own mirrors": Considering colorism within a Sharon Flake narrative – an after-school book club enhanced critical thinking skills for some adolescent girls while leading to insights on gender and race. *Journal of Adolescent Adult Literacy, 51*(8), 660.

Chouliaraki, L., & Fairclough, N. (1999). *Discourse in late modernity: Rethinking critical discourse analysis*. Edinburgh, UK: Edinburgh University Press.

Collins, P. H. (2000). *Black feminist thought: Knowledge, consciousness, and the politics of empowerment* (2nd ed.). New York: Routledge.

Creswell, J. W. (1998). *Qualitative inquiry and research design: Choosing among five traditions*. Thousand Oaks, CA: Sage Publications.

Dewalt, K. M., & Dewalt, B. R. (2002). *Participant observation: A guide for fieldworkers*. Lanham: Altamira.

Dooley, C., Ellison, T., & Welch, M. (2016). Digital participatory pedagogy: Digital participation as a method of technology integration in curriculum. *Journal of Digital Learning in Teacher Education, 32*(2), 52–63.

Ellison, T. (2017). Digital, agency, and choice: An African American youth's digital storytelling about Minecraft. *Journal of Adolescent & Adult Literacy, 61*(1), 25–35.

Ellison, T., & Wang, H. (2018). Resisting and redirecting: Agentive practices within an African American parent-child dyad during digital storytelling. *Journal of Literacy Research, 50*(1), 52–73.

Fairclough, N. (1989). *Language and power*. London: Longman Publishers.

Fetterman, D. M. (2010). *Ethnography: Step-by-step* (3rd ed.). Los Angeles: Sage.

Gee, J. P. (2005). *An introduction to discourse analysis: Theory and method* (2nd ed.). New York: Routledge.

Gibson, S. (2010). Critical readings: African-American girls and urban fiction. *Journal of Adolescent Adult Literacy, 53*(7), 565.

Gibson, S. (2016). Adolescent African American girls as engaged readers: Challenging stereotypical images of Black womanhood through urban fiction. *The Journal of Negro Education, 85*(3), 239–249.

Greene, D. T. (2015). "We need more us in schools": Black adolescent girls' literacy and language practices in out-of-school online spaces, *Journal of Negro Education, 85*(3), 274–289.

Greene, D. T. (2021). (W)rites of passage: Black girls' journaling and podcast script writing as counternarratives. *Voices from the Middle, 28*(5).

Haddix, M., & Sealey-Ruiz, Y. (2012). Cultivating digital and popular literacies as empowering and emancipatory acts among urban youth. *Journal of Adolescent & Adult Literacy, 56*(3), 189–192.

Hall, T. (2011, May). Designing from their own social worlds: The digital story of three African American young women. *English Teaching: Practice and Critique, 10*(1), 7.

Henry, A. (1998). "Speaking up" and speaking out: Examining "voice" in a reading/writing program with adolescent African Caribbean girls. *Journal of Literacy Research, 30*, 233.

Jocson, K. (2005). "Taking it to the mic": Pedagogy of June Jordan's poetry for the people and partnership with an urban high school. *English Education, 37*(2), 44–60.

Kendrick, M., Early, M., & Chemjor, W. (2013). Integrated literacies in a rural Kenyan girls' secondary school journalism club. *Research in the Teaching of English, 47*(4), 391.

Luke, A. (2000). Critical literacy in Australia: A matter of context and standpoint. *Journal of Adolescent Adult Literacy*, 448.

Mahiri, J. (2005). *What they don't learn in school: Literacy in the lives of urban youth.* New York: Peter Lang.

Morgan, D. L. (1997). *Focus groups as qualitative research* (2nd ed.). California: Sage Publications.

Morrell, E. (2004). *Linking literacy and popular culture: Finding connections for lifelong learning.* Norwood, MA: Christopher-Gordon Publishers.

Morris, V., Agosto, D., Hughes-Hassell, S., and Cottman, D. (2006). Street lit: Flying off teen bookshelves in Philadelphia public libraries. *Journal of Young Adult Library Services, 5*(1), 16–23.

Morris, V. I. (2012). *The readers' advisory guide to street literature.* Chicago: ALA.

Muhammad, G. E., Haddix, M. (2016). Centering Black girls' literacies: A review of literature on the multiple ways of knowing of Black girls. *English Education, 48*(4), 299.

Muhammad, G. E., & McArthur, S. A. (2015). "Style by their perceptions": Adolescent girls' interpretations of Black girlhood in the media. *Multicultural Perspectives, 17*(3), 1.

Muhammad, G. E., & Womack, E. (2015). From pen to pin: The multimodality of Black girls (re)writing their lives. *Ubiquity: The Journal of Literature, Literacy, and the Arts, 2*(2).

Patton, M. (1990). *Qualitative evaluation and research methods.* California: Sage.

Price-Dennis, D. (2016, July). Developing curriculum to support Black girls' literacies in digital spaces. *English Education, 48*(4), 334.

Price-Dennis, D., & Matthews, M. (2017). Teacher education in the digital age. *English Journal, 106*(5), 97.

Price-Dennis, D., Muhmmad, G., Womack, E., McArthur, S., & Haddix, M. (2017). The multiple identities of Black girlhood: A conversation about creating spaces for Black girl voices. *Journal of Language and Literacy Education, 13*(2), 1–18.

Richardson, E. (2002). "To protect and serve": African-American female literacies. *College Composition and Communication, 53*(4), 675.

Richardson, E. (2003). *African American literacies.* New York: Routledge.

Richardson, E. (2007). "She was workin like foreal": Critical literacy and discourse practices of African-American females in the age of hip hop. *Discourse & Society, 18*(6), 789–809.

Richardson, E. (2008). African-American literacies. In B. Street (Ed.), *Encyclopedia of language and education* (vol. 2, 2nd ed., pp. 335–346). New York, NY: Springer.

Rogers, R. (2003). A critical discourse analysis of the special education referral process: A case study. *Discourse: Studies in the Cultural Politics of Education, 24*(2), 139–158.

Rogers, R., Malancharuvil-Berkes, E., Mosley, M., & Hui, D. (2005). Critical discourse analysis in education: A review of the literature. *Review of Educational Research, 75*(3), 365–416.

Rubin, H. J., & Rubin, I. (2005). *Qualitative interviewing: The art of hearing data* (2nd ed.). Thousand Oaks, CA: Sage Publications.

Sims-Bishop, R. (1983). Strong Black girls: A ten-year old responds to fiction about Afro-Americans. *Journal of Research and Development in Education, 21.*

Sims-Bishop, R. (1990). Windows, mirrors, and glass sliding doors. *Perspectives: Choosing and using books for the classroom,* 6(3).

Smitherman, G. (2006). *Word from the mother: Language and African-Americans.* New York: Routledge.

Stewart, D. W., & Shamdasani, P. N. (1990). *Focus groups: Theory and practice.* California: Sage Publishers.

Sutherland, L. (2005). Black adolescent girls' use of literacy practices to negotiate boundaries of ascribed identity. *Journal of Literacy Research,* 365.

Vasudevan, L. (2006). Making known differently: Engaging visual modalities as spaces to author new selves. *E-Learning, 3,* 207–215.

Vasudevan, L., & Hill, M. (2008). *Media, learning and sites of possibility.* New York: Peter Lang.

Wissman, K. K. (2011). "Rise up!": Literacies, lived experiences, and identities within an in-school "other space." *Research in the Teaching of English, 45*(4), 405.

## *Young Adult Literature Cited*

Morrison, T. (1994). *The bluest eye.* New York: Vintage International.

Sapphire. (1996). *Push.* New York: Knopf Double Day Publishing Group.

# 12

# A DIGITAL MISMATCH

## Adolescent Black Girls' Perceptions of the Usefulness of Digital Tools

*Autumn A. Griffin*

As literacy educators begin to incorporate technology into classrooms, both researchers and practitioners must begin to understand how, if at all, their practices are facilitating spaces for Black girls to practice digital literacies in authentic ways that allow for both critical discourse and development of their literacies for their future-oriented desires. In response to this need, this chapter explores how six Black adolescent girls at a one-to-one technology school perceive the mismatch between the purposes of their digital literacies and the instruction they receive. As a contribution to the burgeoning knowledge on Black girls' digital literacies, this chapter answers the following questions: *What are the perceptions of six Black girls regarding the use of computers and other digital tools in the context of their one-to-one technology school? How do these girls employ their digital literacies outside of school?*

This chapter seeks to reimagine and reclaim the possibilities of Black girls' literate practices in the digital realm. Specifically, it recasts Anyon's (2014) notion of radical possibilities and applies it to Black girls' digital literacy practices to directly confront the systemic inequity and hegemony Black girls face in classrooms and to reimagine uses for digital technology as a vehicle for literacy development and empowerment. Using case study analysis (Bogdan & Biklen, 2007) informed by critical ethnography (Willis, 2008), I center the voices and knowledge of six Black adolescent girls to understand their perceptions of how the computers the school gives each student are used in classrooms. I explain the details of the project further in the methodology section. I begin the findings with an overview of how the girls engage digital tools for their own purposes, highlighting the important thought work they are doing on their own, without teacher or school mediation. Subsequently, I focus on the issues the girls point out with their school-given computers and conclude this chapter with implications for both practice and future research.

## Black Girls' Literacies and Counter-Storytelling

I draw upon two theoretical perspectives to analyze Black girls' perceived uses for technology in their classrooms. Foundational to this study are Muhammad and Haddix's (2016) Black Girls' Literacies Framework and the Critical Race Theory tenet of counter-storytelling (Decuir & Dixson, 2004).

As argued by Muhammad and Haddix (2016), Black girls' literacies are (1) multiple; (2) tied to identities; (3) historical; (4) collaborative; (5) intellectual; and (6) political/critical. That is, Black girls engage in multiple literate practices, which are directly tied to their identities. In doing so, they draw on the historical traditions of their foremothers and work collectively and collaboratively with their sistas (other Black girls) to develop as intellectual and political/critical beings. Understanding and applying these six tenets to this study allows for a complex and rigorous analysis of how the Black girls in the study engage their unique literacies to make sense of how computers are being used in their classrooms at school.

Counter-storytelling, a tenet of Critical Race Theory, is defined as "a means of exposing and critiquing normalized dialogues that perpetuate racial stereotypes" (Decuir & Dixson, 2004, p. 27). As such, counter-stories amplify the voices of people from marginalized communities, allowing them to "talk back" to narratives steeped in Whiteness (hooks, 1989). Counter-storytelling provides a fuller narrative of literacy than does adhering to definitions of literacy so constrained by conceptions of Whiteness. By detailing the perceptions of the six Black girls in this study, I center their counter-stories, privileging their experiences and interpretations of how technology has been used in their classrooms over those of teachers who may have a different perception of the use of these tools.

## Black Girls' Digital Literacies

The study of digital literacies acknowledges the idea that as society evolves, scholarship must also expand traditional conceptions of literacy to consider its broader sociocultural aspects (New London Group, 1996). Defined here as the "multiple and interactive [literacy] practices mediated by digital tools such as computers, cell phones, and video games that involve reading, writing, language, and exchanging information in online environments" (Lewis, 2013, p. 1), the study of *digital literacies* focuses on the ways people engage in the reading and creation of texts using multiple multimedia technologies (Muhammad & Haddix, 2016). Throughout this chapter, I define *digital tools* as the digital hardware or tools with which the girls engage (e.g. computers, cell phones, etc.).

Understanding that literacy is far more than reading and writing, researchers who study digital literacy often focus on how the use of digital technology and digital modes of communication facilitate the development of critical thinking skills for the purposes of cultivating empowerment, agency, and collaboration

(Haddix & Sealey-Ruiz, 2012; Hall, 2011; Kirkland & Jackson, 2009; Kynard, 2010; Lewis, 2013; Muhammad & Haddix, 2016; Vasudevan et al., 2010). As explained by Muhammad and Haddix (2016), engagement in digital literacies has the potential "to enable collaboration, relationship building, participation in sociopolitical thought, and the vehicle to assert multiple literacies against hegemonic discourses" (p. 309). Thus, it is imperative that educators begin to understand how students engage their digital literacies in order to prepare them for a future where their use is unavoidable.

Unfortunately, however, studies of Black youths' digital literacies have revealed educators' demonization and criminalization due to fear and a desire for control (Haddix & Sealey-Ruiz, 2012). Because digital literacies symbolize and necessitate a redistribution of power with which teachers are often uncomfortable, these practices tend to be relegated to out-of-school spaces, leaving little to no room for students to practice and develop them in classrooms (Haddix & Sealey-Ruiz, 2012). This unfortunate truth is at odds with literature that details the importance of students' development of twenty-first century literacy skills in an age of rapidly expanding technological knowledge and use (Cope & Kalantzis, 2009; Kellner & Share, 2005; Morrell, 2012). For Black girls, who already exist at the margins of society, this type of affect towards their digital literacies works to silence, discourage, and further marginalize them.

Scholars have only recently begun to investigate Black girls' digital literacies. In an exploration of how the contemporary digital literacy practices of Black youth are informed by their historical legacies, Hall (2011) found that through digital co-authoring, the girls used digital tools to engage in practices of resistance and kinship, writing to represent their lived experiences. Likewise, Kendrick and colleagues (2013) found that when digital tools are (re)positioned in an after-school journalism club, Black girls used digital tools and literacies to take on the identities of novice journalists. More recently, Greene (2016) and Muhammad and Womack (2015) posited that Black girls engage digital literacies to (re)present themselves in digital spaces. Greene (2016) examined the language and literacy practices of Black adolescent girls in an online street literature book club and found that the book club allowed girls to use multiple modalities to reimagine representations of themselves. Similarly, Muhammad and Womack (2015) described how Black girls used their digital literacies to "pin" against representations of themselves rooted in hegemonic discourses. Finally, Price-Dennis (2016) reported the potential of curriculum to support the development of Black girls' digital literacies by exploring social issues, practicing agency, and (re)imagining their identities as learners.

As a Black woman and literacy researcher, I am deeply invested in the practice and development of Black girls' digital literacies, not only to contribute to the field of literacy education in general and the burgeoning scholarship on Black girls' literacies in particular, but also to better understand Black girls' *own* perceptions of digital tools in their lives and for their purposes. Because the body of literature around Black girls' digital literacies is fairly new, there is still much to be explored, thus allowing unlimited possibilities to contribute to this ever-expanding discourse. Grounded in aforementioned understandings of digital literacies, the treatment of Black students' digital literacies in general, and Black girls' digital literacies in particular, this study answers the questions: *What are the perceptions of six Black girls regarding the use of computers and other digital tools in the context of their one-to-one technology school? How do these girls employ their digital literacies outside of school?*

## Methods

Data for this project were drawn from a study about the in- and out-of-school digital literacy practices of six Black adolescent girls. I conducted my investigation at Northeast Charter School (NCS; to protect the identity of all participants, all names of people and places hereafter are pseudonyms). NCS is a Title I, charter middle and high school in an urban, mid-Atlantic city. The school is situated in a rapidly gentrifying area and students commute from all over the city to attend. NCS focuses on language immersion in Chinese, Spanish, and French as well as inquiry-based learning. The school offers the International Baccalaureate (IB) Middle Years Program for students in sixth through eighth grades, and is an authorized IB school for students in ninth through twelfth grades. NCS prides itself on its three pillars, which are: (1) advanced language learning in Chinese, Spanish, and French; (2) IB curriculum and programs for all students; and (3) one-to-one technology ratio. In support of their third pillar, the school provides each student with a laptop at the beginning of their NCS career. The school's technology policy states that while students may be asked to use non-computer devices in class (i.e. cameras, tablets, etc.), they are prohibited from using personal electronics during school hours for any reason (i.e. cell phones).

NCS is a racially, economically, and linguistically diverse urban public school. The student population is made up of 37.1 percent Black students, 40.3 percent Latinx students, 13.4 percent White students, 5 percent multiracial students, 3 percent Asian students, and 1 percent Native American students. Over half of the students at NCS have been identified as "economically disadvantaged." Of the students, 11.1 percent are English Language Learners (ELLs) and 16.6 percent have been identified as having special needs. Finally, 48.5 percent of students at NCS have been identified as male and 51.5 percent of students have been identified as female.

Guided by the principles of participatory action research (PAR) and critical scholarship (Willis, 2008), I relied on the local knowledge of experts in the community for participant selection (Brown & Rodriguez, 2009; Herr & Anderson, 2005; Park, 1993). Participants were nominated by the assistant principal of the participating school, a millennial Black woman who has known and worked with the students for five years, first as their middle school math teacher and then as assistant principal of the high school. The principal, Ms. Williams, nominated participants based on three researcher-identified criteria: (1) students must be between the ages of 14 and 18 years old; (2) students must be identified as female on all official school documents;[1] and (3) students must self-identify as Black, African American, West Indian/Caribbean American, or African. Due to the assistant principal's knowledge of and strong relationship and rapport with her students, I accepted all nominated participants for the study. A brief description of each girl and her personal interests as stated by her during the initial interview is presented in Table 12.1.

Data from this study were taken from a larger project where I conducted three semi-structured focus group interviews with the selected six Black girls during the school day. Each day of the focus group revolved around a different topic: (1) getting to know you; (2) in-school digital literacies; and (3) out-of-school digital literacies. This particular study focuses on data from the second and third days of interviews. Importantly, Halle was not feeling well and was absent from the second day of interviews. Thus, she was significantly quieter than her peers throughout the study.

Focus group interviews took place in a small meeting room at NCS during the girls' lunch hour. Students were provided with lunch and snacks for their willingness to participate in the study. During the focus groups, I asked girls questions such as: *How do you use technology in your classes? What do you think is the purpose of using computers and other forms of technology in your classrooms? Why, if at all, do you feel like your use of technology in your classrooms is useful to you? How do you use technology most outside of school? What, if anything, do digital spaces outside of the classroom afford you that those in the classroom do not?* (For a complete list of protocol questions, see Appendix.) All interviews were audio-recorded and lasted approximately 60

**TABLE 12.1** Participant Descriptions

| Pseudonym | Age | Grade | Ethnicity/ Nationality | Interests/Goals |
|---|---|---|---|---|
| Aniyah | 15 | 10 | Black American | Black girls Social justice |
| Ariana | 16 | 10 | Haitian American | Politics |
| Nicole | 15 | 10 | Senegalese | Computer programming Cyber security |
| Arielle | 14 | 9 | Black American | Anthropology Anatomy |
| Chloe | 14 | 9 | Black American | Public work Helping others |
| Halle | 14 | 9 | Black American | n/a |

minutes. I took field notes and memos to ensure a more nuanced and holistic understanding of participants' digital literacy practices.

Focus group interviews were transcribed and cleaned for accuracy. Transcripts were analyzed with a list of preliminary codes that reflected emerging themes in relation to my research question (Corbin & Strauss, 1990). Examples of pre-liminary codes included "surveillance," "benefits of computers," "drawbacks of computers," and "the role of computers in instruction." Multiple phases of data segmentation revealed new insights as to how the participating Black adolescent girls spoke about their digital literacies and the underlying motivations and led to secondary codes. Examples of secondary codes included "power," "issues of equity," "technical difficulties," and "future-oriented digital literacies." I attached supporting quotes to all secondary codes and organized all secondary codes under primary codes to assure relevance of each code and associated quotes. Additionally, I used my field notes from focus group sessions to triangulate all data and gain further insights from coding interviews.

## Limitations

There were several limitations within the present study. First, it is evident that the tenth-grade students (Aniyah, Nicole, and Ariana) were considerably more talkative than their ninth-grade peers. While the reasons behind this phenomenon are beyond the scope of this chapter, it is important to note that some voices were more present in the findings of his research than others. Second, this study focused on two primary aspects of the identity of Black girls: race and gender. However, a deeper analysis of the ways ethnicity and nationality influence Black girls' digital literacies would be useful both for understanding how ethnicity and/ or nationality may influence how Black girls make sense of digital tools and to inform future research. Finally, this chapter primarily focuses on the use of social media and computers. Future research would do well to look more closely at how Black girls use phones and/or other electronic devices in tandem with computers. However, the research questions at hand do not allow us to interrogate how various devices might interact with computers.

## Findings

With this study, I sought to explore perceptions about what the girls thought to be the multiple benefits of computers and other digital tools, as well as the ways those benefits are at odds with the realities of these digital tools and how they are used in their classrooms. The girls articulated that the benefits of digital tools include an outlet for the expression of feelings, the potential for increased confidence to confront bigotry, and the opportunity to develop their digital literacies for their future careers. However, girls also explained that digital tools have the potential to create multiple barriers for learning and that often the ways computers, specifically, are used in classrooms are not in alignment with their own digital literacy practices. Below, I begin with a description of how the girls in this study describe the benefits of their own purposes for their digital tools. I then explicate the ways they perceived those uses to be at odds with issues they have observed in their schools.

## Digital Tools for Our Own Purposes

### Digital Journaling

The girls articulated what they perceived to be the multiple benefits of computers and other digital tools, including expression of feelings and the potential for increased confidence to confront bigotry, and the opportunity to develop their digital literacies for their future careers.

Girls in the study described their use of Snapchat (accessed on their mobile devices) to express feelings they may not feel comfortable sharing in person or may not want to engage by way of face-to-face discourse. In one instance, Nicole explained that she began posting quotes to Snapchat that reflected her mood:

> I was posting very depressing quotes and people were asking me to stop. . . . I tried my best to stop doing that because I figured, why am I posting it? Sometimes I feel like I identify with [the quotes] if it's in the moment, but then I get over it I guess.

Here, Nicole describes the use of her Snapchat account as a type of journal where she can express her feelings by reposting quotes she feels are tangential to her own (see Table 12.2). Additionally, Nicole's comment communicates that through her

**TABLE 12.2** Digital Platforms, Purpose, and Impact

| Platforms | Purpose | Impact |
| --- | --- | --- |
| Snapchat | Journaling—Snapchat allowed girls to express feelings they did not want to engage by way of face-to-face discourse. | The girls engage in multimodal literacy practices, adjusting font color and size as well as the content of the media to suit their purposes. |
| Twitter and Instagram | Talking back—These digital mediums allowed the girls to engage in the Black feminist practice of "talking back" to issues of injustice and to educate their peers. | The mediation of screens provides a layer of safety for the girls to disrupt injustice in ways they may not be protected for doing the same in school. The screens also allow time for reflection rather than an immediate response the way an in-person conversation might. |

use of Snapchat, she is negotiating the complex interplay between engaging with social media for her followers and the broader social media community, and using the medium for her own purposes. She recognizes that it has the ability to suit both purposes and is trying to make sense of how she desires to fit between and within the two.

Similarly, Arielle finds solace in the use of Snapchat to express feelings she doesn't necessarily want to talk about with anyone, but wants to "get out":

ARIELLE: I post depressing stuff. Once in a while I'll be really happy and I'll put a quote or whatever, but usually, it's just when I feel I want to talk about it but I don't want to talk about it at the same time.

AAG: And why do you think you post [these quotes]?

ARIELLE: Just to . . . I don't know to be honest. I kind of want to get it out, but not really get it out if that makes sense.

AAG: Ok, so it's like a journal?

ARIELLE: Yeah.

ARIANA: Are your quotes where you make them really tiny?

ARIELLE: Yeah, so that no one can read them.

ARIANA: I'm looking at a whole paragraph and I'm like "I don't want to screenshot it because I don't want to look like a creep, but I want to know if something is wrong."

NICOLE: And I told you I couldn't read it and you were like, "that's the point."

ARIELLE: Yeah, that's the point.

When I asked about how the girls *do* respond in the event that a friend replies to something they've posted, Nicole responded by explaining, "I'm like, 'thanks for caring.' Most of the time nobody replies, but I'm cool because I don't want to keep explaining myself." The responses of both girls express that while they do want an outlet in which they can share their feelings, they don't necessarily want to engage in dialogue with anyone about how they're feeling or why they may be feeling that way. Arielle uses the font feature on Snapchat to play with the size of her content so her followers are unable to read what it is she's posted. In this way, Arielle is employing her multiple literacy skills to bend her practices towards her own purposes. Arielle's use of Snapchat is multimodal, employing matters of textual content and font to convey a very specific message. Because of its ability for users to manipulate content, Snapchat provides both Arielle and Nicole with an opportunity to digitally journal and selectively share pieces of their thoughts and feelings.

## Talking Back

The girls also used Twitter and Instagram to speak directly back to ideas that perpetuated injustice and to educate their peers. For instance, Aniyah explained that in the past she has used Snapchat to respond to bigoted ideas about sexual harassment:

AAG: What are some ways you all feel empowered to combat the issues you see?

ANIYAH: I yell at a lot of people. Just kidding (coughs playfully). But on Snapchat people will be like . . . the other day this guy was like "oh, all these women are coming out against men saying it's sexual harassment, they have been sexually harassed. There's too many women. Blah blah. This has to be fake." When I tell you I swiped up and put the little chat button and I was like "type, type, type . . . paragraph. No." Because a lot of people are more willing to say that over social media. . .

NICOLE: . . . than in person.

ANIYAH: Than in person. So when you see that then you can confront it. And you can also change minds. Because when you see something written by a friend then you can read that and actually absorb it. When you see the person, I probably would've yelled and it's kind of difficult to listen to people when they're in your face with trouble comprehending, but . . . yeah. So I think that way is a way I feel empowered. Like when I see something I say something over social media.

Aniyah explains how social media allows her to confront issues and people she may not feel as comfortable or prepared to respond to in person. Mediated by screens and not limited to the constraints of time that face-to-face interaction often demands, social media allows Aniyah an opportunity to "read and actually absorb" information so she can later have a conversation that "changes minds." Thus, digital tools allow Aniyah to engage in the intellectual work of reflecting on and seeking to understand her online interactions so that she can grow in her criticality and ability to respond using sound arguments. Because she doesn't feel the pressure associated with responding to a person in the moment, Aniyah is able to reflect and craft a response that will have a greater influence on her reader.

Likewise, Ariana details how she has used her digital tools to speak to injustices like bullying:

> Last year because I had a hard time and it would upset me so much. Especially when someone would tell someone else to kill themselves. I would be like "well, you really shouldn't say that because you don't know what that person is going through. You could be the reason that person potentially tries to commit suicide.

Like Aniyah, Ariana uses the tools at her disposal to speak to a known injustice—bullying. However, rather than speaking of the reflection she does herself, Ariana encourages others to reflect on the potential harm they could be inflicting upon others with their words. Additionally, Ariana describes how the use of digital tools allows for the opportunity to disseminate her message broadly:

> Social media is a great thing because you can just tell a big group of people not to do something and I didn't realize that people actually listened to me or read my stuff on social media because they actually absorb what I'm saying and actually chew it.

Like Aniyah, Ariana recognizes the benefits of digital tools to allow people to "chew on" or reflect on information they receive in order to craft a thoughtful response and builds on Aniyah's argument by explaining that social media can be used to speak to a large audience of people. Invoking the criticality of her multiple literacies, Ariana recognizes that there is power in both her words and the use of social media to articulate her message. Because of their ability to mediate time and space, digital tools provide the girls with an opportunity to develop the confidence to confront issues of injustice they otherwise might not.

## Developing Skills for Future Careers

Lastly, the girls explained how digital tools provide them an opportunity to develop necessary digital literacies for their future careers. As stated earlier, *digital literacies* refer to the "multiple and interactive [literacy] practices mediated by digital tools such as computers, cell phones, and video games that involve reading, writing, language, and exchanging information in online environments" (Lewis, 2013, p. 1). Aniyah explained the importance of her computer in facilitating the development of skills for her future:

> As someone who would like to go into the humanities, I need to be able to get news and connect to people. Even if you're not in the STEM field things are still online. And also there's so many law cases that revolve around something online. There was just the case with Apple versus the government about whether or not they could access their phones. And also there's all these human rights violations issues where you can make a case for . . . I don't know.
>
> There's a lot, but then even if you're not doing anything with computers in the law field, you're still going to have to research. Research is so important and it's so much easier to access things online than it is to read or flip through a book. And if you want to get things done quickly, it's the way to go. Also, typing up your notes for something or making a presentation. Everything that you can do in a notebook you can do on a computer and it will be faster and more legible.

Here, Aniyah explains how digital literacies—namely using her digital tools to stay up to date on current events, and conducting research and creating presentations for her future career—will be important for engaging in the future. She begins by explaining that the necessity and practical application of digital literacies extends beyond STEM fields into careers in humanities as well. Her explanation points to multiple skills necessary for a career, including staying up to date on news, social networking, research, taking notes, and creating presentations. Aniyah's explanation engages the multiplicity, intellectuality, criticality, and political nature of Black girls' literacies in obtaining and sustaining a future career. Furthermore, she articulates her vision of how phones will continue to be relevant in the future and can and should be leveraged for professional purposes.

## Barriers for Learning

Although they pointed out several benefits of digital tools, girls in the study also detailed the multiple barriers digital tools have the opportunity to create, especially in classrooms. Barriers the girls described dealt with issues of surveillance and technical difficulties due to issues of equity.

### Blocking Content

The first issue of digital tools in classrooms came up fairly early in my interviews. One of the first questions I asked involved the use of their school-provided computers. Immediately, Nicole responded by telling me that teachers have the power to block students from content on their computers:

AAG: So, one of the things I know is different about this school is that everyone gets a computer. Can you tell me a little bit about that just to open up?

NICOLE: A lot of the things on the computer are blocked. Restricted. So, sometimes that can affect our learning, but not all the time. Like in chemistry, when we were doing our projects I wanted to search for a recreational drug and what it was Importantly, Nicole felt it was necessary that the first thing she told me about students' use of computers at school was that administrators and teachers have the power to restrict student access to certain websites, and that sometimes, this can impinge upon their learning. Nicole later went on to explain that ultimately, if a teacher or administrator deems a student's use of their computer to be inappropriate in any way, they also have the power to completely surveil and control students' computer use:

NICOLE: They could also ex out your tabs and stuff like that, and send you notes if you're off task and also, report it. They also can get you on restricted access. Because there are different types. The regular one where some things are blocked. Then there's the one that's taken a step further. It's already restricted, but you can't even access it at that type of restriction. And then the next one is the maximum one, which is where you literally have to have a teacher sign in for you and you can't do anything else but Google Classroom. Even research, you can't do.

AAG: And they can control that by student?

NICOLE: Yeah.

Here, Nicole's comments reinforce that she understands the overregulation of digital tools to be an impediment to student learning. She explains that in many cases, restricted access to websites blocks students from accessing and utilizing vital tools for research across contents. Further, her comments depict the ways teachers' enforcement of rules regarding technology can and sometimes do mimic that of a prison structure (from minimum to "maximum" security).

Interestingly, Aniyah later explains that although teachers attempt to block student access, students inevitably find ways around these restrictions:

ANIYAH: They block stuff, we figure out a new way around it. They block stuff, we figure out a new way around it.

AAG: Ok, how do you figure out a way around it?

NICOLE: It's like simple things that they overlook like settings.

Aniyah and Nicole explain that students engage in hacking activities to regain access and agency to various tools necessary for learning. They not only recognize the necessity of various digital tools for their academic success but are also able to engage their literacies around the use and management of these tools to overcome educator-induced barriers.

### School-Supplied Digital Tools as Barriers

The girls in the study also explained the ways school-supplied digital tools can serve as barriers because of the various technical difficulties that arise due to issues of equity. When asked about some of the challenges of attending a one-to-one technology school, Nicole and Ariana explained:

NICOLE: If you don't have Wi-Fi, you're screwed.

AAG: So the Wi-Fi goes out at the school sometimes?

CHORUS: No.

ARIANA: At home.

NICOLE: You have to be able to have Wi-Fi at home, or you'll have to go to the—

ARIANA: I didn't [have Wi-Fi] for seventh and eighth grade. I didn't.

AAG: So what happens with your schoolwork then?

ARIANA: I mean, I would connect to my mom's hotspot, but like I did most of my homework in school or whatever.

AAG: Was there ever a time where it affected you? And were teachers understanding of that?

ARIANA: No. I mean, I always figured out a way to get my homework done, but in my observations teachers in the past weren't generally understanding if students didn't have Wi-Fi.

NICOLE: They were like, "Go to the library."

Girls explained that students who are unable to access Wi-Fi outside of the school walls were sometimes unable to complete assignments or were asked to find various locations where they could access Wi-Fi in order to complete the assignment. Ariana's and Nicole's responses suggest that teachers were sometimes unsympathetic to this barrier.

Additionally, Nicole and Chloe explained that the use of computers posed financial burdens for students:

CHLOE: I've had to pay like over four hundred dollars for computers.

AAG: Oh, wait, they charge you?

NICOLE: Seven computers! How am I supposed to pay for seven computers? Even to this day I don't have my own Chromebook. This is a loaner. So that means after summer and during any major holidays, I have to turn it back in. And it's been happening for three years that I've never had my own Chromebook since the seventh grade.

Both Chloe and Nicole explain that their use of computers at the school has been financially costly, as they have had to pay for the repair of broken computers. Because computers are integral to the design of NCS, choosing not to use the computer is not an option for students.

Overall, the girls' comments suggested that the use of computers in school often reinforces the real-world surveillance of Black bodies and activity and reinscribes issues of academic inequity.

## Misalignment With Our Literacies

Lastly, analysis of the data revealed that the use of computers in classrooms was often misaligned with the ways the girls employed their digital literacies outside the walls of the classroom. Earlier, I detailed the ways the girls use their digital tools to express their feelings, confront bigotry, and prepare for their future careers, all of which require collaborative methods of engagement with technology. However, the girls described classroom experiences with computers as individualized and isolated:

AAG: Ok. So, do you all use the discussion setting for collaboration or help from your peers?

CHORUS: No.

NICOLE: It's just mostly a "do now," like in English class, when they're like you have to write your answers and then answer somebody else's question or add on to it.

The girls explained that most of their computer usage in classes is to complete individual work. In an effort to understand how this might vary across classes, I asked the girls to explain their usage of computers in the class where they felt they used them most:

AAG: Is there a class where you use computers most?

CHORUS: History.

AAG: Ok, so tell me what all of this looks like in History class.

ARIANA: Research. Because you walk in, your "Do Now" on the computer, then we watch a video, and then we do our independent practice on our computers and that's for basically the rest of the class.

AAG: And that's the same every day?

ARIANA: Yeah, unless we're doing presentations or something.

ANIYAH: Which are done on the computer and then presented. You talk and then you have your slideshow behind you.

AAG: Ok, so is most of this work, then, in History independent?

ARIANA: Yeah.

ANIYAH: Uh huh.

ARIANA: I don't think we've done a group project this year. Yeah, no we haven't.

Girls explained that overall teachers require them to work independently on their computers during class, which is antithetical both to what research says about the potential of digital literacies in learning environments and how the girls described their use of digital tools. This individualized use of digital tools in the classroom aligns with White standards of rugged individualism and neglects the collaborative nature of Black girls' literacies.

## A Digital Mismatch

Throughout the focus group interviews, participants in the study narrated their counter-stories (Decuir & Dixson, 2004), which highlighted the disconnect between their own purposes for digital tools and the realities of how those tools are used in classrooms. The girls' purposes for digital tools fell within the tenets of the Black Girls' Literacies Framework (Muhammad & Haddix, 2016).

Their explanations of utilizing digital tools to craft journal entries highlighted both the multiplicity and the identity-centered nature of their literacies. Using multimodal methods of creation, girls constructed digital entries that allowed them to discreetly share pieces of themselves in an online forum. Additionally, the girls employed the critical nature of their literacies on Snapchat. When Ariana notified Arielle that she couldn't read what she'd posted, Arielle responded by stating, "that's the point," signaling to her audience that she was asserting her agency to manipulate the platform towards her purposes for writing.

Further, the girls employed their Black girls' literacies when using digital platforms to speak back to ideas that perpetuate injustice. Namely, they drew on the intellectual tradition of their foremothers (i.e. Maria Stewart, Ida B. Wells, Fannie Lou Hamer, etc.), using their literacies to call out and challenge misrepresentations of themselves and people from other marginalized communities in public spaces (Collins, 2002; Richardson, 2002; Royster, 2000; Waters & Conaway, 2007). Summoning all six tenets of the Black Girls' Literacies framework (Muhammad & Haddix, 2016), the girls worked to speak up and speak back to these ideas in ways that promoted critical reflection and dialogue both within their peer groups and in their broader social networks. Finally, the girls drew on their digital literacies to make sense of the digital skills they will need in their future careers, tying their use of digital tools to both their current and future identities. Thus, the girls articulated the multiple ways they will have to engage digital tools in the future (to read news, conduct research, take notes, etc.) and are actively working to develop those skills now.

However, findings also revealed several mismatches between how Black girls employ their digital literacies and how digital tools are used in their school. First, girls in the study explained the emphasis on independent work on computers at school. Research on Black girls' digital literacies has revealed that curriculum revolving around digital tools has the potential to provide Black girls with spaces to facilitate the development of their digital literacies (Price-Dennis, 2016). Specifically, curriculum involving digital tools should allow Black girls to explore social issues that affect their lives, provide them opportunities to allow them to exercise agency and confidence, and create space for them to (re)image what it means to be a learner (Price-Dennis, 2016). Additionally, according to the student standards posed by the International Society for Technology in Education (ISTE) (2007), the use of technology in classrooms should facilitate the creation of: (1) empowered learners; (2) digital citizens; (3) knowledge constructors; (4) innovative designers; (5) computational thinkers; (6) creative communicators; and (7) global collaborators. Unfortunately, girls in this study revealed that the lessons they receive rarely allow them to develop as these kinds of learners in the classroom. Rather, teachers often use computers as digital variations of textbooks and worksheets. If students are only ever asked to work independently on computers to complete rote tasks, how are they to become empowered learners, digital citizens, creative communicators, or global communicators?

Additionally, the girls' description of how computers pose barriers for learning and conflict with their own literacies echoes the work of Vickery (2017) and Haddix and Sealey-Ruiz (2012), who explained that because of teachers' fear of relinquishing control and discomfort with digital tools themselves, they often neglect to develop students' digital literacies, and rather stunt their growth and infringe upon their creativity and academic development. In this way, children are silenced in classroom spaces. For Black girls in particular, this surveilling, silencing, and focus on power and punishment is closely tied to issues of policing (Crenshaw, Ocen, & Nanda, 2015; Epstein et al., 2017; Morris, 2016). The girls in the present study revealed the ways that computers are currently being used to perpetuate this problem within the walls of their classrooms. Currently at NCS, teachers use surveillance techniques to restrict student access to various tools for learning. Interestingly, however, this teacher-created barrier seems to present an opportunity for the development of another digital literacy skill set— hacking. Girls used their knowledge of the capacity of their tools to circumvent teacher-sanctioned restrictions to access needed information. To be clear, this is not to suggest that the over-regulation of Black girls' digital literacies is by any means productive, but rather to highlight the ways the girls are creating their own opportunities to develop their literacies *in spite of* teacher and administrator regulations. Instead of overregulating the use of student technology, teachers should be seeking to understand how students are using digital tools outside of the classroom. In doing so, we would learn much about the skills these digital natives have developed on their own and perhaps think more critically about how to incorporate rather than prohibit the use of personal electronics and other digital tools in the classroom.

## Implications and Conclusion

The present research has several implications for practice. At this point, we have both theoretical research and practical research that includes student voices to support the need for a reconsideration of the ways educators currently integrate digital tools into their lessons and use digital tools as a means to police the consumption, creation, and actions of students. If we are to truly aid in the development of students who are bearers of twenty-first century skills, we must begin to critically assess the role of technology in classrooms. As well, the voices of the Black girls in the study suggest that administrators may need to reconsider the use of "personal electronics" in their technology policies. If students are doing work that facilitates intellectual and critical growth, perhaps we should revisit the value of these tools in the learning process.

Furthermore, we must consider the implications for how computers are being used to create an atmosphere of control and surveillance, a practice almost exclusively reserved for schools where Black and Latinx students are among the majority. What is the purpose of giving students' computers if we are to hyper-regulate how they use them? What does this kind of hyper-security mean for digital literacy development? What does it mean about the kinds of literacies they intend for students' development? What are the purposes of regulating the *types* of digital tools students engage? How can we think about productive use of personal electronics without overregulating students? Future research should begin to ask these questions in order to inform the ways teachers develop pedagogical practices and curricula that support the development Black girls' *own* digital literacies.

Finally, as we continue to consider the purposes of digital technology in classrooms, we must consider the financial and logistical costs for students in order to determine ways to proactively navigate around them. Students from families unable to afford Wi-Fi or data plans are at a disadvantage in a school where access to Wi-Fi is key. How might we manage to support them in gaining access, to alleviate any barriers to academic and social success? Future research should perhaps investigate the development of potential programs that alleviate the financial burden of attending a school that centers the use of twenty-first century technology.

# APPENDIX

## Interview Protocol Questions

### Interview 1:

- Can you tell me a bit about yourself?
- Who is the most important person in your life? Why?
- What is your favorite thing to do? Why?
- Can you tell me a little about your school?
- What is your favorite class and why?
- What is your least favorite class and why?
- What kinds of things are you interested in learning more about?
- What do you want to do when you grow up? What is it going to take to get there?

### Interview 2:

- How do you use technology in your classes?
- What kind of programs do you use?
- What is the purpose of computers and technology in your classes?
- What do you mostly use technology for in your classes?
- Is there a class where you use technology most? What is it? How, if at all, has the use of technology in that class helped you to make sense of that subject area?
- Why, if at all, do you feel like your use of technology in your classes is useful?
- How, if at all, do the ways you use technology in your classes help you understand the world around you?
- Do any of your teachers require you to use technology to take social action? If so, which teachers? What effect does this have on your learning?

## Interview 3:

- How do you use technology most outside of school?
- What technological or digital platforms do you use most outside of school?
- How do you use those platforms outside of school? Why do you use those platforms in that way?
- Do you have a digital or online persona? If so, how would you describe her?
- What, if anything, do digital spaces outside of the classroom afford you that those in the classroom do not?
- What, if anything, have you learned using technology outside of school that you wish you would learn more about in school?

## Note

1 Given that IRB requires participants had to have a permission slip signed to participate, this choice was made to protect any students who may identify as trans or gender nonconforming at school but may not have come out to their parents or families at home.

## References

Anyon, J. (2014). *Radical possibilities: Public policy, urban education, and a new social movement.* Routledge: New York.

Bogdan, R. C., & Biklen, S. K. (2007). *Qualitative research for education* (5th ed.). Boston, MA: Pearson.

Brown, T. M., & Rodriguez, L. F. (2009, Fall). Editors' notes. *New Directions for Youth Development*, 1–9.

Collins, P. H. (2002). Black *feminist thought: Knowledge, consciousness, and the politics of empowerment.* Routledge: London.

Cope, B., & Kalantzis, M. (2009). "Multiliteracies": New literacies, new learning. *Pedagogies: An International Journal, 4*(3), 164–195.

Corbin, J. M., & Strauss, A. (1990). Grounded theory method: Procedures, canons, and evaluative criteria. *Qualitative Sociology, 13*(1), 3–21.

Crenshaw, K., Ocen, P., & Nanda, J. (2015). *Black girls matter: Pushed out, overpoliced, and underprotected.* Center for Intersectionality and Social Policy Studies, Columbia University.

DeCuir, J. T., & Dixson, A. D. (2004). "So when it comes out, they aren't that surprised that it is there": Using critical race theory as a tool of analysis of race and racism in education. *Educational Researcher, 33*(5), 26–31.

Epstein, R., Blake, J., & Gonzalez, T. (2017). *Girlhood interrupted: The erasure of Black girls' childhood.*

Greene, D. T. (2016). "We need more 'us' in schools!!": Centering Black adolescent girls' literacy and language practices in online school spaces. *The Journal of Negro Education, 85*(3), 274–289.

Haddix, M., & Sealey-Ruiz, Y. (2012). Cultivating digital and popular literacies as empowering and emancipatory acts among urban youth. *Journal of Adolescent and Adult Literacy, 56*(3), 189–192.

Hall, T. (2011). Designing from their own social worlds: The digital story of three African American young women. *English Teaching, 10*(1), 7.

Herr, K., & Anderson, G. L. (2005). *The action research dissertation: A guide for students and faculty.* Thousand Oaks, CA: Sage Publications.

hooks, b. (1989). *Talking back: Thinking feminist, thinking black.* South End Press.

Kellner, D., & Share, J. (2005). Toward critical media literacy: Core concepts, debates, organizations, and policy. *Discourse: Studies in the Cultural Politics of Education, 26*(3), 369–386.

Kemmis, S., McTaggart, R., & Nixon, R. (2013). *The action research planner: Doing critical participatory action research.* New York: Springer Science & Business Media.

Kirkland, D. E., & Jackson, A. (2009). "We real cool": Toward a theory of Black masculine literacies. *Reading Research Quarterly, 44*(3), 278–297.

Kynard, C. (2010). From candy girls to cyber sista-cipher: Narrating Black females' color-consciousness and counterstories in and out of school. *Harvard Educational Review, 80*(1), 30–53.

Lewis, T. Y. (2013). "We txt 2 sty cnnectd": An African American mother and son communicate: Digital literacies, meaning-making, and activity theory systems. *Journal of Education, 193*(2), 1–13.

Morrell, E. (2012). 21st-Century literacies, critical media pedagogies, and language arts. *The Reading Teacher, 66*(4), 300–302.

Morris, M. (2016). Pushout: *The criminalization of Black girls in schools.* New York: The New Press.

Muhammad, G. E., & Haddix, M. (2016). Centering Black girls' literacies: A review of literature on the multiple ways of knowing of Black girls. *English Education, 48*(4), 299–336.

Muhammad, G. E., & Womack, E. (2015). From pen to pin: The multimodality of Black girls (re)writing their lives. *Ubiquity: The Journal of Literature, Literacy, and the Arts, 2,* 6–45.

National Educational Technology Standards for Students, Second Edition. (2007). *International society for technology in education.* www.iste.org

New London Group. (1996). A pedagogy of multiliteracies: Designing social futures. In B. Cope, & M. Kalantzis (Eds.), *Multiliteracies: Literacy learning and the design of social futures* (pp. 9–37). London: Routledge.

Park, P. (1993). What is participatory research?: A theoretical and methodological perspective. In P. Park, M. Brydon-Miller, B. Hall, & T. Jackson (Eds.), *Voices of change: Participatory research in the United States and Canada* (pp. 1–2). Toronto: The Ontario Institute for Studies in Education.

Price-Dennis, D. (2016). Developing curriculum to support Black girls' literacies in digital spaces. *English Education, 48*(4), 337–361.

Richardson, E. (2002). "To Protect and Serve": African American female literacies. *College Composition and Communication,* 675–704.

Royster, J. J. (2000). *Traces of a stream: Literacy and social change among African American women.* Pittsburgh, PA: University of Pittsburgh Press.

Vasudevan, L., Schultz, K., & Bateman, J. (2010). Rethinking composing in a digital age: Authoring literate identities through multimodal storytelling. *Written Communication, 27*(4), 442–468.

Vickery, J. R. (2017). *Worried about the wrong things: Youth, risk, and opportunity in the digital world.* Cambridge, MA: MIT Press.

Waters, K., & Conaway, C. B. (2007). *Black women's intellectual traditions: Speaking their minds.* Burlington, VT: University of Vermont Press.

Willis, A. I. (2008). *On critically conscious research: Approaches to language and literacy research.* Teachers College Press: New York.

# KITCHEN TABLE TALKS

## Digital Literacies and Black Girlhood

*Delicia Greene, Autumn Griffin, Tonya Perry, and Detra Price-Dennis*

> When I began presenting evidence on the ways that Google was misrepresenting women and girls of color in particular, nobody really cared except women and girls of color.
>
> —Safiya Nobel

The kitchen table represents physically and symbolically an inclusive space for Black girls and women to come together, to be seen, to be heard, and to just be. The kitchen table signifies the rich history of our foremothers and grandmothers who sat at the kitchen table where, beyond gossip and social talk, women bared their souls and received healing and affirmation in the company of their sisters. We embrace the notion of "sitting at the kitchen table" as a reflection of our collective desire to transform spaces by sharing our experiences and asserting our voices.

The authors in this section gathered around a virtual kitchen table, using the online platform Zoom, to engage in conversation around shared ideas and guiding questions about Black girls' digital literacies practices. They participated in a conversation where they talk across their respective work as literacy educators and scholars who foreground Black feminist/womanist epistemologies in their personal, social, and professional lives. This kitchen table talk is organized around these sub-questions:

- Why is it critical that all educators acknowledge Black girls' literacies in their work?
- Why do digital literacies matter(s) for Black girls?
- How are Black girls' digital literacies honored in your work?

- When you think about how Black girls are represented in the literature about digital literacies, what are important considerations for the field of literacy education and classroom practice?

In the sections that follow, we highlight our dialogic exchanges in response to these questions and conclude with final words of wisdom. To recreate our kitchen table talk, we video-recorded our Zoom chat and transcribed the video. Each section that follows captures key points transcribed that were made to address the guiding questions.

## Acknowledging Black Girls' Literacies

### Why Is It Critical That Educators Acknowledge Black Girls' Literacies in Their Work?

DELICIA: If we acknowledge and make spaces for Black girls, in essence, everyone will benefit.

AUTUMN: I think Black girl literacies are critical for educators to recognize Black girls as fully human. We know that literacy has historically been used to martial power and determine who's human and who's not. Who's a citizen and who's not. So, when we think about Black girls' literacies from the historical and political standpoint, we know that acknowledging someone as a literate being means, in part, acknowledging them as fully human. And when you see someone as human and deserving of all the love and rights that you have yourself, you're better able to empathize with them when you see them being mistreated. So, you're not able to drag Black girls out of the classroom for texting then, right? Or you're not able to arrest a 6-year-old for having a tantrum because you understand that her outburst is an expression.

TONYA: You know Autumn, you really have said that beautifully. But I was just thinking, I found this quote this morning out of something I was reading. And it says, "We need to deconstruct what we're asking of leaders. We need to create a culture where we're asking other people to step up." We ask women of color to do more with less. That's actually what we do every single time. We've always created change with less and imagine what Black women could do, and girls, if we were truly supported?

This made me think about this idea of being fully human and being seen as human. This idea of not being seen as someone who can always has to make a meal out of nothing or somebody who has to learn with few resources. But what does it mean for Black girls and Black women to be fully supported and have the resources and be seen fully for her body, mind, and her spirit? And having all of those things come together, so pedagogically, looking at teaching the wholeness of the Black girl. And what would happen if Black girls' literacies were actually supported? What if we had the resources to take care of the whole Black girl?

## Digital Literacies in Action

### *Why Do Digital Literacies Matter(s) for Black Girls?*

DELICIA: I think there's this misconception that Black girls are not even using technology. I think so many people will say, "Oh, there's this digital divide," and, "Black girls are not even—they can't afford access to technology." But Black girls are finding ways to very much be present in a digital space, not only as users but also as composers.

It also about addressing the narrative around what it means to be Black and female. Black girls are always having to navigate and balance and disrupt the ways in which they're seen. However, I also feel like it creates a space for them to speak back. In that way digital literacies are an emancipatory tool. And, I think, in a lot of ways, digital technologies creates this pedagogy of healing for them. It creates an opportunity for them to release, to really disrupt, but to also address something that they're trying to figure out or negotiate to deal with traumas in their lives.

TONYA: Okay. So once again, it goes back to this pedagogy of wholeness for Black girls. And this idea that digital literacies actually provides Black girls some. Engaging in digital literacies allows Black girls to not to have to wait for those parsed out pieces that sometimes the world gives them, right? So, it's this kind of pedagogy of wholeness. It's this digital world that would allow for us to participate in a way in which we can really do heart work, do mind work, and do the kind of soul work that I think is not just internal, but it can be external as well. We can share it with each other and be able to have that kind of collaboration and communication the way we want to and have some control. And Autumn, you may pick up more on that as well, but I love that idea's looking at ourselves as fully human, not pieced together, not just parts, which sometimes the world will say, "We're just our body" or "Look at that on her." I just love this idea of wholeness for Black girls and a way to be able to use that through literacy.

AUTUMN: Yeah. And to speak back to that, I think one of the things you said about how digital literacies allow Black girls the space to be in collaboration with one another. I've been thinking a lot about what it means for Black girls to be agents of power in digital spaces. We see them forming communities in these digital spaces and doing things like digital counter-stories creating websites that represent themselves in ways that they see fit to again represent themselves as fully human and control their own narratives. And I think it's also important that we think about how Black girls are taking these new technologies through the use of digital literacies to build on what others did. The literacy practices are not new. What's new is the technology. So, these digital literacies are allowing Black girls to explore new frontiers and take up space.

TONYA: Yeah, I agree. I was thinking of the idea of taking something that we've always done to tell our story, to collaborate, to put something together, to make something, and how technology allows us to do the same practice in a different way. And I think the practice of quilting could be akin to digital literacies, right? A place, a gathering space. Where Black girls are working and creating together.

AUTUMN: And I mean, that even makes me think of things like Instagram, right? And even the layout of Instagram, right? And how you're actually putting together this digital quilt that tells a story.

## Honoring Black Girls' Literacies

### How Are Black Girls' Digital Literacies Honored in Your Work?

DETRA: These ideas push us to think about how our Black girl literacies are honored in our work. All of you do a beautiful job talking about that in your chapters, but I wonder if there's more you would like to elaborate on from your chapter or your work in general. How do you honor Black girl literacies?

AUTUMN: In my work, it's important for me to create space for Black girls to talk about how they're exercising their literacies. It's one thing for me to put together a study and to kind of observe. It's another to give them space to say this is what we're doing and this is why we're doing it and this is how we're doing it. And then to kind of talk collaboratively about what that means for the classroom, and how their digital literacies can be brought into and honored in the classroom so that they are partners in this work.

When I was thinking about this, it made me think of how Ruth Nicole Brown talks about dance a lot in her work, right? And how dance is this expression of Black girlhood and joy and liberation, right? And so, it almost feels like this dance that we're doing together where I'm like, "You're going to talk to me about what it is you're doing, and then together we're going to dance to create this new type of pedagogy where you and I are partners in creating what goes on in the classroom."

DELICIA: One of the things that I try to always do is to get a sense of the experiences of Black girls. But as Autumn had mentioned, I always want to be a learner in the process, and allow them in a lot of ways to lead, even if I may have questions that I'm interested in. I allow that process to continue because I don't want to be just someone who is a scholar that says Black girls have this autonomy that takes place, and then I don't allow that autonomy and creativity that comes from them leading in a very authentic way.

And then I also try to really focus on their social-emotional well-being. I'm always looking at the ways in which Black girls use technologies that are therapeutic and free flowing. I also want to always be engaging in the ethic of care and the pedagogy of healing in any approach that I take so that I am creating the type of experiences for Black girls that they don't necessarily have in schools. I'm always looking at how can I help Black girls? How can I be a copilot as they start to navigate and get to the other side of whatever experience that they have? And then not only that, I also don't want to, at the same time, feel like Black girls are always downtrodden and have downtrodden experiences. I want to acknowledge that there are times when they are having challenges, but I also want a space that honors and celebrates Blackness and females and I want them to be the leaders and pilots in that narrative.

TONYA: As I think about what we want our students to be able to do, our girls be able to do, with the digital literacies, I think that we cannot ignore what Delicia alluded to, which is the importance of talk. In my work that kind of collaboration education is important. And, I think in spaces where we don't honor that, Black girls probably feel as if they don't have a place. So, in the spaces we create, dialogue and collaboration are very important. I also believe that it is important for Black girls to feel like they are part of something, have some buy-in, and have some leadership in those spaces.

## Considerations for the Field of Literacy Education

### When You Think About How Black Girls Are Represented in the Literature About Digital Literacies, What Are Important Considerations for the Field of Literacy Education and Classroom Practice?

TONYA: So, in my best mind as a teacher practitioner, I would love to see teachers design lessons that speak to the heart, mind, and body of our Black girls. I'd love to see a section in the lesson plan like:

"What are you doing in your development of classwork and experiences when you're with Black girls."

Not dismissing anybody else, but, "What are you doing in your class every day that speaks to this practice that raises up Black girls, their abilities and capabilities so that you can get the most from them in your classroom practices?"

"What are you doing for your Black girls to meet the needs of their body, mind, and the spirit?"

"What do you do?"

"What does this look like?"

"What is it that you don't understand?"

And then, "How does that translate into them being able to use their digital literacies in a way that is respectful and honored?"

The goal is the creation of spaces that honor Black girls every day in the classroom.

AUTUMN: I think, in terms of research, I think about what it would mean to knock down the walls of the ivory tower and to consider how we're thinking about Black girls' literacies and how we know that Black women's knowledge has often not existed within academia. I think about, what does it mean to bring other voices into the conversation? Specifically, the voices of Black women and girls who are not academics? So, I wonder, what does it mean to bring the voice of Marley Dias into scholarship? What does it mean to bring the voice of Solange, who is physically disrupting white spaces, into conversation? What does it mean to bring Jada Pinkett-Smith and her Red Table Talk into conversation with the academy, not just as examples of people who are doing this work but as people who, as Black girls are knowledge bearers who have something to contribute to the conversation. And then I think about what it would look like to bring them into conversation with women who are academics. For example, women like Kimberle Crenshaw and Patricia Hill Collins; those are voices that are also important. And if we're thinking about this holistically and thinking about recognizing Black girls as fully human that means also being practical and recognizing that our girls are looking at these other women and girls too.

This kitchen table talk reflects our investment in Black girls and our deep appreciation for ways they express their creativity, joy, hopefulness, and pain through their multimodal literacy practices in sociotechnical spaces. Our collective work and scholarship about the brilliance of Black girls and women emphasizes how digital literacies empower Black girls to counter dominant narratives within mainstream spaces and to generate knowledge outside of school-sanctioned expectations. We concluded this generative and affirming discussion by sharing how proud we are to be Black women who are invested in uplifting Black girls and creating spaces for them to thrive!

# AFTERWORD

## Artist, Survivor, Academic, Activist

*Elaine Richardson*

To my knowledge, there is no other full-length book dedicated to Black girls' literacies. The title of this collection, in and of itself, signals a serious pursuit of freedom that honors Black girls' lives and ways of being in this world. We've known for quite some time that the autonomous model of literacy erases Black social reality and diminishes Black lives. African American and Black literacies seek to create free spaces for Black lives. As I wrote in *African American Literacies* (2003):

> For people of African descent, literacy is the ability to accurately read their experiences of being in the world with others and to act on this knowledge in a manner beneficial for self-preservation, economic, spiritual, and cultural uplift. African American literacies are ways of knowing and being in the world with others. When we think of African American cultural practices as literacy technologies or literacy practices, we see reading, writing, speaking, storytelling, listening, rhyming, rapping, dancing, singing, computing, phoning, mopping, ironing, cooking, cleaning, performing . . . among other activities as vehicles for deciphering and applying knowledge of public transcripts to one's environment or situation in order to advance and protect the self.
>
> (Richardson, 35)

I sketched the development of African American-centered rhetorics and literacies through the eras of enslavement, Reconstruction, "separate but equal" racial segregation, Harlem Renaissance, Civil Rights Movement, Black Power Movement, and Hiphop. I argued that African American experience and culture provide rhetorical models and literacies that demonstrate Black people's negotiation of life in a hostile society.

Paying attention to a wide range of Black women and girls' experiences and social situatedness, in "To Protect and Serve: African American Female Literacies," I set out to understand how we saved our own lives, our particular points of vantage, our special ways of knowing, and how we developed language and literacy practices to resist White supremacist, hegemonic, patriarchal, and dehumanizing stereotypes and ideologies (Richardson, 2002). I wanted to showcase our skills—vernacular expressive arts and crafts that Black females use to advance and protect ourselves. Though I mainly focused on the U.S. context, I argued that African American and Black diasporic women and girls' contribution to knowledge creation should be central in our literacy education.

In other words, if somebody is teaching reading and writing the world out of context to students' lived experiences, out of context to the macro levels and political workings of society, and how these affect us in our everyday lives, somebody is teaching us to comply with social inequality, to be docile. There is no such thing as neutral language or neutral text, or apolitical reading of the world. Everyone is always reading, writing, speaking, living in context and in particular ways of making meaning that make a difference in the world. With our legacy of Black girlhood and womanhood, Black women and girl-identified people have the authority, agency, and authenticity to accurately read and write our life experiences, and to act on behalf of ourselves for social transformation. When we stand on Blackness as hope, when we stand with Black girls' lives and literacies as sacred (Morris & Atlas, 2019), when we repudiate hegemonic standard/neutral/colorblind claims to language, literacy, and life, we intentionally reject anti-Black girl ideologies, practices, and pedagogies.

There is currently a smoldering of simultaneous movement afoot of educators, social activists, scholars, and community members. This movement demands more adequate and relevant social, political, educational, and economic policies that address impoverishment, the new jim crow, the prison industrial complex, educational failure, access to quality affordable mental and physical healthcare, childcare, housing, healthy food, and other conditions and tools that the sovereign uses to oppress Black people. Black girls' literacies studies is part of this work as it converges or intersects with movement such as #BlackLivesMatter, #BlackGirlsMatter #AllBlackLivesMatter, #sayhername, #metoo, queer of color critique, reproductive justice, Black (and Hiphop) feminisms, and Black girlhoods.

Black girls' literacies work is about interrupting systems of oppression with hope, Black joy, and healing, in spaces meant to erase or at best assimilate. Investing in Black girls' literacies aligns with Black optimism. Moten (2008, p. 1745) writes:

> In contradistinction to skepticism, one might plan, like Curtis Mayfield, to stay a believer and therefore to avow what might be called a kind of metacritical optimism. Such optimism, black optimism, is bound up with what it is to claim blackness and the appositional, runaway, phonoptic black

operations—expressive of an autopoetic organization in which flight and inhibition modify each other—that have been thrust upon it. The burden of this paradoxically aleatory goal is our historicity, animating the reality of escape in and the possibility of escape from.

Like Moten, I, along with Black girls' literacies workers, refuse to totally surrender to the structural impossibility of Blackness although Black life is under constant threat. Black literacies represent a space of Black creativity "in the underground, quotidian, and even joy-ful expressions of performative blackness that form the fabric of a black life less captured by white sovereignty" (Linscott, 2017, p. 115).

Black girls' literacies are embodied, multiple, layered, complex, collaborative, historical, performative, political, written, digital, and otherwise signaled modes of being, making meaning, knowing, and doing (Muhammad & Haddix, 2016). Black girlhood is a space of creativity and freedom generated from Black girls themselves, their literacies and productions, from Black girls' knowledges (Brown, 2009, 2013). This creative potential of Black girlhood is the organizing principle of their lives. Brown's interdisciplinary and foundational work with Black girls underscores that centering Black girls' knowledge creates the context for self-recognition that Black girls can be accountable to; and that we, as facilitators, build trusting relationships with them that hold them accountable. The work in this collection, like Brown's work, centers Black girls in their own complex experiences, humanity, their intellect, their beauty, their survival/thriving strategies. This conceptualization flies in the face of monolithic, pathological representations of Black girls' literacy undergirded by the White supremacist capitalistic patriarchal settler gaze.

Black Girls' literacies, as one of the chapter author's asserts, seeks to transgress the "boundaries of realism." The research, teaching, and community-engaged practice shared in these pages represent a sampling of the state of the art of Black feminist literacies work that collectively presents a challenge to all (educational) endeavors undergirded by state-sanctioned anti-Blackness. The work represented here is about ending all forms of violence against all Black girl-identified people and their communities, one space at a time. I am proud and humbled to have the last word in this collection of creative and critical scholars who have built on my work and taken it upward and onward, representing hope in action.

## References

Brown, R. N. (2009). *Black girlhood celebration: Toward a hip-hop feminist pedagogy.* New York: Peter Lang.

Brown, R. N. (2013). *Hear our truths: The creative potential of Black girlhood.* Urbana: University of Illinois Press.

Linscott, C. P. (2017, Spring). "Close-up: #Black lives matter and media: All lives (don't) matter: The internet meets afro-pessimism and Black optimism" *Black Camera: An International Film Journal, 8*(2), 104–119.

Morris, M., & Atlas, J. (2019). *Pushout: The criminalization of girls in school. The film.* Women in the Room Productions. https://pushoutfilm.com/film

Moten, F. (2008). Black Op. *PMLA*, 123(5), Special Topic: Comparative Racialization, (October), 1743–1747.

Muhammad, G., & Haddix, M. (2016, July). Centering Black girls' literacies: A review of the literature on multiple ways of knowing of Black girls. *English Education*, *48*(4), 299–336.

Richardson, E. (2002). "To Protect and Serve": African American female literacies. *College Composition and Communication*, *53*(4), 675–704.

Richardson, E. (2003). *African American Literacies.* New York & London: Routledge.

# IN DIALOGUE

## Collectivities

### *The Black Girls' Literacies Collective Statement*

> We realize that the only people who care enough about us to work consist-
> ently for our liberation are us.
> —The Combahee River Collective Statement, April 1977

We are Black women literacy scholars who formed the Black Girls' Literacies
Collective (BGLC) in 2015, though our relationships have evolved over many
years. The purpose of the BGLC is to support, uphold, and advance the literacies
and well-being of Black women and girls. The BGLC is a space for resistance and
a site for possibility in literacy and English education research, theory, and practice. We are actively committed to bringing to the forefront research and practice
that call out and work against educational harm toward Black women and girls,
while simultaneously promoting their social and academic success.

Following the rich traditions of Black women's literary societies, the Combahee River Collective, the Third World Women's Alliance, and the Crunk Feminist Collective,[1] we use a Black womanist lens to define our understanding of
collectivity, describe the work of the BGLC, and discuss how we work toward
transformation and equity. We understand the work of collectivity through Black
women's ways of knowing and being that are intersectional, that promote an ethics of care, and that require hope for the future.

A Black womanist lens informs our understanding of collectivity and why
we bring people together to think collectively about issues of marginalization

in literacy research that disproportionately affect Black women and girls. As we create spaces that honor the inclusion of identities and perspectives that represent the full spectrum of Black girlhood and womanhood, we draw upon ways of knowing that are steeped in an intersectional framing to make sure we account for the multiple ways of being a Black girl or woman in a variety of contexts. Our understanding of collectivity rejects monolithic treatment of Black girlhood and womanhood and celebrates the cacophony of race, gender, sexuality, religion, class, language, ethnicity, and other identities coming together. We believe in making connections with and among interdisciplinary groups of people in ways that honor past movements for equity, that work in solidarity with current movements, and that create opportunities for future movements to emerge. Fostering collectivity through a Black womanist lens across these networks also centers the practices of an ethics of care. These practices include our being transparent and honest with one another, desiring and seeing each other's differences as a source of strength, flushing out sources of tensions and dealing with them, and making choices that honor individual needs while acknowledging the needs of the collective. It is our intention that our embodiment of these practices will serve as a model for future collective movements to consider. Therefore, collectivity through a Black womanist lens honors the past and prepares for the future.

As Black women scholars, we recognize that our presence in the Academy is a disruption. Given that, we emphasize sisterhood and engage in self-care in service of our scholarly pursuits, which focus on advancing the well-being of Black women and girls. The work of the BGLC includes writing and thinking collaboratively about our research and community-engaged work; presenting at national and international conferences; attending and participating in public forums sponsored by the Congressional Caucus on Black Women and Girls; designing and coteaching graduate courses; providing professional development and consultations for K–12 schools and districts; preparing preservice and in-service teachers; developing and facilitating literacy curricula, after-school programs, and summer institutes for Black girls; mentoring doctoral students and early-career scholars; and creating spaces to foster ongoing dialogue about Black girls' literacies via social media. We are strategic about publishing Black girls' literacies research, individually and collectively, for both researcher- and practitioner-focused audiences (Haddix & Sealey-Ruiz, 2016; Price-Dennis et al., 2017). While academia prides itself on individualism and competition, we stress collectivity, even when it is not highly rewarded. We recognize the potential impact our work could have on the field of literacy research, and that gives us resolve to support each other in the work we are doing to advance our humanity. Thus, our approach is community-focused—keeping our eyes on the communities we create, those we serve, and those that serve us.

Moving forward, our collective goal is to advance toward transforming educational spaces for Black women and girls. Classrooms and schools remain ahistorical, unresponsive to their identities, and emotionally and physically oppressive. Importantly, curricula and instruction do not largely advance achievement to match the potential of Black girls. In order to move through equitable practices, we advocate for schools and classrooms to adopt the Black Girls' Literacies Framework (BGLF; Muhammad & Haddix, 2016), which can be used to frame pedagogy and professional development. The BGLF addresses the histories, identities, criticality, intellectualism, collaboration/collectivism, and multiple literacies of Black girls. Further, practices must incorporate digital literacies and be grounded in sociopolitical movements from the past and present. We contend that work that benefits Black girls can consequently benefit everyone. When we survey professional development sessions, they tend to center Black boys, and funding rarely and unequally focuses on Black girls. Black girls must be in the conversation. Black women and girls have a rich and lengthy history of literacy and literary excellence. There is no reason why this excellence should not be extended into classroom spaces today. As we continue our work as a collective, we will insist on Black women and girls' inclusion in any movement toward educational equity for all.

## Note

1. We are writing this column in the spirit of these collectives of Black women and women of color that have come before us. Following in their footsteps, we recognize the significance of leaving a historical record for future generations of Black women literacy scholars to understand our commitments, our challenges, and our aspirations. To learn more about Black women's literary societies, refer to McHenry (2002). To read the entire Combahee River Collective statement, refer to Combahee River Collective (2014). To learn about the Third World Women's Alliance, refer to Ward (2013). To learn about the Crunk Feminist Collective, go to www.crunkfeminist collective.com/about/

   This statement was drafted by Marcelle Haddix, Gholnecsar E. Muhammad, Detra Price-Dennis, and Yolanda Sealey-Ruiz on behalf of the **Black Girls' Literacies Collective**. The BGLC is an expansive collective of Black women literacy scholars at different stages of their careers, from doctoral students to leading voices in the field. BGLC sista scholars include Marcelle Haddix, Gholnecsar E. Muhammad, Detra Price-Dennis, Yolanda Sealey-Ruiz, Sherell A. McArthur, Carmen Kynard, Elaine Richardson, Erica Womack, LaToya T. Sawyer, April Baker-Bell, Tonya Perry, Bettina Love, Tamara Butler, Delicia T. Greene, Reba Y. Hodge, Fahima Ife, Maima Chea Simmons, Dywanna Smith, Stephanie P. Jones, Stephanie Toliver, Em A. Kirkwood, Autumn A. Griffin, and Ebony Elizabeth Thomas. It is our hope that the collective continues to expand its affiliations as the field of Black girls' literacies research advances.

## References

Combahee River Collective. (2014). A Black feminist statement. *Women's Studies Quarterly, 42*(3–4), 271–280. http://www.jstor.org/stable/24365010

Haddix, M., & Sealey-Ruiz, Y. (Eds.). (2016). Black girls' literacies [Special issue]. *English Education, 48*(4).

McHenry, E. (2002). *Forgotten readers: Recovering the lost history of African American literary societies.* Durham, NC: Duke University Press.

Muhammad, G. E., & Haddix, M. (2016). Centering Black girls' literacies: A review of literature on the multiple ways of knowing of Black girls. *English Education, 48,* 299–336.

Price-Dennis, D., Muhammad, G. E., Womack, E., McArthur, S. A., & Haddix, M. (2017). The multiple identities and literacies of Black girlhood: A conversation about creating spaces for Black girl voices. *Journal of Language and Literacy Education, 13*(2), 1–18.

Ward, S. (2013). The third world women's alliance: Black feminist radicalism and Black Power politics. In P. E. Joseph (Ed.), *The Black Power movement* (pp. 131–166). London: Routledge.

# INDEX

Black African immigrant girls' literacy experiences 105–107; Black girlhood in literature and 131, 132, 134–136, 147, 149–150, 155–156, 166–167; critical media literacy as 44–54; digital literacies and 185, 204–205, 210–213, 214, 232; in literacy collectives 31–32, 34, 36–43; in placemaking study 74, 78, 80; social activism and 44–54 (*see also* social activism)
preamble writing: defined 35; in literacy collectives 33–43; sample 35, 37, 38, 40
Price-Dennis, Detra 1, 170, 182, 203–204, 215, 220, 239
*PUSH* (Sapphire) 206, 208–213

racial identity 21, 23, 52; *see also* identity
racism: Afrofuturism re-envisioning 154, 163–164; Black African immigrant girls experiences of 98–99, 100–102, 107, 110; Black educators addressing 89; Black girlhood in literature addressing 124, 125, 147; critical media literacy countering 44–45, 48, 51, 54; literacy collectives addressing 31–32, 37, 39; mapping and 76; out-of-bound spaces for resistance to 14, 23, 26; social activism against 44–45, 48, 51, 54
radical democracy 49
reading about Black girlhood *see* Black girlhood in literature
representation: of Black girlhood in literature (*see* Black girlhood in literature); of Black girls in literature about digital literacies 243–244; Black women educators as 83–84, 87, 94–95; false (*see* misrepresentation of Black girls); of identity in literacy collectives 32–43; importance of 172–173, 203; in media (*see* media); of self in out-of-school digital multimodalities 208–213, 220
resistance: digital literacies as tool for 200, 210, 220; literacy collectives for 31–32, 36, 38–43, 109, 249; out-of-bound spaces fostering 14, 16–17, 26, 27; placemaking for 71; *see also* social activism
respectability politics 125
Rhodes, Jewell Parker, *Bayou Magic* 142–151
Richardson, Elaine 8, 202, 245
Riessman, C. 18

Robeson, Paul 170
Rollins, Charlamae 123
Rountree, W. 124, 135
Royster, J. J. 2

safe spaces: for Black African immigrant girls' literacy experiences 105; classrooms restructured as 15, 26–27; literacy collectives as 31–32; out-of-bound spaces as 13–14, 17, 26
Sanders, Sam 132, 134, 137
Sapphire, *PUSH* 206, 208–213
Saving Our Lives Hear Our Truths (SOLHOT) after-school program 16
Savoy, Lauret 71, 72, 79
Schmidt, R. R. 15
Schomburg Center for Research and Black Culture 83
schools: academic literacies for 185, 192, 193; Black African immigrant girls' experiences in 98–111; Black educator representation in 83–84, 87, 94–95; Black girls' literacies in and beyond (*see* Black girls' literacies); critical media literacy in 45, 46–47, 48–49, 52–54; disrupting traditional digital literacy models in 200–201; gratitude fostered in 90; gratitude journaling for work in 83–96; literacy as digital practice in 213; literacy as socio-political act in 214; literacy collectives vs. 36–37, 42–43; negotiation of self in context of 129–131; out-of-school digital multimodalities vs. 200–215, 220; Pedagogy of Confidence in *183*, 183–184; perception of digital tool usefulness and use in 218–236; placemaking for Black girls fostered in 68–69, 73–80; practical recommendations for educators of Black girls in 62–63, 118–119, 175–178, 243–244; safe spaces in 15, 26–27, 105; school-to-prison pipeline 4; seeing Black girls in 85–86, 90, 92, 94–95; social activism fostered in 45, 49; STEM in 181–182, 186, 189–190, 193; urban Black girls' digital media practices applied in 190–194; violence in 4, 47
science, technology, engineering, and mathematics (STEM) 181–182, 186, 189–190, 193
Sealey-Ruiz, Y. 94, 232